Who Rules the Police?

WHO RULES THE POLICE?

Edited by

Leonard Ruchelman

Lehigh University

New York: New York University Press   1973

6/27/79 Beehoort Tayler 12.50

To Lauren Rose

TABLE OF CONTENTS

EDITOR'S NOTE

Police reform in the United States has been instituted from out of an unduly narrow frame of reference. Preoccupied with methods which would reduce police laxity or corruption and increase "efficiency," civic leaders and public officials who helped make the rules have underestimated the significance of the policeman's own special values and interests. The idea of police politics in any manner or form has generally been considered anathema.

Such attitudes, unfortunately, tend to distort the contemporary police role and bind the policeman in contradictions. Caught between what he is supposed to do as a matter of "sound administrative principle," and what he actually does in light of prevailing circumstances, the law officer is often converted into an early cynic. As societal problems have increased and as the politics of communities have become more intense—even violent —the police officer has tended to respond through political stratagems of his own. Contrary to what was intended by the reformers, it appears that many of the very procedures they recommended have contributed to the spread of police politics.

In light of this, the present volume seeks to probe the realities of the police officer's job in the context of community affairs. The essential interest is to examine the subject of civil accountability and control of the police in its more trenchant dimensions. As a means of best achieving such goals, the case material selected for reading concentrates primarily on the nation's largest cities where the pressures have been greatest. Hopefully, through such exposition, we can begin to set the stage for a more responsible law enforcement process which can better assure "liberty and justice for all."

Leonard Ruchelman
Lehigh University
Bethlehem, Pennsylvania

In the readings, some material and footnotes have been omitted which were not necessary to the purpose of the present work. Editor's omissions in the text are indicated by five points (. . . . .); where necessary, footnotes have been renumbered for this volume and appear at the end of each article.

Who Rules the Police?

INTRODUCTION: THE POLICE SETTING

√The current widespread anxiety over public protests, violence, and crime, particularly in our largest cities, has placed a heavy burden on the police. Because they are the most visible part of the law enforcement process, the American public has great expectations about what the police can do in preserving order and social stability. Yet, as the Task Force Report on The Police explains, the ability of the police to achieve these objectives is limited. "The police did not create and cannot resolve the social conditions that stimulate crime. They did not start and cannot stop the convulsive social changes that are taking place in America. They do not enact the laws that they are required to enforce, nor do they dispose of the criminals they arrest." [1]

The sense of frustration which grows from the contradictions of their daily work, however, has contributed to feelings by the police that they are alone and unappreciated. A 1968 survey of 437 policemen in 11 different cities shows that fifty-four percent were dissatisfied with the respect they received from citizens; and thirty percent believed that the average citizen in their patrol precincts held the police in some degree of contempt. It was also found that while the police are generally dissatisfied with the external rewards of their job, over eighty percent of them were most happy with their colleagues. [2]

Not only do the police manifest insularity, but they have become activist as well. A recent inquiry into five cities found that police "are coming to see themselves as the political force by which radicals, student demonstrations, and Black Power can be blocked." [3] And as the readings in this book will show, the police are quite capable of acting on such beliefs.

Here, then, is the challenge presently being posed in many of the nation's cities. When one views the record of the largest cities, moreover, it becomes clear that incidents of police activism are not isolated events. In places like New York City, Chicago, Los Angeles, Philadelphia, Detroit, Cleveland, Boston and San Francisco, elected public leaders have all experienced some degree of police testing and resistance.

It is to such matters that the present volume addresses itself. The purpose is to convey some clearer perspective into what appears to be a new kind of relationship between law enforcement and the polity. By way of preparing for the reading selections which follow, it would help to ponder the following questions: Is police politics a temporary phenomenon or is it the manifestation of a long-term trend? What underlying structural factors are responsible? What implications does this bear for the political system and the question of civil accountability and control of the police?

The Reform Ethos

Because of its role as community watchdog and law enforcer, the police have always been subject to pressures and temptations from a host of special interests. Most prominent in this regard have been the political parties and the racketeer organizations. When metropolitan police forces were developing in the nineteenth century, police jobs and promotions were often influenced by party leaders who had political as well as pecuniary stakes in the quality of law enforcement.[4] Similarly, the prohibition and depression days of the 1920's and 30's demonstrated how bootleggers, gamblers, and traffickers in prostitution require tolerance and even support by the police if they are to prosper.

In view of this, civic groups and reformers have long argued for procedures which would restrict police collusion with "outside" forces. Reacting to such demands during his administration, President Herbert Hoover appointed a commission to study the problem and make recommendations. Known as the Wickersham Commission after its chairman, its report of 1931 set the tone for police reform throughout the country. "The chief evil," it was explained, "lies in the insecure, short term of service of the chief or executive head of the police force and in his being subject while in office to the control of politicians in the discharge of his duties." [5] Among those singled out as the cause of poor law enforcement was the mayor:

The chief is usually appointed by the mayor. . . . Such appointment is, however, never a guaranty of competency for the place of the person appointed, but is simply an assurance that he is the personal appointee of the mayor and subject to his arbitrary control, or, more likely, that he is satisfactory to the party politicians whom the mayor felt obliged to consult before he dared risk confirmation of his nominee. [6]

We should also note that the Commission did not seem to have any great faith in the workings of democracy:

Limiting the powers of the police executive by placing absolute control of police under the mayor, commissioners, or city manager has opened the door for every conceivable type of incompetency, political corruption, and organization demoralization. The theory that the mayor, representing the people, will exercise wisdom in conducting the business of the city and, being directly responsible to the electors, will do his utmost to protect lives and property of inhabitants and preserve the peace, has been badly shattered, judged by the caliber of police service which is to be found in the majority of the communities in this country. [7]

Thus the elected officials were seen as bunglers or corrupters of efficient police operations. In this light, their role in police affairs was to be limited while the police were to be made as "professional" as possible. To abet this, the Commission proposed new and improved training methods as well as civil service to recruit better policemen.

Such forms of prescription have had an important impact on the contemporary police role. For one, rules which were intended to make the police professionally independent also permitted them to become politically independent—something the reformers never quite anticipated. By the 1960's, the growing bureaucratization of the police launched them as an independent political force. Through their guilds and associations, as we shall see, police personnel have become contenders in referendum battles, election campaigns, and in debates over broad issues of public policy.

Another consequence of reform prescription is the persisting confusion over the proper role of elected leaders in police affairs. If the mayor and city councilmen are viewed primarily as "politicians," and if the police are viewed as "professionals," any action taken by the former can be labeled "political interference." Thus vagueness surrounds questions of police accountability and control. The police can use this as protection against "outsiders" even as they engage in political activism. Mayors can use this also when they want to avoid responsibility or blame for police behavior.

The Governmental Framework

In most large cities, the police operate in a governmental environment which can be characterized as diffuse. This is attributable to the wide variety of public institutions, agencies and offices which have some impact on the police role.

At the farther corners of the police setting are units of the federal government: courts, congressional committees, U.S. attorneys and administrative agencies. Reacting to the rising urgency of the law and order issue during the 1960's, the federal government has come to intervene more intensively in what has traditionally been considered a state and local function. Laws recently passed by Congress now require greater intergovernmental law enforcement cooperation in such areas as drug abuse, riot control, organized crime control, civil rights and juvenile delinquency. Of additional significance in weighing the federal role have been new Supreme Court decisions on police practices. In rulings which have become familiar through such names as *Miranda v. Arizona, Escobedo v. Illinois* and *Mapp v. Ohio,* the Court has mandated that the due process guarantee of the 14th Amendment binds state and local policemen, as well as federal officers, to obey the various procedures established by the Bill of Rights. On such matters as interrogation of suspects, seizure of evidence, electronic eavesdropping, and lineup procedures, the police must now tread carefully.

While federal involvement is relatively new, state government has always played an important role in structuring police affairs. During the nineteenth century, state lawmakers often assumed major responsibility for prescribing police organization and procedures. In 1857, for example, the New York legislature passed the so-called Metropolitan police bill which consolidated the police districts of the cities of New York and Brooklyn and the counties of Kings, Westchester, and Richmond under a board of five commissioners appointed by the governor; and for a number of years thereafter the state continued to control the policing of the entire area. This precipitated a new approach to police control throughout the United States and traces can still be found in a number of localities. In Baltimore, St. Louis, and Kansas City, for example, it is still the state governor, rather than the mayor, who appoints the police commissioner.

What is more important, in terms of contemporary concerns, is that it is the state policy making institutions which still set much of the agenda for what the police are expected to do—i.e., enforcement of state laws which regulate the health, welfare, safety, and morals of the people; and, to a large extent, the state courts sit in judgment of such activities. Furthermore, in spite of "home-rule" guarantees which assure powers of local self-government, the state capitals can still control many of the things that the police need or want, e.g., rates of pay, pensions, hours of work, collective bargaining.

For the most part, however, it is the municipality which structures the police function and it is on this level where inter-action between the police and other public actors is most intense. Crucial, in this regard, are relations with the mayor. The person who holds the mayoralty office, after all, is the chief executive and ultimately responsible for administering the many needs of the city. Primarily because of the reform ethos, however, mayor-alty command in most places is problematic. To illustrate, while the mayor can usually appoint the police commissioner, recruit-ment and promotion of most of the remaining personnel, usually up to the rank of captain, is subject to the civil service laws as administered by the local civil service commission. In some places, the mayor's power over such matters is even more limited. The Police Superintendent of Chicago is appointed by the mayor from among three candidates suggested by a police board of five members. In Los Angeles, a Board of Police Commissioners not only appoints the Commissioner, but it also exercises broad supervisory powers over all police operations. Under such con-ditions, where the mayor is not adept at using other means of influence—i.e., budgetary powers, persuasion, patronage—the police are able to resist his leadership.

Occupying a position of command between the mayor and the police bureaucracy is the police commissioner. As such, the commissioner is almost always caught in a situation of conflict. Does he look to the mayor, his immediate overseer and bene-factor, or does he take his cues from the men whom he com-mands? Is he to be the "mayor's cop" or is he to be a "cop's cop"? An even more difficult role, which few commissioners have mas-tered successfully, is the "professional cop"—i.e., a commissioner who insists on independence from mayor and bureaucracy alike. As community pressures for "law and order" have continued to build, and as the police environment has become increasingly politicized, the major task for the commissioner has been to maintain internal control over the men he commands. How well he manages this depends on his ability to deal with key partici-pants in the police environment: this usually includes the mayor and other elected officials, the party leaders, the police constituency, and, most important, the organized police bureaucracy.

√Because their work is so closely related, the police must also come to terms with others in the criminal justice system: notably the local district attorney and the city judges. Relations with the former are usually much more cordial than they are with the latter. The district attorney and his staff generally share the desire of the police to prevent the imposition of restrictions on arrests, interrogations and trial procedures. And while the district attorney needs effective police work to secure convictions, the police must rely on the district attorney for the prosecution of those whom they arrest. Police dealings with the courts, however, have become much more tacky, often leading to public recriminations.⌋ Much of this results from the frustration of the police in having to work around judicially imposed restrictions. While the Warren Court has been identified as the prime source of their difficulties, the local judiciary has come to serve as the most readily available target for allegations of "coddling" criminals.

Other local units which participate in the police environment are the overhead agencies—e.g., budget, law, personnel—and the line agencies—e.g., fire, health, sanitation, welfare, housing, recreation, public works. The special kinds of relationships which develop between these units and the police are too complex to generalize about; but the degree to which there is either cooperation or rivalry has significant bearing on how the police carry out their responsibilities in the community. As the local law-making body, the city council also plays a role though there is evidence of indecisiveness in the police policy area—the hotter the issue, the greater the inclination to pass the buck to the mayor. In none of our case readings does the council appear to play a prominent role.

The Police Constituency

Since just about everyone, from time to time, is subject to law enforcement, the groups and organizations to be found in the police environment are as varied as society itself. Some groups, of course, have greater stakes in the police role than others and consequently it is to their interest to strive for good police relations if not more permanent forms of alliances. Merchant and automobile associations, underworld elements, political parties, and those who are dependent upon police licensing and inspection procedures (e.g., nightclubs, building contractors, taxi companies) pursue such goals with varying degrees of success. The communications media, and particularly the press, play a more ambivalent role; for while they rely on the police for crime news, they are often just as happy to report on police corruption and violence—it all makes good copy.

Like the other city bureaucracies, the police are unlikely to discourage clientele relations because they can in many ways make their jobs easier (e.g., as a source of criminal information not otherwise available). Even more important, group connections can provide the police with outside support for their own special goals. Yet, the police also realize that any attempt to achieve and perpetuate such connections bears great danger; for where they are not careful, the special interests can become dominant just as the party machines dominated in former days. Furthermore, where the police are in collusion with outside interests, they can then be accused of favoritism and even corruption from such others as the bar associations, civil liberties groups and some of the news media. Thus, the police are usually defensive in their dealings with potential support groups. Any mutuality of interests must be nurtured guilefully and, as a rule, surreptitiously. The police constituency, then, has tended to be low-keyed and fragmented, unable to offer much help during times of stress.

The growing public concern over riots, demonstrations, and crime during the 1960's, however, has served to change the established patterns of police support. To illustrate, a survey of fifteen major cities conducted in 1968 for the National Advisory Commission on Civil Disorders shows that when white persons were asked to suggest "the most important thing" their city government can do to prevent racial disturbances, they are likely to think in terms of proposals for stronger police action.

"This view, held by nearly half the white population, was expressed in various ways; enlarge the police force, give police the power to shoot, arrest agitators, pass stricter laws, separate blacks from whites, and the like." [8] In his book *The Hidden Crisis in American Politics,* Samuel Lubell documents the growing anti-black, pro-police attitudes to be found in the white worker neighborhoods of places like Cleveland, Gary, Philadelphia and New York.

In the country at large, national leaders have been able to sense the growing influence of a new hard-line coalition of rural persons, blue-collar workers, and middle-class suburbanites—all predominantly white. Upon assuming office in 1968, the Nixon administration took the position that it had a popular mandate to deal vigorously with crime. Accordingly, new proposals which have since been passed into law give the police a freer hand under certain circumstances—what may be considered counterweight to earlier Supreme Court limitations. Included are the following provisions: a federal drug control measure permitting "no-knock" police entry into private quarters; "no-knock" police entry and preventive detention in the District of Columbia; expanded use of evidence acquired by wiretapping in dealing with organized crime. Here, now, is a new police-control model being copied and expanded upon by state and local governments.

The Pursuit of Police Autonomy

Along with other participants in city politics, the police bureaucracy seeks to influence government policy making. The greater part of their energies have been directed towards influencing policies which affect their conditions of work. As pressures on the police have continued to build, however, and as they have come to sense new threats in their immediate environment, their range of policy interests have increased as well. With support from their newly strengthened constituency, the police now openly address themselves to broad questions of social concern: radicalism, patriotism, free speech, the Supreme Court, Black Panthers are all part of the agenda.

To better effect themselves on such matters, the police have come to place great weight on their own organizational capabilities. Though tending to eschew labor unions because of the need to project an image of neutrality, policemen's associations and fraternal orders serve almost as well. In this way they are not only able to consolidate resources, but they can better perpetuate their own system of norms: by espousing the virtues of "professionalism," the organization works to limit the influence of "outsiders." Analyzing this in New York City, Wallace Sayre and Herbert Kaufman observe:

> With the aid of the state legislature, the approval of civil service reformers and the newspapers and other communications media, the indulgence of the Civil Service Commission, and the gradual concessions of hard-pressed Mayors, (the leaders of the police and fire associations) have succeeded, perhaps even beyond their own expectations. The two departments are now closed in the most exact sense. The police and fire bureaucracies are supervised and directed by officers and officials whom they recognize and regard as "their own." . . .[10]

What they consider as "their own" usually includes the police commissioner as well as ranking supervisory staff. The expectation is that commissioners will be appointed from the police ranks or at least be selected from among those who manifest long-time experience in police work—a sign of having been socialized to police norms. In just about every city, furthermore, the only point of entry into the police department is at the bottom, so that all those in the higher ranks are officers who have worked their way up. This affords a long period of indoctrination in which the nonconformists can be discouraged or weeded out. It is from this pool of talent, also, that the commissioner is expected to select his top commanders.

In their pursuit of self-directing autonomy, the police bureaucracy manifests other characteristics. William A. Westley's

classic case study of the police in a middle-sized industrial community reveals how sensitive they are towards anything that
might downgrade their self-respect.[11] He finds that in situations
where they are likely to be criticized, such as in their use of
force, the police try to protect themselves through secrecy.
Westley elaborates in the following way:

> Like other men, the police were sensitive to the
> demands of their occupational audience. Their work
> tended to make this audience hostile, so they tried to hide
> what they were doing, to counter the hostility of the pub-
> lic with a negative definition of human motives, and at
> the same time, wherever possible, to seek ways of getting
> public approval. The norms of the police (emphasizing
> secrecy, the use of violence for arrests, and the mainte-
> nance of respect for the police) represented a solution to
> the threats to their self-respect posed by the nature of
> their occupation.[12]

Today, when policemen are being injured in riots, shot at
by snipers, and criticized by student and minority groups, they
are indeed reacting with anger, violence and secrecy. Not only
do they try to protect themselves through greater insularity,
but in many places they have launched a counterattack through
direct involvement in the political process. The fragmented governmental framework, moreover, provides them with a mul-
tiplicity of decision-making centers by which they can better
carry out their strategies.

An important consequence of such development is that we
are no longer sure who it is who actually reviews police action
and can hold them responsible for their behavior. If society is
to cope with this problem more effectively than it has in the past,
we must try to break through the doctrinal cobwebs of reformist
thinking at the same time that we strive for a perspective which
can begin to meet present-day conditions. To begin this endeavor
is the basic purpose of the present volume.

Our approach is to gauge significant dimensions of police

behavior in the largest cities—primarily New York, Philadelphia, Chicago and Detroit. The first chapter sets the stage by presenting basic standards of conduct that society holds for its constabulary, and then, as a related phenomenon, the means by which society hopes to achieve these standards. Because the standards are often vague or unrealistic in light of existing circumstances, we see in the second chapter that it is the individual policeman, deciding a course of action by himself, who is the key variable. The third chapter shows that where the means of civil accountability and control are ineffectual, the police are capable of abusing their decision making authority. The last chapter gives us some taste of a new feature in our cities: political struggle between civil authority on the one hand and the organized police on the other. Most important in the readings which follow is the lesson that power relations are fundamental to a realistic assessment of the contemporary police role. To ignore this, or to be presumptuous about it, means that attempts to reform the system are likely to be superficial at best.

NOTES

1. The President's Commission on Law Enforcement and Administration of Justice, *Task Force Report: The Police* (Washington, D.C.: U.S. Government Printing Office, 1967), p. 1.
2. The National Advisory Commission on Civil Disorders, *Supplemental Studies for the National Advisory Commission on Civil Disorders* (Washington, D.C.: U.S. Government Printing Office, 1968).
3. *San Francisco Chronicle*, December 16, 1968. Quoted in *The Politics of Protest*, Staff Report to the National Commission on the Causes and Prevention of Violence (Washington, D.C.: U.S. Government Printing Office, 1968), p. 210.
4. Two useful historical treatments of this subject are Roger Lane, *Policing the City, Boston 1822-1885* (Cambridge, Mass.: Harvard University Press, 1967); James F. Richard-

son, *The New York Police* (New York: Oxford University Press, 1970).

5. The National Commission on Law Observance and Enforcement, *Report on the Police* (Washington, D.C.: U.S. Government Printing Office, 1931), p. 1.
6. *Ibid.,* p. 2.
7. *Ibid.,* p. 49.
8. Angus Campbell, *White Attitudes Toward Black People* (Ann Arbor, Michigan Institute for Social Research, 1971), p. 28.
9. Samuel Lubell, *The Hidden Crisis in American Politics* (New York: W. W. Norton and Company, 1970), chapter four.
10. Wallace Sayre and Herbert Kaufman, *Governing New York City* (New York: W. W. Norton and Company, 1960), p. 429.
11. William A. Westley, *Violence and the Police* (Cambridge, Mass.: The MIT Press, 1970). First published as a Ph.D. dissertation in 1951.
12. *Ibid.,* pp. xiv, xv.

I. ACCOUNTABILITY AND CONTROL OF THE POLICE

This first chapter sets the tone by focusing on two fundamental questions: What are society's standards for police behavior? What assurances do citizens have that police will act in
compliance with these standards? Such concerns go to the very
heart of a democratic system where public employees and officials
are presumed to be held accountable for their actions. Such concerns are even more crucial where, in the course of carrying out
their duties, public employees and officials are legally authorized
to arrest people and exercise coercion.

In the first two selections, we get some understanding of
what is usually meant by "responsible" police behavior. The
"Law Enforcement Code of Ethics," promulgated by the International Association of Chiefs of Police, illustrates forms of
behavior which the police profession expects of itself. (This code
is typical of police codes in most cities.) "Police Justice," as
reported for the City of San Diego, shows what society requires
through constitutional provisions.

To the average policeman, however, professional rules and
Supreme Court interpretations of the Constitution can give the
appearance of an obstacle course. Not only do they make his
job complicated, but they can make him look inefficient—criminals can evade conviction when the policeman fails to comply
with the intricacies of due process. Consequently, unless the
mechanisms of civil accountability and control are in good working order, we cannot be sure that the police, or at least all

police, will abide by established standards. The remainder of the readings treat just this problem. In "Sources of External Control," prepared by a Presidential task force, we get an overview of some of the traditional controls as administered by governmental institutions—i.e., mayor, city council, prosecutors, judiciary—as well as suggestions for new approaches. More important, however, is the argument that the present institutional framework does not sufficiently assure law enforcement which is consistent with democratic values. In recent years, minority groups have been especially vehement in urging new procedures for channeling citizen grievances against alleged police misconduct. The merits of external or "Civilian Review" versus internal review of police behavior are examined in the fourth selection as based on experiences in Philadelphia, the first city to adopt a civilian complaint review board. "Community Control" of the police is another proposal which has not yet passed beyond the discussion stage. This is analyzed in the last piece by Alan Altshuler. Here he tackles the very difficult question of how this would work in the inner-city and whether it would or should detract from concepts of police professionalism.

1. LAW ENFORCEMENT CODE OF ETHICS

International Association of Chiefs of Police

As a Law Enforcement Officer, my fundamental duty is to serve mankind; to safeguard lives and property; to protect the innocent against deception, the weak against oppression or intimidation, and the peaceful against violence or disorder; and to respect the Constitutional rights of all men to liberty, equality and justice.

I will keep my private life unsullied as an example to all; maintain courageous calm in the face of danger, scorn, or ridicule; develop self-restraint; and be constantly mindful of the welfare of others. Honest in thought and deed in both my personal and official life, I will be exemplary in obeying the laws of the land and the regulations of my department. Whatever I see or hear of a confidential nature or that is confided to me in my official capacity will be kept ever secret unless revelation is necessary in the performance of my duty.

I will never act officiously or permit personal feelings, prejudices, animosities or friendships to influence my decisions. With no compromise for crime and with relentless prosecution of criminals, I will enforce the law courteously and appropriately without fear or favor, malice or ill will, never employing unnecessary force or violence and never accepting gratuities.

Issued by the International Association of Chiefs of Police, Training Key #15, 1965. Reprinted by permission.

programs and goals of another agency, or of the process as a whole.

In the United States, it is assumed that the courts will occupy a dominant position in the administration of criminal justice. It is the courts, in particular the appellate courts, which interpret the meaning and scope of such principles as due process of law, the presumption of innocence, the reasonableness of searches and seizures, etc. Few of our citizens, however, come into any contact at *any* time during their lives with the functioning of our appellate courts. If citizens are to have dealings with any of the agencies of justice, then this contact for most of them will come about as the result of their dealing directly with lower, magistrate-level courts, or with the police.

Justice, for the most part, can be measured by the actual contact which the average citizen has with the police or lower courts. The enunciations of the highest courts notwithstanding, the content of justice, the real meaning of justice, is determined by the types of relationships the individual can consistently expect to receive when he deals with these two lower-level agencies. If the average citizen—one without personal power or influence—can reasonably expect to receive fair and sympathetic treatment from the police and from the lower courts, then justice to him is both fair and sympathetic. It is for these reasons, therefore, that the operating policies and procedures of the police are of crucial importance. Contacts with the police, more than any other matter, determine citizen evaluation of the administration of criminal justice, as a whole. Justice, in fact, consists of those rights which the average citizen enjoys "out on the streets."

The role of the police in the administration of criminal justice can be divided, basically, into six parts. They are as follows:

1. The prevention of crime.
2. The detection of crimes which have been committed.
3. Identification of the person or persons responsible for crimes.
4. Apprehension of the person or persons responsible.
5. Detention of the person for processing by the judiciary; and
6. Presentation of the evidence to the prosecutor.

Throughout the performance of these functions, any attempt to deprive a person of any of the rights guaranteed him by law represents a violation of due process.

Police violation of due process may take the form either of technical legal violations or they may, in fact, be more subtle violations of the "spirit" of due process. Technical legal violation of due process may take a variety of forms. The police may falsify the evidence which they present, or they may be guilty of illegal arrests or detention. On the other hand, the police may have used an excessive amount of force in apprehending or detaining the person accused of the crime; or they may have performed unreasonable or illegal searches or seizures. In addition, they may have used physical or psychological coercion in extracting a confession or admission, or they may have inflicted all sorts of other punishments upon the person which are prohibited by law. Police violations of due process, therefore, may take many forms. Consequently, a careful examination of the practices employed by the San Diego Police Department was made in an effort to determine possible violations of due process. If violations were found, procedures were established by the research team which would enable a distinction to be made between random or accidental individual violations and those which took the form of a traditional and systematic organizational violation of due process. The rationale for this orientation by the research team was that it is just as important to uncover propensities toward the violation of due process as it is to uncover the actual violations. A report of our findings in this regard is submitted.

It is noteworthy that nowhere in the findings of this study were allegations of the falsification of evidence or the forcible extraction of admissions and confessions advanced by any person interviewed; nor were they otherwise suggested by observation and investigation. It can be assumed, however, that the high judicial standards which prevail today would make the exercise of these unconstitutional acts meaningless in the accomplishment of the police purpose. Accordingly it is not expected that any law enforcement agency would subscribe to technical practices which may have been more common in earlier times.

Allegations of unreasonable search have been implied by

accounts of persons concerning officers making their field interrogations, particularly of juvenile subjects. Similarly, this kind of
violation of due process, if substantiated, would be related to that
of illegal detention, and, possibly, actual arrest not in conformity
with the law. In addition, complaints of the use of excessive
force, carrying the inference of an exactment of a kind of punishment outside the authority of law enforcement officers, were
examined. All of these charges of due process violation were
subjected to careful scrutiny.

First, it must be noted that the San Diego police officer is
well indoctrinated in the principles of law and in their application to modern police practice. The manual of instruction placed
in the hands of each officer lays great stress on the rights of the
police and the restrictions placed upon them in accomplishing
their mission. The text includes elaborate coverage of both federal and state court decisions which define the proper exercise
of the duties imposed upon the police agency. A recent device
for familiarizing all members of the Department with the evolv-
ing law on human rights is a three-hour classroom presentation
on the subject. This training is prescribed for all police
personnel.

Next, the matter of field interrogation presents itself. This
is a field patrol procedure entailing the stopping and questioning
of persons on the streets and in public places with the purpose
either of disclosing criminal activities or of making a record of
information to be employed in a later investigation of crime.
Approximately 200,000 field interrogations are made annually.
The majority of these apparently are directed towards juveniles.
The manual of training for recruits devotes much space to the
purpose and manner of making the field interrogation. Legal
justification stemming from case law is presented in exacting
form. While the Department makes a uniform denial that specific quotas are imposed upon the policeman to make field interrogations, it is apparent that the Patrol Division officers are
required to submit a "fair" volume of reports on their activity
in this regard. Departmental supervisors determine what is an
appropriate number of field interrogations.

California law does not require that information be given to a police officer by a citizen *except* under very limited circumstances. Section 647 of the Penal Code, for example, prescribes that information as to identity and presence must be given only when one:

> . . . loiters or wanders upon the street or from place to place without apparent business . . . if the surrounding circumstances are such to indicate to a reasonable man that public safety demands such identification.

Evaluation of whether the San Diego Police Department abuses its authority in field interrogations is individualized. Certainly, there is much resentment over the practice.

While the resentment against the field interrogation embraced by certain persons may be high, there is no evidence that the widespread practice represents a violation of due process. That the field interrogation can be subject to abuse, that it can be employed to hurt one's dignity, that it may be at the core of a deficient (aspect of) relationship between the citizenry and the police must be recognized, and it will be dealt with elsewhere in this report. However, it can be labeled as being either unconstitutional or otherwise illegal—*only* if it is used excessively or as a tool of harassment.

Unlawful arrest by the San Diego Police Department does not appear to be a major concern of citizens. There are few complaints charging false arrest, and no allegation has been made of such illegal action in the interview of any official involved in the administration of justice. Therefore it can be concluded that the action of the San Diego police officer in making arrests is usually in accord with the law.

Finally, there is the matter of undue force. One aspect of this is the policy of handcuffing all adult prisoners and many older juveniles. This policy was constantly mentioned by members of the Police Department, itself. It was also a matter of strong complaint by many citizens. The procedure is to handcuff persons' wrists behind their backs when transported from the

scene of arrest to jail. The protection of the arresting officer—
in most cases alone at the wheel of his vehicle—is repeatedly
given by superior officers as the reason for this restraint. Since
Sections 835 and 835a of the California Penal Code authorize
the use of "reasonable" force and restraint, it would appear that
the practice of handcuffing everyone represents no illegality or
other violation of due process. The Department provides further
precautions inasmuch as all patrol cars are equipped with heavy
wire screens between the front and back seats in order that no
physical assaults may be made by prisoners. Also, every officer
is outfitted with a helmet, which he must wear at all times. The
negative implications of a practical nature will be commented
upon elsewhere.

Excessive physical force is the subject of widespread charges
and sometimes concrete complaints. In a sample of eighty [80]
complaints made by citizens against members of the Patrol Division in the first six months of 1966, there were sixteen which
charged some degree of physically abusive behavior. In addition,
the commonly accepted use of the "sleeper hold" and the temporary use of pressure on the vessels of the neck to deprive the
brain of its blood supply might be considered as measures possibly implying a use of force in excess of that permitted by law.

Nevertheless, there is little substantial evidence of actual
physical brutality by San Diego policemen. Department administrators are emphatic in their pronunciations that it will not be
tolerated. Policemen deny its exercise. Representatives of other
agencies engaged in the administration of justice, and members
of the bar, discount rumors of its use. Even the most vociferous
critics of the police attest to the absence of any regular exercise
of physical abuse of persons by the police. Examination of the
few actual complaints of physical brutality presented for our
consideration offered little to substantiate the charges.

It can be said that technical-legal violations of due process
by the San Diego Police Department are isolated. When they
exist, they are individual acts and cannot be fairly interpreted
as representing the consequence of a pattern of organizational
attitude and practice. It is not part of the administrative style

of the San Diego Police Department to encourage technical-legal violations of due process.

Due process, however, has another face, i.e. the "spirit" of due process, the spirit of fair play. In order to gain an insight into this aspect of due process, it is advisable to examine the role which the San Diego Police Department has set for itself and for its members. In this way, one can delineate the dominant concept of due process which characterizes members of the Department. It is necessary to determine if there is only a grudging acceptance of the "rules of the game," or if, in fact, the members of the Police Department use certain restrictions as a necessary and vital part of democratic policing. Begrudging adherence to the letter of due process may have a different social effect than willing, wholehearted acceptance. Much of the latter is dependent, of course, upon the top leadership of the Department. These high-ranking officers set the administrative and organizational tone and style with which the police mission is accomplished.

Comments by police officers upon the judicial process came to the attention of researchers in a variety of ways. Interview schedules, of course, were designed to elicit the attitudes and comments of policemen about the process. Data which were accumulated on this point did not come, however, solely in response to specific questions by researchers on the point. Much of the data was volunteered or initiated spontaneously by officers prior to any specific question by interviewers. Comments were also accumulated during parts of random observations, in patrol cars, in headquarters, on the streets, etc. In addition, comments were accumulated as a result of panel method sessions which were held with members of the Police Department.

Of all the data, the striking characteristic is its uniformity. From the data accumulated in this research one could easily make the observation that policemen in San Diego represent almost a monolithic structure when they express an opinion about due process, the judicial process, the administration of justice, etc. There certainly must be exceptions to this typical attitude within the Police Department; but the research staff simply did not come into contact with them! Typical of responses which

the staff encountered is this direct quotation which poses the
question as a moral issue:

> I fail to see the moral rightness in allowing a killer to
> walk free because of technicality. I feel that in some
> ways this country has gone overboard in protecting the
> rights of the individual and lowering the rights of the
> general public as a whole.

Resentment over recent appellate court decisions is posed not
only in moral terms, but also in political terms.

> . . . if the courts want to release dangerous rapists and
> murderers because of technical problems related to arrest
> procedures that is the problem of the country and not
> really a problem of the police because the people are
> going to suffer as a result.

Our data demonstrate that officers throughout the San Diego
Police Department, from the highest to the lowest ranks, are
intensely concerned about the effect which recent appellate
courts decisions (state and federal) have had upon their ability
to do their work. High-ranking officers express particular concern
over the effect they suppose these decisions will have on the task
of apprehension. Officers on all levels point to these decisions
as being a major factor in police morale.

Credit can be given Departmental leadership for having
created an internal working environment which sustains high
morale, a condition which prevails despite the supposed dele-
terious effect of court decisions. Patrolmen also point to recent
court decisions as having an effect upon morale, and those able
and willing to make projections predict that police morale will
be even lower five years from now precisely because the court
will impose "further restrictions" on police agents.

It is obvious from the various data collected that the police officer in San Diego is comparatively well trained in the technical aspects of criminal law, procedure, and related portions of constitutional law. These matters are stressed throughout the Department in a variety of ways. They are covered extensively in both recruit and in-service training programs; legal matters are regular subjects of staff conferences, Department training memos, and in roll-call training. Data leaves little doubt that the police in San Diego are well-prepared in these areas of technical-legal knowledge. However, little emphasis is ever given to the theoretical framework upon which the laws are based.

On the other hand, it seems equally clear that little is done in the way of instilling knowledge and values of "American Institutions." Insufficient attention is apparently given to the matter of pointing out the social and democratic importance of due process, the presumption of innocence, and other legal theories which are basic components of a democracy. In no place does the data demonstrate that attention is given to such matters as the powerlessness of most persons when they are confronted by the legal resources of government. In no place does the data reveal that the "perspective" of the accused is dealt with in any form in Departmental training, supervision or leadership. Rather than this perspective, emphasis throughout the Department is upon techniques and methods of improving efficiency in such matters as investigation, apprehension, patrol procedures, etc.

This observation may seem to be petty or of minor significance to police officials. To the research staff, however, this matter may be of crucial importance and central to at least a portion of the police-community relations problem. Just as a teacher who ridicules the academic process or who is anti-intellectual may have a dysfunctional effect upon the educational process for children, so too, a policeman who is "anti-process" may have a dysfunctional effect upon persons he encounters in his official capacity.

Ranking officers in San Diego, for example, are indignant when the Department is accused of "harassment." This is a charge which is often leveled at the Department by minority group persons. The Department denies the charge and takes the posture that such practices are specifically guarded against by close supervision. This enunciation of policy is, however, at variance with statements (and justifications) made by personnel on the operational level. Many officers stated in private conversations, for example, that motorcyclists are controlled by rigid vehicle "inspection" practices. These inspections are justified socially on the ground that they keep "undesirables" from congregating in the city and creating disturbances.

Other officers admit the practice of concentrating Departmental resources in sections of the city where "trouble-makers" are known to congregate. Although the deployment and procedures used are admittedly "harassing," they are rationalized on the ground that they are preventive in result. According to some police, they do keep the problems, which inevitably occur, from occurring, and this is the presumed social goal of police action. Furthermore, these practices are seen as being particularly effective in controlling juveniles, at least, harassment bordering upon "verbal brutality" is rationalized by some officers. To quote one officer who justified the practice:

> . . . Sometimes it is necessary to embarrass, let us say, one teenager in front of his friends. If, for example, he can be verbally put down, no matter how this was done, the rest of his friends will sometimes then follow his example, once he has been put in his place. This is a tactic used by the Police Department, it is necessary, and it is comprised of things that a person would not normally say, but he feels that it was necessary to resort to.

The policeman in San Diego, therefore, is dedicated to doing things which experience tends to demonstrate have an effect upon his work-load and overall mission. He tends to resent those practices, complaints, or rules which restrict his application of "proven" methods. In San Diego, according to his folkways, the effectiveness of field interrogations, a show of force, selective enforcement, etc., has been "proven" to his satisfaction. To him, these methods work and he resents persons from the "outside" who question these methods.

It may be that the policeman is impressed more by utilitarianism than by the theoretical or symbolic implication of certain matters. He sees his job and his role in a particular way. He seems much less concerned about the theoretical function he may serve in the administration of criminal justice than he is by the ever-present danger that awaits him and the general society.

B. *Differential Standards of Enforcement*

It is not surprising that the minority community feels that the degree of law enforcement to which it is subjected differs from that exercised in parts of the city predominantly occupied by Caucasians.

Persons interviewed make conflicting allegations of too much and too little enforcement in minority group neighborhoods. For example, emphasis was placed by many on gross toleration of vice in the parks of Logan Heights. Heavy concentrations of rowdy youngsters, glue sniffing, gambling, and drinking—these were practices described as persisting in the Negro community while these same practices were being suppressed in the white neighborhoods.

On the other hand, there is a feeling in some quarters that the police do not respond to calls for assistance made by Negroes. At the same time, the police are presumed to go out of their way in enforcing the law against members of the minorities.

A widespread allegation made by both whites and Negroes is that the San Diego Police Department does discriminate against juveniles of all races. According to this belief, the juvenile is the chief target in traffic enforcement, and he is the most frequent subject of the field interrogation. The screening at the Mexican border check station also is directed at the juvenile. The heavy policing of high school sporting and social events is designed to cope with his supposed propensity to violate the law.

The expressed feeling that there is differential treatment of the young person is too common to be ignored. Like the Negro, the juvenile is highly visible and is easily singled out for enforcement attention. However, the incidence of crime and traffic violation committed by him, coupled with the youthful propensity of becoming involved in disturbances, makes a higher degree of enforcement directed at him easily explainable. The adult community readily accepts the screening to which the juvenile is subjected at the Tijuana border. Adults view the device as one designed for the juvenile's protection.

It is not the purpose of this study to pass on the merits of the police technique employed in juvenile enforcement. It may be questioned, however, whether the enforcement policy is sufficiently understood, in view of the undercurrent of thought which holds the young person to be the object of discriminatory police practice. Perhaps the Department is deficient in enunciating the significance of its enforcement policy as it relates to the young subject.

While the Department disclaims any official policy of double standards in law enforcement it, nevertheless, is manifested by many individual policemen. Thus, the minority community has gained the impression that the Department condones discrimination. Also, the increased incidence of vice activity and the added difficulty in suppressing it may have led to the assumption that it is condoned. The relatively high incidence of crime in the minority community are Departmental reasons for stepped up police activity which may be mistakenly considered discriminatory.

Concerning any lack of zeal in handling the request for police assistance made by the Negro, neither the study of complaints against police personnel, nor the personal observations of the researchers bears out this contention. There is no indication that the San Diego Police Department renders less service to the Negro complainant than in cases where it deals with the Caucasian. That an individual officer may exercise differential treatment of a race in occasional or several contacts must, however, be recognized.

3. SOURCES OF EXTERNAL CONTROL

Task Force on the Police

The operations of the police, like the operations of any other administrative agency that exercises governmental authority, must be subject to effective legislative, executive, and judicial review and control. This is important when the police are called upon to carry out specific legislative, executive, or judicial mandates. It is doubly important in areas in which the police are left with discretion to develop their own policies within broad legislatively or judicially fixed limits.

Methods of External Control

While there is a very strong formal commitment to local control of law enforcement in this country, the actual means for exerting control has become quite obscure. To whom is a police agency responsible? By what means may citizens influence its functioning?

By City Councils and Mayors. Ultimate control, in local government, is normally exerted through the ballot box. But efforts to protect the police from partisan political influence have, in many jurisdictions, made the police immune from the local elec-

From *Task Force Report: The Police,* The President Commission on Law Enforcement and Administration of Justice, pp. 30-35. Published by the United States Government Printing Office, 1967.

tion processes. Early efforts to assure popular control of the police did include provisions in some cities for the chief of police to be elected. In others, the police were made responsible to the local legislative body. It became quickly apparent,, however, that such direct control led to a pattern of incompetence, lax enforcement, and the improper use of police authority. Elected office holders dictated the appointment and assignment of personnel, exchanged immunity from enforcement for political favors, and, in some cities, made use of the police to assist in the winning of elections.

In more recent times there has been a continuing effort to compromise the need for popular control with the need for a degree of operating independence in order to avoid the undesirable practices that have generally resulted from direct political control. Election and city council supervision of the police function gradually gave way to the establishment of administrative boards, variously constituted, in an effort to assure both independence and some semblance of civilian control.

These organizational patterns have, in turn, often led to an obscuring of responsibilities, resulting in a swing back to more direct control in the form of a movement for the appointment of a single executive, directly answerable to the elected mayor or, more recently, to a city manager who in turn is responsible to a city council. Variations of each of these arrangements, including some attempts at State control, continue to this day, with periodic shifting from one organizational pattern to another in response to a community's conclusion that its police force has too much or too little independence.

The record of involvement by elected officials in police operations, to the detriment of both the efficiency and effectiveness of the police establishement, has had a lasting and somewhat negative impact on the lines of control between the citizenry and the police. In cities in which the desire to isolate the police from political interference led to the adoption of special organizational patterns, the change in some instances has had the effect of making the police impervious to citizen demands of a legitimate nature. Although the organizational structure provides for direct control, the results have nevertheless been somewhat similar even in those cities in which the police administrator is directly responsible to an elected mayor.

Fear of being accused of political interference and an awareness of the sensitive nature of the police task have often resulted in the mayor abdicating all responsibility for police operations by granting complete autonomy to his police department. Indeed, the mayors of several of the largest cities, considering police department autonomy to be a virtue, have campaigned for reelection on a platform stressing the independence which they have granted to their police agencies. A mayor's apprehensions are created by his knowledge that any action on his part affecting the police, no matter how legitimate, may be characterized as political or partisan interference. The consequence is that we are now in a period of uncertainty as to the best relationship between police and the city government, the issue aggravated by the situation of unrest in large urban areas.

By Prosecutors. The prosecutor, State's attorney, or district attorney is designated as the chief law enforcement officer under the statutes of some States. However, despite this designation he is not generally conceived of in this country as having overall responsibility for the supervision of the police. His interest in police operations is usually limited to those cases likely to result in a criminal prosecution, thereby excluding the non-prosecution-oriented activities that constitute so high a percentage of the total police effort.

Practices vary significantly from one jurisdiction to another as to the degree of involvement on the part of the prosecutor in the review of police procedures and actions in those cases in which the police objective is prosecution. While some cases are subject to review prior to the effecting of an arrest, the vast majority of arrests by municipal police officers are made prior to consultation with the prosecutor. Some prosecutors establish procedures for the review of all arrests prior to their presentation in court, while others do not become involved until the initial hearing is begun before a magistrate. Systematic review of all cases prior to their presentation in court tends to result in the adoption of standards that are informally and sometimes formally communicated to the police agency. Police practices may be criticized or changes suggested, but such criticism and suggestions are not generally viewed as a form of control. Rather, they are seen as being primarily motivated by a desire on the part of the prosecutor to facilitate his task in the review and prosecution of cases. Where there is no prior review, the staff of the prosecutor in large cities often routinely presents in court cases in which the practices by the police were clearly illegal, apparently feeling no responsibility for reacting to the police practice, either in the form of a refusal to prosecute or in the form of a communication through appropriate superiors to the administration of the police force.

In general, instructions or guidelines issued by the prosecutor relating to procedures for the prosecution of criminal cases will be accepted and followed by the police, particularly if the prosecutor is viewed by the police as seriously interested in an effective presentation of the case in court. But neither the police nor the prosecutor assume that the prosecutor has the responsibility either to stimulate or to participate in the development of administrative policies to control the wide range of police practices.

By the Judiciary. In many jurisdictions the trial judge has acted as a sort of chief administrative officer of the criminal justice system, using his power to dismiss cases as a method of controlling the use of the criminal process. But except in those cases in which his action relates to the admissibility of evidence, this has been done largely on an informal basis and has tended to be haphazard, often reflecting primarily the personal values of the individual trial judge.

In contrast, the function of the trial judge in excluding evidence which he determines to have been illegally obtained places him very explicitly in the role of controlling police practices. However, trial judges have not viewed this role as making them responsible for developing appropriate police policies. Many trial judges, for example, when asked if they would explain their decision to the police, indicate that they have no more responsibility for explaining decisions to police than they have with regard to private litigants. When asked whether they would suggest to the police proper ways of acquiring evidence in the future, some judges assert that it would be unethical for them to do so unless they also "coached" the defense.

Occasionally a judge will grant a motion to suppress evidence in order to dismiss a case he feels should not be prosecuted because the violation is too minor or for some other reason. Use of a motion to suppress evidence in this manner serves to confuse the standards that are supposed to guide the police, and has a destructive effect upon police morale.

Most often, the process of judicial review is seen as a decision about the propriety of the actions of the individual officer rather than a review of departmental administrative policy. Judges seldom ask for and, as a consequence, are not informed as to whether there is a current administrative policy. And, if there is one, they seldom ask whether the officer's conduct in the particular case conformed to or deviated from the policy. As a result, police are not encouraged to articulate and defend their policy; the decision of the trial judge is not even communicated to the police administrator; and the prevailing police practice often continues unaffected by the decision of the trial judge.

The effectiveness of trial court review is further complicated in courts of more than a single judge by the disparity of their views about the propriety or desirability of given police practices. Ordinarily the prosecution has no opportunity to appeal adverse decisions. And where appeals are allowed, prosecutors seldom view them as a way of resolving conflict between trial judge rulings. As a result police often tend to ignore all of the decisions, rationalizing that it is impossible to conform to conflicting mandates. While increasing attention has been given to minimizing sentencing disparity through such devices as sentencing institutes, designed to minimize disparity, no similar attention has been given to disparity in the supervision of police practices.

Finally, the effectiveness of the exclusionary rule is limited by the fact that it deals only with police practices leading up to prosecution. Many highly sensitive and important practices are confined to the street and are not reflected in prosecuted cases.

Civil Liability of the Police Officer. One much discussed method of controlling police practice is to impose financial liability upon the governmental unit as well as the police officer who exceeds his authority. A somewhat similar approach is provided for under the Federal Civil Rights Act.

The effect of the threat of possible civil liability upon police policy is not very great. In the first place, plaintiffs are seldom able to sustain a successful lawsuit because of the expense and the fact that juries are not likely to have compassion for a guilty, even if abused, plaintiff. Insurance is also now available along with other protective methods that insulate the individual officer from financial loss.

The attitude of the police administrator is to try to protect his man or the municipality from civil liability even though he may privately be critical of the actions of the officer. Usually legal counsel will instruct the police administrator to suspend departmental disciplinary proceedings because they might prejudice the litigation.

Even in the unusual case where an individual is able successfully to gain a money judgment in an action brought against a police officer or governmental unit, this does not cause a reevaluation of departmental policy or practice.

In general, it seems apparent that civil litigation is an awkward method of stimulating proper law enforcement policy. At most, it can furnish relief for the victim of clearly improper practices. To hold the individual officer liable in damages as a way of achieving systematic reevaluation of police practices seems neither realistic nor desirable.

By Citizen Complaint. Complaints alleging police misconduct may relate to an isolated incident involving the actions of a specific officer or may relate to a formal or informal practice generally prevailing throughout a department. However, the citizen complaint process, like the civil action, is typically limited, in its effect, to the specific case which is subjected to review. Experience has shown that most complaints come not from the ghetto areas where there may be most question about police practice, but rather from middle income areas where an articulate citizen becomes irate over the actions of an officer which deviate from prevailing police practice in his neighborhood.

Most attention in recent years has focused upon the means for investigating such complaints, with public discussion concentrated upon the relative merits of internal departmental procedures versus those established by a form of citizen complaint board functioning in whole or in part outside the department. Whatever the method for conducting an investigation, there is no evidence that the complaint procedure has generally served as a significant vehicle for the critical evaluation of existing police practices and the development of more adequate departmental policies.

Proposed Improvements in Methods of External Control

The primary need is for the development of methods of external control which will serve as inducements for police to articulate important law enforcement policies and to be willing to have them known, discussed, and changed if change is desirable. There is obviously no single way of accomplishing this.

The task is complicated by the fact that popular, majority control over police policy cannot be relied upon alone. Often the greatest pressure for the use of improper police practices comes from the majority of articulate citizens who demand that "effective" steps be taken to solve a particular crime, to make the streets safe, or to reverse what is often seen as the trend toward an increase of lawlessness.

Effective response to crime is obviously a proper concern of police. But it is also apparent that police policy must strive to achieve objectives like consistency, fairness, tolerance of minority views, and other values inherent in a democratic society.

The creation of an institutional framework to encourage the development and implementation of law enforcement policies

which are effective and also consistent with democratic values is
obviously difficult. To achieve this requires a basic rethinking of
the relationship between the police and legislatures, courts, prosecutors, local government officials, and the community as a whole.

The Legislature. Adequate external control over police policymaking requires first an explicit recognition of the necessity and
desirability of police operating as an administrative policymaking
agency of government. One, and perhaps the best, way to accomplish this is through legislative action which will delegate an
explicit policymaking responsibility to police in areas not pre-
empted by legislative or judicial action. Often it is neither feasible nor desirable for the legislature to prescribe a specific police
practice; there is a need for administrative variation, innovation,
and experimentation within limits set by the general legislative
purpose and such legislative criteria as are provided to guide and
control the exercise of discretion.

Legislative recognition of the propriety of police policymaking should encourage the development of means to develop enforcement policies and their subjection to adequate external
control. It should also encourage flexibility and innovation in
law enforcement while at the same time providing some guidance
to police policy-making through the prescription of appropriate
legislative standards or criteria.

Judicial Review of Police Policymaking. Given explicit legislative recognition of police policymaking, it ought to be possible
to develop effective methods of judicial review which will not
only serve to minimize the risk of improper police practices but
will also serve to encourage the development, articulation, defense, and, if necessary, revision of police policies.

If there is legislative acknowledgment of the propriety of
police policymaking, it would seem to follow that it would be
appropriate for a person, with proper standing, to challenge
existing policy, formal or informal, on the ground that it is
inconsistent with general legislative policy. Where there is challenge, courts would have an opportunity to require the law

enforcement agency to articulate its policy and to defend it, and, if the challenge is successful, to change the policy.

It is possible and certainly desirable to modify the current system of judicial control and to make it consistent with and, in fact, supportive of the objective of proper police policymaking. To accomplish this would require some basic changes in judicial practice:

(a) When a trial judge is confronted with a motion to suppress, he, and the appellate court which reviews the case, should request a showing of whether the conduct of the officer in the particular case did or did not conform to existing departmental policy. If not, the granting of such a motion would not require a reevaluation of departmental policy. However, it ought to cause the police administrator to ask whether a prosecution should, as a matter of police policy, be brought when the officer violated departmental policy in getting the evidence.

If departmental policy were followed, the judge would be given an opportunity to consider the action of the individual officer in the light of the overall departmental judgment as to what is proper policy. Hopefully, a judge would be reluctant to upset a departmental policy without giving the police administrator an opportunity to defend the reasons for the policy, including, where relevant, any police expertise which might bear upon the reasonableness of the policy. To do this will slow down the proceedings, will take judicial time and effort, but if judicial review of police policy is worthwhile at all, it would seem that it is worth doing properly.

(b) Trial judges in multijudge courts should develop appropriate formal or informal means to avoid disparity between individual trial judges in their decisions about the propriety of police policy. The Sentencing Council, created in the Eastern District of Michigan to minimize judicial disparity in sentencing, would seem to be a helpful model. This council uses a panel of judges to consider what is an appropriate sentence rather than leaving the decision entirely to a single judge. The panel serves to balance any substantially different views of individual judges, and results in a more consistent judicial standard. Again, this involves cost in judicial time.

(c) It seems obvious that judicial decisions, whenever possible, ought to be effectively communicated to the police department whose policy was an issue. Yet it is common in current practice for the police administrator to have to rely primarily upon the newspaper as a source of information about judicial decisions, even those involving an officer of his own department. One way of achieving effective communication might be through making the police officer commonly assigned by departments to regular duty in the courtroom responsible for reporting significant decisions to the police administrator. This would require a highly qualified, legally trained, court officer. In addition, trial judges would have to be willing to explain their decisions at least orally, if not in writing.

(d) If the exclusionary rule * is to be a principal vehicle for influencing police policy (as distinguished from disciplining an individual officer who acts improperly) then it seems apparent that the appellate process must be accessible to the prosecution as well as the defense so that inconsistent or apparently erroneous trial court decisions can be challenged. It is nonetheless often urged that allowing appeal in a particular case is unfair to the particular defendant. Moreover, where the authority to appeal does exist, prosecutors often limit appeals to cases involving serious crimes rather than systematically appealing all cases in which an important law enforcement policy is affected.

Other Forms of External Control Over Police Policymaking. Even with carefully drafted legislation and a more adequate system of judicial review, there will still be wide areas of police practice which give rise to very important issues which must be resolved by administrative action without specific legislative or judicial guidance. This is particularly true with regard to the wide range of police contacts with citizens on the street, contacts which usually do not result in criminal prosecution but which do have a major impact upon public order and upon the relationship between police and the community. It is very impor-

* In *Mapp v. Ohio,* decided in 1961, the Supreme Court held that evidence derived from an illegal search and seizure could not be admitted in evidence in state criminal proceedings.

tant that these practices be the subject of careful administrative policymaking and be subject to appropriate methods of external control.

It has been said that one of the major current challenges to our system of governmental control is to devise appropriate methods for safeguarding the exercise of discretionary power by governmental agencies in situations where judicial review is not feasible or not desirable.

Because there is no "best" answer to the question of control over the exercise of discretionary power, it seems obviously desirable to encourage a multifaceted approach, stressing innovation and experimentation, with the hope that, in the process, enough will one day be learned to afford an adequate basis for deciding what methods are best.

The basic need can be stated briefly, though at some risk of oversimplification. It is for giving police policymaking greater visibility, so that the problems and current police solutions are known to the community; to devise methods of involving members of the community in discussion of the propriety of the policies; and to develop in police a willingness to see this process as inherent in a democratic society and as an appropriate way of developing policies which are both effective and supported by the community.

There are some worthwhile alternatives which can be identified:

The Involvement of the Mayor or City Council in Policymaking. It may be helpful, in the long-range interest of law enforcement, to involve local officials in the process of developing enforcement policies, particularly those which have an impact upon a broad segment of the community. If, for example, a police agency is to adopt a policy to govern individual officers in deciding what to do with the down-and-out drunk, it would seem appropriate and helpful to report that policy to the mayor and city council in order to see whether there is opposition from the elected representatives. Where the issue is significant enough, a public hearing may serve to give an indication of the community response to the particular policy being proposed. Although this involvement of city government may give rise to concern over "political influence," the risk of improper influence is minimized by the fact that the involvement is open to view. The vice of political influence of an earlier day was that it tended to be of a personal nature and was secretive.

The Involvement of the Prosecutor and Trial Judiciary. Where a police policy deals with an issue such as investigative practices, which have impact upon the arrest, prosecution, and conviction of offenders, it would seem desirable to involve those other criminal justice agencies which also have policymaking responsibility.

This will require, in practice, a greater interest by the prosecutor who often today conceives of his role as limited to the trial and appeal of criminal cases rather than the development of enforcement policies which anticipate many of the issues before they arise in a litigated case.

The participation of the trial judge on an informal basis in policymaking raises more difficult questions. In theory, the judge is the neutral official not involved until an issue is properly raised in the course of the judicial process. In fact, some trial judges do act as if they are the administrative head of the criminal justice system in a particular community, and do deliberately try to influence policy with regard to when arrests are to be made, who is to be prosecuted, when charges are to be reduced, and other matters which vitally affect law enforcement.

Citizen Involvement in Policymaking. In some areas of governmental activity, there is increasing utilization of citizen advisory committees as a way of involving members of the community in the policymaking process. In some cases, the group may be advisory only, the governmental agency being free to accept or reject its advice. In other instances, the group is official and policies are cleared through the committee as a regular part of the policymaking process. The advantages of both methods are that they serve as an inducement for the police administrator to articulate important policies, to formulate them, and to subject them to discussion in the advisory group. How effective this is depends upon the willingness of the group and the police administrator to confront the basic law enforcement policy issues rather than being preoccupied with the much easier questions of the mechanics of running the department. Where there is a commitment to exploring basic enforcement policy questions, the citizens' advisory group or policymaking board has the advantage of involving the community in the decision-making process, thus giving a broader base than would otherwise exist for the acceptance and support of enforcement policies.

Official or Unofficial Inquiry Into Police Practices. In some other countries of the world there is a greater commitment to continuing inquiry into governmental activity designed to learn and assess what is going on. Thus, in England a royal commission has, on several occasions, been based as a vehicle for helpful inquiry into the state of police practice there. In other countries, especially in Scandinavia, there has been reliance upon the ombudsman, not only as a way of handling complaints, but also as a vehicle for continuing official inquiry into governmental practice, including the practices of police.

There has been less tradition for systematic, official inquiry into governmental practice in this country. Where there has been inquiry into police practice it has commonly been precipitated by a crisis, has been directed toward finding incompetence or corruption, and, whatever the specific finding, has failed to give attention to the basic law enforcement issues involved.

It would be helpful to have systematic legislative inquiry into important police practices at the local, state, and federal level. If devoted to an effort to learn what the existing practices are and to give the police an inducement to articulate their policies and a forum for explaining and justifying them, the process of legislative inquiry can have a positive impact upon the long-range development of the police as a responsible policymaking agency. To achieve this obective, the short run price which police would have to pay in criticism and controversy would be well worth it.

Unofficial studies of law enforcement practices can also be helpful. For example, a bar association may make an important contribution by the maintenance of a standing committee with

important law enforcement policies. The police field would, in
the long run, be aided by the critical, but at the same time sympathetic, interest of the organized bar.

There is also need for greater involvement of universities
and especially social science research into the basic problems
which confront police. Continuing university interest is itself a
form of inducement to confront some of the basic policy questions; and by reporting and critically evaluating current law
enforcement practices research can serve as a method of review
and control in the same way that law review comment has
served this function with regard to the appellate judicial process.
Greater involvement of the university would also serve as a basis
for the development of badly needed social science courses which
deal adequately with the tasks confronting police and the role
which police play in our society. This in turn should increase
the number of educated and articulate citizens who are knowl-
edgeable about and interested in the important problems of law
enforcement and who thus hopefully will constitute a support
for proper police policies.

*Establishing Communication With the Inarticulate Segments of
the Community.* One of the most important ways of asserting
appropriate control over police practice is to have an informed
and articulate community which will be intolerant of improper
police practice. A difficulty in the law enforcement field is that
the groups which receive most police attention are largely inarticulate, and no formal system for the expression of views will
be utilized by the groups. There is need, therefore, for development within the minority community of the capacity and willingness to communicate views and dissatisfactions to the police.

Fulfillment of this need would not only be in the interests
of the community, but is desirable from the police standpoint.
If the minority community could better articulate its needs, a
more balanced community support for the role that the professional police administrator sees himself as filling in a democratic
society would be provided. A stronger minority voice would also
serve to offset some of the pressures brought to bear upon the

police to adopt policies and engage in practices that are of questionable nature.

Secondly, the police have a very practical reason for wanting to be informed about what is bothering the residents of an area. However narrow a focus a police administrator may assume with regard to the development of the police function, it seems apparent that if he is to take seriously his responsibility for preventing outbreaks of violence in his community, he must undertake programs which will keep him informed of the basis for unrest.

There has been substantial progress toward meeting this need through the establishment of a wide range of police-community relations programs. The success of these is in large measure dependent on the degree to which they serve as a vehicle for enabling the otherwise unorganized citizenry to make themselves heard. It seems apparent that programs which rely primarily upon contact with well established and organized interest groups, while of value in their own right, do not serve to meet the kind of needs that are most critical. Properly developed, police-community programs afford an opportunity for police to take the initiative in soliciting the kind of insight into their own operations and the way they affect a community, which should in turn contribute to the development of more adequate police policies.

Total dependence obviously cannot be placed upon the police to assist the minority community in articulating its needs. Indeed, the lack of sensitivity to the problem on the part of the police in some jurisdictions may place the entire burden on other methods, such as the development of community action programs and neighborhood law offices. Services of this kind, which are becoming increasingly available, are likely to bring demands upon the various governmental agencies, including demands that the police review some of their policies for dealing with problems encountered in the ghetto area. A sensitive police administrator ought to recognize that such groups can contribute to a process of development and continuing evaluation of important law enforcement policies.

4. CIVILIAN REVIEW—PHILADELPHIA

Joseph D. Lohman and Gordon E. Mismer

The Formative Years

Establishment of the Board and the first year. The Philadelphia Police Review Board was created on October 1, 1958 by Mayor J. Richardson Dilworth. Mayor Dilworth appointed five community leaders and charged the first Board with:

> The responsibility of considering citizens' complaints against the police where the charges involve brutality, false arrest, discrimination based upon religion or national origin or other wrongful conduct of police personnel toward citizens.[1]

A long tradition of citizen concern for the public weal may account in part for Philadelphia's receptivity to the concept of civilian review earlier than most other major cities faced the question. The presence of a large and active Quaker community has given a tone of responsible public service to concern with the operation of public agencies. Then in the early 1950's the

From *Police and the Community*, A Report Prepared for the President's Commission on Law Enforcement and Administration of Justice, Vol. II, pp. 213-218, 246, 249, 253-266, 270. Published by the United States Government Printing Office, October 1966.

Republican political machine was defeated after 67 years, opening the city government to the introduction of many reforms and innovations. A number of signs of community re-vitalization marked the administrations of Mayor Joseph S. Clark, Jr., (1952-1956) and Mayor Dilworth (1956-1962).

The appointment of the Review Board came after a long period of citizen dissatisfaction with existing avenues for redress of grievances against policemen and followed a struggle by advocates of a review board against those who opposed any review of police work by civilians. Spencer Coxe, since 1952 the Executive Director of the Greater Philadelphia Branch of the American Civil Liberties Union, reports the circumstances leading to the foundation of the Board. According to him, his office received numerous appeals from citizens of Philadelphia alleging misconduct on the part of policemen and summary treatment of their complaints to the Police Department. During the six years prior to the founding of the Board the A.C.L.U. knew of no instance where a member of the Philadelphia Police Department had been disciplined for a wrong done to a civilian as a result of a complaint that originated by a civilian. Within the Police Department the existing avenues of redress were the Commissioner's Office and the Police Board of Inquiry. Coxe reports:

> When the Commissioner's office ordered an investigation complainants found that the matter was likely to peter out; they were usually not notified of any conclusion unless they pressed for a report, when they would be told that the investigations showed that the complaint was without jurisdiction. Complaints referred to the Board of Inquiry turned out the same way.[2]

The A.C.L.U. itself reportedly took a number of these complaints to the Police Department and became convinced that such action led nowhere.

Therefore, the A.C.L.U.'s Board of Directors passed a resolution at their meeting on June 7, 1957, recommending the es-

tablishment of a civilian tribunal to hear complaints of citizens
against the police. The A.C.L.U. took its proposal to the Philadelphia Fellowship Commission, an organization concerned with
inter-ethnic group relations, and to the Philadelphia Bar Association. The Bar Association took no official action, but the Fellowship Commission developed a similar proposal of its own.

In December, 1957, the A.C.L.U.'s President, Attorney
Henry W. Sawyer III, then a member of City Council, proposed
an ordinance "to create a police review board to receive, hear and
determine complaints against personnel in the Police Department." [3] Meanwhile, other members of the City Council became
concerned about "the excess zeal being showed by policemen in
searching houses for numbers-writers—often without warrants, or
with warrants obtained too readily." [4] At the insistence of Councilman Gastano Giordano, hearings were scheduled by the Council's Committee on Law and Government to investigate the
problem of illegal entry. The hearings received wide publicity
and served as a springboard for organizations like the A.C.L.U.
and the N.A.A.C.P. to press for alleviation of all types of citizen
abuse by police that had been brought to their attention.

When Councilman Sawyer's proposed ordinance died in
committee, and no further Council action seemed likely, he took
the case directly to Mayor Dilworth. The hearings had called the
Mayor's attention not only to some possible abuses of police
power but also to the extent of community discontent with the
current modes of redress. Additionally, the A.C.L.U. and the
Fellowship Commission recommendations and Sawyer's proposed
ordinance provided suggestions for possible reform. When Sawyer appealed to Dilworth to establish the review board by executive order, therefore, he found the Mayor sympathetic.

Using the powers of appointment vested in his office under
the City Charter, Mayor Dilworth appointed five citizens to the
first Board. The letters of appointment were accompanied by no
specifications of rules and procedures, nor were funds provided
for expenses or remuneration of appointees. No provision was
made for an office. The Board began to operate very quietly; the
pace of its initial activities reflected the Board members' uncertainty about what they could do and what they should do, given
the generality of their mandate. The Board's records suggest, and

those close to it at that time confirm, that it was cautious. Coxe reports that "during the first eight months, it received few complaints, and disposed of none." [5]

The pace of Board activity quickened in the summer of 1959, when Thomas B. Harvey, Jr., then a law student and now Assistant Director of the Philadelphia A.C.L.U. served as a volunteer executive secretary for the Board. Harvey recalls that when he came to the Board there were no procedures for dealing with complaints or conducting hearings. Working with Board Secretary William T. Coleman, Jr., Harvey was able to begin more systematic methods for handling the Board's business. He took fact-finding initiative on new cases, interviewing the complainants and investigating the incidents that led to complaints.

The late Allen B. Ballard, then Chief Inspector in charge of the Community Relations Division of the Police Department, interviewed the policemen involved and provided the Board with careful prompt reports. Inspector Ballard, a Negro, described as "a man of unusual objectivity, friendliness, and tact," [6] was devoted to improving police-civilian relations and felt that the Board could serve this goal. His cooperation undoubtedly helped the Board gain momentum smoothly.

The Board also enjoyed the strong backing of Mayor Dilworth, who was prepared to give his appointees vigorous moral support, if not money or staff. A report reached the Mayor, for instance, that a policeman whose conduct had been reported to the Board was harassing the complainant. Dilworth fired off a very sharp letter to Commissioner Gibbons, informing him that such retaliation must be halted. Presumably it was.

When Mr. Harvey returned to his studies in the fall of 1959, the Police Review Board had been in existence for nearly a year. While it had not been aggressive nor tremendously active, the Board had moved some distance toward clarifying its responsibilities. The First Annual Report to the Mayor was able to claim a modest start toward fulfillment of its mandate.

> The Board has so far received 29 complaints against police conduct alleged to be within its jurisdiction. . . . Of the 29 complaints, the Board has completed investigation and

rendered decisions in 18 of these cases. Of the remaining
11, six are in the process, one public hearing was continued in order to take further testimony, in two of the
cases public hearings have been held and only the Board's
decision is pending, and there are two other cases on which
the Board is about to hold a public hearing.

Very few recommendations adverse to police officers, were made,
and none was particularly severe. A five-day suspension was
recommended, for example, for a policeman charged with
brutality.

*Some distinguishing characteristics of the Philadelphia
Board.* The Philadelphia Police Review Board (now the Police
Advisory Board) is clearly political in organization. Its creation
and continuation can be traced directly to political pressure from
certain segments of the community. Contrary to popular opinion,
support of the review board among minority groups in Philadelphia has come chiefly from what must be regarded as the moderate side. Members of some of the more militant organizations
do not believe that a review board—as an agent of established
authority, the Mayor's office—can effectively eliminate abuse of
police power.

As an advisory board to the Mayor, serving at his pleasure,
the P.A.B. is unattached to any other bureaucratic agency of the
city government. Therefore, it can act with dispatch and with
regard for the distinctive circumstances of each case without en-
cumbering red tape. The present Executive Secretary maintains
this is a great advantage, enabling the Board to get things done
quickly without following elaborate rules and procedures. Nevertheless, there is always the danger in this arrangement that a
Mayor may decide to disband the Board or to weaken it by
allowing vacancies to persist or by ignoring the Board's recommendations.

The Board members have been outstanding citizens from the
beginning. It has been impossible, however, to match the pres-
tige of the first appointees including the late Clarence Pickett,

holder of a Nobel Peace Prize, and Thorsten Sellin, an internationally recognized student of criminology. Sociologists with an appropriate specialty and at least one attorney have always been included in Board membership. Recently, Mayor Tate appointed two retired police officers in response to the criticism that Board members are ignorant and unappreciative of police operations and procedures.

The initial Board membership was selected with the intent of establishing a balance of representation from various community groups and interests. Vacancies have been filled to the present time in accordance with this policy.

It is reported, for instance, that the Mayor was slow in filling a recent vacancy because he was looking for a qualified man from organized labor. One result of the Mayor's success in maintaining a balanced membership has been a dearth of objections that the Board favors one group to the detriment of others.

As the original statement of the Police Review Board mandate implies, there is no category of complaint to which the Board has been unreceptive. Complaints are not limited to the most blatant misconduct, such as unwarranted physical abuse. Rather, complaints encompass harassment, illegal search and seizure, racial or religious slurs, etc. This policy of inclusion enables the Board to fulfill a broad function for the Mayor and the community-at-large.

Some of the actions the Board has taken were probably not envisioned by its founder. For example, one complaint concerned damage by policemen to the door of a home. The complainant only wanted repairs, and the P.A.B. was able to secure funds for this.

The great variety in types of complaints received by the Board necessitates the flexible handling of individual problems that has always characterized it. There is no predetermined succession of steps through which each case must pass. Sometimes cases are settled without a hearing, sometimes only after an investigation, hearing, and determination by the Board. Some complaints are withdrawn; others are dropped in fact, without formal withdrawal. The Executive Secretary has a considerable role to play in judging whether some informal efforts on his part can effect the redress the complainant seeks. If it is a matter of explaining police rights and procedures, or asking a policeman for an apology, the complainant may be satisfied without the formality of investigation and hearing.

Although investigations follow formal Police Department protocols, and hearings are conducted according to a regular pattern, the hearings have always been relatively informal in comparison to normal courtroom procedures. The tone of Board members at the hearings is sympathetic, tolerant, and solicitous, giving the impression that the Board is more interested in hearing both sides completely and fairly than in enforcing procedural rules. For example, if a complainant is cut off by counsel for the police, the Board gives him a chance to say what he wants to, even though the questioner may have been looking for a simple affirmation or denial. In the same way, police officers are allowed to complete statements and qualify them, expanding or explaining testimony as they desire. The hearings have always been public, although during the last six months very few citizens have attended a hearing unless they were there as witnesses to testify. . . . .

A significant minority of cases, well over one third, are closed without settlement. Many reasons exist, e.g., death of the complainant, inability of the P.A.B. to deliver notice of hearing to the complainant, resignation of the officer, etc. By far the largest number of cases are closed because the complainant fails to pursue the case. He either withdraws the complaint, fails to appear at a hearing, or does not answer the Board's communications. More people have failed to pursue complaints of brutality than all other types combined, even though the majority of individuals do not allege brutality. It is hard to account for this, but it may be that the delays in Board functioning, especially prolonged inability to hear cases, are particularly detrimental to the complainant alleging brutality. The other complaints often can be settled informally without hearing by a letter of apology, expunging a record, etc. But usually the form of redress sought in a brutality complaint is discipline of the officers involved. To arrive at a recommendation of disciplinary action, the Board *must* have a hearing.

Undoubtedly, a large proportion of these complainants who fail to follow through on their initial complaint have become discouraged with the amount of time taken by the whole process of investigation and hearing. Those which have been closed within twenty days are usually cases in which the complainant requests the file closed. At the other extreme, most delays resulted from one of two types of situations. Some were carried as open cases because of the Board's inability to find the complainant after the complaint was filed. Other cases, due either to a F.O.P. court case or to the absence of an Executive Secretary, were carried until the Board resumed normal operations.

Expectations for the Board and its accomplishments. When the Police Review Board was advocated ten years ago and whenever subsequently the matter has been discussed, some very specific hopes for it have been expressed or implied by the supporting arguments. Certainly after eight years it is appropriate to inquire how well the Board has lived up to expectations. But it must be emphasized that evaluations of this sort are extremely precarious. It is nearly impossible to know "what-would-have-happened-if." Furthermore, the P.A.B. records were not kept from the beginning with the intent of facilitating evaluative research, so there are gaps in the information we might have had to help analyze the effects and significance of the Board's work.

Of primary interest are the characteristics of citizens who have complained to the Board. What is the evidence that the P.A.B. serves the disadvantaged members of the community, inhabitants of slums and ghettoes, who in the past have had the most frequent complaints of discriminatory, illegal, or otherwise unjust treatment at the hands of the police officers? Non-Caucasians constitute a larger proportion of the complainants served by the P.A.B. than would be expected, given their proportion in the populations of the city as a whole.

Unfortunately, it is not as easy to tell whether Puerto Ricans utilize the Board. The records do not consistently indicate whether a complainant speaks Spanish or English or another language. A reading of the closed files reveals more than an occasional Spanish name, and from time to time it has been necessary to use interpreters in conducting investigations and hearings. The Mayor's appointment of a Puerto Rican minister to membership on the P.A.B. suggests that these citizens use the Board. In addition, Mr. Farmer has noted during his tenure that many complainants live in the sections of the city inhabited by Puerto Ricans.

There are more non-Caucasian men than any other category of complainant and very few Caucasian women. Some other characteristics of complainants, such as their ages and occupations, are unknown in one third or more of the cases, primarily because the current records system is relatively new. . . . .

The Police Advisory Board was established and supported in the hope that it would assist in relieving hostility and resentment against the city government for wrongs suffered at the hands of the Police. According to the Third Annual Report of the P.A.B.:

> No longer is it necessary for a citizen who has felt himself wronged by police action, to harbor resentment within himself, or to spread his hostile feelings throughout the Community. The Board is at their disposal, ready to receive their problems in a mature and constructive manner.

Yet no one really knows whether citizens who come to the Board are satisfied with the results. Some may return to their homes more frustrated than before. One indication that the Board does relieve individual frustrations emerged from observing and interviewing a number of citizens who have filed complaints and who have had public hearings. Usually they were favorably impressed with the treatment they received in the P.A.B. office.

The citizen who appeals to the Board must be able to trust that it will protect him. Nothing could be more damaging to the individual citizen's morale and faith in his government than systematic—or even random, but frequent—retaliation against complainants. There have been at least three cases of intimidation reported over the years. None of these allegations has been documented, but the occurrence of such reports from time to time leads to the suspicion that now and again some policeman has acted to discourage complaints to the Board.

The existence of the Board may also be reassuring to those who know about it but have never had occasion to use it. Since most of the Board's publicity has centered around the controversy of the court cases, it is difficult to know how widespread knowledge of the P.A.B. is. It is also difficult to know whether its functions are known in the community at large. Self-referrals have not noticeably increased with the passage of time, as might be expected if word were spreading about the Board.

It may not be necessary that many citizens know of the Board personally, however, if those who have a complaint are referred to the Board by community leaders and organizations. Referrals have come in the past from churches, civil rights groups, politicians, other agencies of government, and now and then from the Police Department itself. Perhaps the most noteworthy trend is the growth of referrals from public agencies, while the private groups declined both in absolute numbers and in the percent of all complainants referred. This is another indication of the P.A.B.'s integration into city government.

The relief of community tensions is a responsibility of community organizations as much as it is a responsibility of individuals. The civil rights and civil liberties organizations that originally backed the P.A.B. have for the most part remained concerned about its operations. Whenever the P.A.B. has been under attack from the F.O.P. (Fraternal Order of Police) or whenever the Mayor has failed to fill empty positions, groups like the A.C.L.U. and the Fellowship Commission have been quick to come to the Board's support. Maurice B. Fagan, Executive Director of the Fellowship Commission, in testimony offered during the September 1966 hearings, stated unequivocally that the P.A.B. has rendered great service in reducing community tension. When they send individuals to the P.A.B., these same organizations take an active interest in the case and follow it through.

Their continued use of the Board over its eight-year history, as well as their leaders' responses to interview questions, suggest that they have been satisfied with the results of their referrals.

Obviously, no such Board could please segments of the community. Those individuals and militant civil rights organizations who want a swift, major overhaul of the rules of police practice have not been satisfied with the Board. For example, Cecil B. Moore, President of the Philadelphia Chapter of the N.A.A.C.P., stated during an interview that the Board *does not* serve any important function in the community, not even the function of relieving community tensions. He advocates a more vigorous use of existing channels, in particular the courts, pointing out that recent civil rights laws provide a basis for court action in some types of cases the Board now hears. Moore does not believe in creating special channels, like the P.A.B., for resolving the problem of abuses of police power. "There should be no special court for policemen. If they have done something wrong, you should lock them up like everybody else." His attitude toward the Board is reflected in the decline of referrals to the P.A.B. from the N.A.A.C.P. The P.A.B. serves established authority and is aimed at alleviating strains and untangling problems rather than promoting radical reform. The Board can function on the former level, but it has no power on the latter.

As Mayor Dilworth intended, the Board has also been able to provide the Mayor with useful information on police practices. For example, in the Second Annual Report the following observations appeared:

> It has been noted by the Board that inter-racial gatherings have on occasion been the subject of mass arrests. These arrests usually result in all parties being discharged the following day either as a result of no charges being filed against the parties or, where the charges are filed, on discharge by the magistrate . . . where an arrest is made without legal provocation, then the Police Department as a whole suffers by gaining a bad

reputation and the tensions that exist within the community are multiplied.

In the same report, as well as in subsequent reports, the Board has commented that it found "no general pattern of officially condoned police brutality or discrimination based upon race, creed or national origin." Nonetheless, individual incidents *do* occur, and where they are reported to the P.A.B., the Mayor learns of them. The aggregate statistics are sent to him in the annual reports along with the Board overall observations and analyses. The Mayor also receives copies of Board recommendations in specific cases.

Each year the P.A.B. continues to supply the Mayor with information on the problems it receives from complainants. The Annual Report for 1962, for example, carried a recommendation on the use of handcuffs. The report noted that in some cases policemen were required to use force to overcome resistance in order to effect an arrest, and after the arrest had been made, the individual was not handcuffed. Often, the report stated, the officers later had to use *additional* force to subdue the individual again; this endangered not only the person being arrested but the officers, as well. On the other hand,

There was a case where the officers handcuffed an elderly woman who was arrested for writing numbers and according to the arresting officers did not resist arrest. This was humiliating to the woman who was paraded in handcuffs in front of her neighbors.

The report concluded:

Additional emphasis should be placed in training officers to use handcuffs at the *proper* time—and to use them es-

pecially with belligerent prisoners as a method of reducing violence towards the individuals and towards the
police officers.

Another example of the P.A.B.'s function of supplying the
Mayor with pertinent information about police operating methods is the following observation contained in its most recent
(1965) annual report.

> During 1965 it came to the attention of the Board that
> in a few police district station houses there seemed to be
> some pattern of violence toward and physical mistreat-
> ment of apprehended persons and discourtesy toward
> civilian inquiries. The Board therefore feels that it would
> would be desirable to have an examination conducted,
> preferably by the Police Department itself, into existing
> practices at such police district station houses with a view
> toward ways of improving
>> (a) the avoidance of violence toward and physical
>>   mistreatment of apprehended persons;
>> (b) courtesy toward citizens who make inquiries; and
>> (c) promptness in handling apprehended persons and
>>   citizens' inquiries.

These recommendations are interesting because they show the
P.A.B.'s general interest in seeing police services *improved.* Even
more important, however, is the fact that these recommendations
contain the implicit assumption that the police, themselves, are
quite capable of bringing about needed reform. Recommendations would seem to refute the charge that the Police Advisory
Board is attempting to extend its authority into areas which are
the administrative prerogative of the Police Department. Additionally, these recommendations would seem to demonstrate the
fact that the P.A.B. attempts to be supportive of the Police in
the exercise of their *proper* functions.

Unanticipated ancillary functions of the Board. The Philadelphia Police Advisory Board began with a very broad mandate that specified as the duty of the members only investigation of citizen complaints against the police, followed by recommendations to the Mayor. While accomplishing this task, the Board has provided other opportunities and services to citizens and also to the Police Department. Each of these has further enhanced its effectiveness.

The man or woman who comes as a complainant to the P.A.B. participates very directly in city government. Seeking a Board hearing is calling for an accounting from government employees. Municipal machinery does respond to an *individual* appeal. The citizen's role in the whole procedure is active, rather than passive. Most often he is not represented by counsel. Therefore, it is he who initiates the complaint, presents his case before the Board, and solicits a response from the police. The Negro and Puerto Rican communities in Philadelphia are discovering legitimate and effective avenues to fair treatment, and this may relieve some of the tension in that city. It hopefully helps to reinforce the ideals of a democratic society.

Democracy is only possible, however, where the citizenry understands how the government operates and what its privileges and responsibilities are. Unfortunately, education and information are not universally distributed in our society. Much of the inner core of cities is populated with citizens who are ignorant or bady misinformed about the operations of the major governmental apparatus. The Police Department must be counted as an institution whose *proper* functions are, indeed, poorly understood. Having encountered many citizens who are woefully uninformed about the powers of police officers, the Executive Secretary of the P.A.B. has found that explaining the rights and responsibilities of the police force constitutes a major part of his work.

The Secretary has been successful in interpreting to citizens more clearly what the police are permitted to do, as well as what they are not permitted to do. He has also found himself acting as a link between units of the Police Department. Some citizens apprehended or arrested by the police, for example, have had

their cars impounded. According to their reports, requests to
recover their vehicles were not given prompt or courteous attention at the district police station where they had been taken
originally. Sometimes they were referred to some other station or
to another bureau within the Police Department. The Executive
Secretary has been able to give the citizen the information he
needs and has sometimes acted as a go-between with the Police
Department. Some information the P.A.B. dispenses is probably
available to the citizen elsewhere; indeed, he might obtain it
from the local District Station. As a rule, however, the citizen
is more willing to accept the word of the P.A.B., since it has
no apparent stake in indiscriminant justification of police
actions.

These "service" activities are certainly not central to the
P.A.B.'s mandate, but probably they relieve some hostility toward
the police. Since citizens do not usually file a complaint when
their problems are addressed expeditiously, the P.A.B.'s informal
assistance is not reported as complaints. The Board for its part
has given no evidence that it is eager to process complaints that
are without substance; apparently it does not wish to hold a
hearing just to have the rights of policemen reiterated to a
citizen. Nor does it wish to hold hearings that serve no other
purpose than railing against the police. Furthermore, where it
can provide information to a citizen that will help him get good
service from the police, it creates more amicable relations both
between the citizen and the police and between the Board and
the police.

The Police Department itself has given the Board a role
not originally envisioned for it. Commissioner Brown in 1962
asked the Executive Director to give a course on the P.A.B. to
rookie policemen at the Police Academy. The course has been
offered continually since then. It provides an opportunity for
explaining the Board's functions to new police officers. Among
other things this may help neutralize the propaganda directed
against the P.A.B. by its antagonists.

The Police Commissioner has also received an important
service from the Executive Secretary through the informal liaison
they have personally developed. To be sure, the Commissioner

receives all recommendations made by the Board at its formal hearings. In addition, however, almost daily telephone calls and frequent personal meetings with the Executive Secretary give the Commissioner a number of insights into what takes place within his Department, particularly the nature of citizen grievances against his department.

The information from the P.A.B. is especially useful because it is not the product of the internal communications system of the Police Department. Information generated in large organizations—especially that of a negative or critical nature—faces certain inherent difficulties. A District captain may be cautious about reporting the inadequacies of one of his men simply because any weakness in his command is a reflection on his own capabilities. If reports generated within the Police Department are to be circulated to a wider audience, e.g., the Mayor, the City Council, or the press, emphasis will most assuredly be on the positive side and some information will be suppressed or disguised. The P.A.B. need not worry about such bureaucratic implications of its information, and the Police Commissioner can do with it what he will because he is in no way responsible to the Board.

As an example, at one point the Executive Secretary had received over a period of several months information about a certain police officer assigned to an ethnically homogeneous neighborhood. The police officer, himself a member of the ethnic group, was accused of being too vigorous in carrying out his duties. He maintained to his neighbors, however, that he had to be "tough" to prove himself in the eyes of the other policemen. The situation, if it had persisted, might have become ugly. When the Executive Secretary passed this information along to the Police Commissioner, the officer was re-assigned to a post that would not require his proving his capabilities in a manner detrimental to the neighborhood and to the force.

It should be noted that police departments are not the only public bureaucracies that suffer from this information gap between policy-making and policy-implementing levels. However, since the very nature of police work involves a high degree of efficiency on the part of the individual officer, it is especially

crucial that the Police Commissioner receive as much reliable
information as possible about how policemen are performing
their duty and how departmental practices affect the public.

Restrictions and limitation of the P.A.B. The budget still
severely limits the services which the Board can perform. This
is true despite the annual increases the Board has received. Lack
of money generally leads to delays and poor services with the
possibility that a citizen may feel he is not receiving that attention he deserves. Likely he will hold the Board or its officers
responsible, although "austerity" is not any fault of either the
P.A.B. or its Executive Secretary. That the Board could expand
its services if it had a larger staff and better facilities is obvious.

In particular, the P.A.B. is handicapped because it must
rely upon the Police Department to conduct investigations,
rather than hiring independent investigators. The growth of the
Board's work and the vigorous administration of the present
Executive Secretary tax the one secretary to her capacity. Incom-
ing telephone calls, preparations for the weekly hearings, typing
out complaint sheets, and keeping abreast of necessary corre-
spondence amount to more than one full-time job. From time to
time, as a result, cases get "lost" or delayed for a few days. Furthermore, any errands that take the secretary out of the office
leave the telephone unattended. If the Executive Secretary is
there alone with a complainant, it means that he must interrupt
his interview to answer the telephone.

Lack of adequate facilities also imposes certain limitations
on the operations of the Board. The office itself is small, and
there is no privacy for complainants during interviews. When
the Executive Secretary has a complainant in his small corner of
the office and there is another complainant waiting, the office is
too crowded and confidentiality is jeopardized.

When the Board requested the Department of Records in
1963 to conduct an analysis of the filing system and the general
office procedures, the findings and suggestions indicated that the
Board had been operating on a shoestring. One recommendation
illustrates the conditions of the P.A.B. office:

Exchange one of the legal cabinets for a letter size cabinet, preferably one in better condition than the marginally serviceable cabinets on hand. (Ideally, both legal size cabinets on hand would be replaced by letter size cabinets whose appearance would create a better image of the organization among the many members of the public who come to the office.)

While the situation has improved somewhat since 1963, the filing cabinets themselves are now overflowing into cardboard boxes, making it quite difficult to keep records in suitable condition.

All these restrictions on the Board's activities seem needless. The Board is a service to the public. As long as it is not well staffed, as long as there is insufficient space for persons and records, in fact, as long as the P.A.B. does not have adequate support of all forms, the public will not receive the best consideration and investigation of its complaints.

It should also be noted that the P.A.B.'s effectiveness is dependent upon citizens to bring complaints. The ultimate responsibility for the Board's operations rests with the citizens. Even if the Board believes the police have overstepped their authority, they have no way to initiate action without a complaint. Having no power to subpoena, the P.A.B. must depend upon the cooperation of complainants, witnesses, and members of the Police Department in its investigations and hearings.

Its slow evolution and periodic disruptions have hampered the Board in its role as a link between the citizen and his municipal government. Some cases have been delayed or withdrawn and some complainants have lost touch with the Board when it was enjoined by the courts from holding investigations and hearings and when the position of Executive Secretary was vacant. Presently the P.A.B. is faced with another court case brought by members of the Fraternal Order of Police. If an injunction should be granted against the Board, it will again be restricted from requesting investigations and hold hearings. These breaks in the continuity have a debilitating effect upon citizens who seek to use the P.A.B. The Board needs stability and legitimation if it is to rank among the options a citizen has for redress of grievances.

The Police Advisory Board, as the name now indicates, is an *advisory* group only in fact, it has *never* had power to enforce its findings and recommendations. With the exception of a few cases in the first five years of its operations, the Board has seen its recommendations to the Mayor implemented by the Police Department. The Police Commissioner now reports to the Board on his actions in cases it has heard. This is done, however, only as a matter of courtesy.

Philadelphia has been very fortunate that men and women of high quality and dedication have been appointed to the Board. All members of the P.A.B. serve without compensation, usually while pursuing full-time occupations in the community. If demands on Board members' time become much greater, however, it seems likely that it will be necessary to offer some compensation for the hours spent on P.A.B. business, for service on the Board is time-consuming. During recent months the Board has been meeting for two to three hours weekly simply to catch up with its backlog of hearings. There are also other P.A.B. matters, which take up time in business meetings. For example, the agenda may include the disposition of current cases, a review of the rules and procedures, relationships with other agencies, and organizations or new actions being taken by the F.O.P.

A comparison between the minutes of the Board in 1959-61 and 1965-66 reveals that the Board, when first founded, reviewed each complaint, whereas today the minutes are concerned almost exclusively with business and policy matters. One result of this shift in emphasis is that a great deal of work is delegated to the Executive Secretary. This includes responsibility for decisions that formerly were made by the Board, e.g., whether or not a given case justifies holding a hearing. The administrative reforms introduced during Dr. Gray's tenure are effective only if the Board can utilize the improved records system and exercise its right to review the actions of the Executive Secretary. Because of the increase in the case load, the Board must now accept from the Executive Secretary most of its information about day-to-day business of the P.A.B. without any independent checks.[7]

The present Executive Secretary has developed a very close working relationship with the Police Commissioner. Many of the complaints that come to the P.A.B. can be settled without a hearing, although in some instances this requires the Commissioner's cooperation. As the relationship now stands, the integrity and independence of the Board do not appear to be in jeopardy. On the other hand, organizational studies suggest that the possibility of the P.A.B.'s cooperation by the Police Department is always present.

Arguments against Civilian Review Boards

Introduction. Our presentation thus far has emphasized the conditions and arguments in favor of civilian review. The existence of organized and determined opposition to the principle can be ignored, however, neither by administrators nor politicians nor by anyone attempting to understand the functions of the civilian boards. The opposition is concentrated primarily within organizations of police officers; this is reasonable enough, given the mandate of these boards.

Most of the arguments against civilian review are found, couched in terms specific to Philadelphia, in the petitions of members of the Fraternal Order of Police filed in December 1959 and September 1965. Certain arguments of the petitions pertain specifically to the legality of the Board as presently constituted in Philadelphia. It is likely, however, that arguments with parallel intent are possible in any particular case. There are finally several assertions found occasionally in the public media or in the journals of law enforcement organizations.

General counter-arguments from F.O.P. petitions:

Both petitions claim that police review boards are redundant in functions, that there are other adequate means to gain redress for any citizen who has a legitimate complaint of abuse by the police.

> 1. Police departments themselves have investigative oper-
> ations that handle such complaints, e.g., the Police Board
> of Inquiry, in Philadelphia.
> 2. The courts have amply demonstrated their willingness
> to review police procedures, e.g., the Supreme Court de-
> cisions regarding the right of suspects to legal counsel and
> the right to avoid self-incrimination.
> 3. The Federal Bureau of Investigation also is able to
> investigate cases in which individuals' civil rights may
> have been violated.[8]

Evidence that, at least in some cities, internal administrative review boards are inadequate, mistrusted, or both, has been presented in previous sections of this chapter. Although the Philadelphia Police Board of Inquiry existed in the 1950's, adequate redress of citizen complaints was apparently virtually impossible to obtain. Given their experience, a number of citizens of Philadelphia were not convinced that there *were* adequate avenues for addressing complaints. Similarly, we have pointed out the practical, financial, and legal difficulties which stand in the way of utilizing the courts to obtain the assistance complainants are seeking.

The second petition filed against the Philadelphia Police Advisory Board stated that:

> The existence of the defendant Board has lowered the
> morale of the Policemen;
>
> has tended to undermine the respect of the Policemen for
> their superior officers;
>
> and has resulted in some necessary arrests being avoided

because of fear of retaliative action before the said defendant Board.[9]

What is more, the police claim to have been confronted by individuals who have threatened to take them before the P.A.B. if they were arrested.

Judging morale is an elusive enterprise. Nevertheless, it is doubtful that the existence of the P.A.B. perceptibly influences it, except perhaps in the cases of individual officers who have had to appear before the Board to answer complaints. Recruitment and retention of personnel is, if anything, more successful in Philadelphia than in other large cities. Low pay, occasional periods of extra duty, the tensions associated with the job, and a number of other well-known characteristics of police work in large cities are the first problems to tackle if morale is judged poor. The formal relations between officers and their superiors have not been affected by the Board. Board recommendations, if accepted by the Police Department, are still carried out by normal Departmental procedures.

Given limited community knowledge of the P.A.B. and its work, one is skeptical that more than an isolated few cases can be found of citizens threatening an officer with a complaint to the Board. Even so, if such complaints are deemed threatening, why not the prospect of a court case or a complaint to the Police Board of Inquiry? Unless the plaintiffs are willing to assert that the Board favors citizens over policemen or that the courts and P.B.I favor the policemen—and neither claim is made—then the argument appears inconsequential.

According to many policemen, the members of civilian review boards do not have sufficient understanding of police procedures to judge them. The theory is that police work is a difficult and arduous task and only those who are intimately connected with it can appreciate what is involved. No matter how well meaning the citizens selected for these boards, no matter how impartial they believe they can be, they just do not know enough to make judgments on police practices. Both petitions have made the argument directly or by implicaion.

The allegation has limited validity. After all, how many judges, whose verdicts the petitioners are apparently willing to accept, can claim any background in police work? Nevertheless, the Board and the Mayor have been concerned to improve the experience available to the P.A.B., as the recent appointment to the Board of two retired police officers demonstrates. As has been already argued, the more fundamental question of the right of citizens to review cannot be shunted aside because police work is particularly sensitive and sometimes dangerous.

The second petition for an injunction states:

> The actions of the defendant Board in numerous cases have violated the constitutional rights of the Philadelphia police officers who, after having been found innocent by our courts of alleged felonies or misdemeanors as a result of their conduct in making arrests, have had to again be subject to public hearings before the defendant Board for the same alleged offense.

The policeman, in short, considers himself threatened with double jeopardy by the existence of the Police Advisory Board. Other constitutional issues were raised in the first petition, including the lack of a jury or an appeal from the Board's recommendations. The constitutional question of double jeopardy must be settled by the courts and the legal authorities. It is doubtful, however, that the claim will withstand scrutiny according to traditional constitutional interpretations of the double jeopardy safeguard.

The second petition also claims that the Philadelphia Police Advisory Board has not been able to demonstrate that it serves the functions for which it was created. Over its eight-year history, the petition contends, few instances have been found where the police actually have been at fault. Consequently, very few adverse recommendations have been made. In the few cases where the citizen might have had a valid complaint, the argument goes, the matter could have been settled by going to the Police Com-

missioner in the first place. The P.A.B., therefore, has not contributed much to the task for which it was ostensibly created.
At the same time its operations—the investigations and the hearings—have been costly in terms of man-hours of police effort.
This time could better be used enforcing the law than in defending past enforcement.

As the previous section made plain, there are certainly
limitations on the Board's functioning. Indeed, the restrictions
caused by the petitions of the F.O.P. members curtailed the
Board's activity at least seven months. The remedies hardly lie,
however, in the abolition of the Board. More staff and space,
money to hire its own investigators (thus releasing back to the
Police Department some time now spent in investigation), and
wider publicity in the community seem to hold greater promise
for the Board's fulfillment of its mandate.

Parenthetically, the second petition claims that the Board
has "held extensive hearings" on over 600 cases and recommended suspension in only three instances. This claim is simply
false. As of November, 1965, the Board has recommended fifteen
suspensions, twelve of them prior to August, 1963. The exact
number of hearings is difficult to know, but it was not more
than 375 by November, 1965, according to the report of the
P.A.B. itself. Research for this report suggests that the complaints of about 150 individuals were heard; there were fewer
separate hearings, since sometimes the complaints of two persons
about the same incident would be heard simultaneously.*

Legality of the Philadelphia Board. The establishment of
the Philadelphia Police Advisory Board is called in the second
petition "an unlawful attempt by the Mayor to extend or delegate" the police powers of the city as set forth in the Charter.
Furthermore, the City Civil Service Commission has the power
to advise the Mayor on problems of personnel administration
"and to establish a system for the 'demotion, transfer and dis-

---

* In its nine years of active existence, the Philadelphia Police Advisory
Board handled 932 cases. A total of 521 of them were withdrawn or settled.
Only one dismissal, 20 suspensions and 30 reprimands were recommended
to the police commissioner from 1958 to 1966.—Ed.

cipline of police personnel." The Board is said to be usurping
these powers. Finally, the petition states:

> Plaintiffs believe and aver that the duty to discipline and
> punish members of the Police Department for infractions
> of the Department's rules and regulations, confers upon
> the Mayor and Managing Director and on the Police Com-
> missioner, judicial functions, and that judicial functions
> cannot be delegated.

The Mayor and the City Attorneys clearly do not believe that
the P.A.B., constituted as an advisory committee to the Mayor,
violates the provisions of the Charter. The question of the
Board's legality must be settled by the court.

Other arguments against civilian review:

It is argued that law enforcement is becoming a professional
occupation. The establishment of civilian review boards threatens
this positive development, for one mark of a profession is the right
to discipline its own members without interference from outside.
No doubt the educational achievements of many officers, particularly some of high rank, improvements in training, career
possibilities within the field, and the outstanding administrations
of leading police executives deserve recognition as progress bene-
ficial to all citizens. Nevertheless, rigorous specialized training
is by no means required of all applicants for admission into
police work. The field is not yet, and likely never will be, of
professional character comparable to law and medicine.[10] Unless and until that time should come, policemen can make no
valid claim for the right of internal professional discipline of
members. Furthermore, even the recognized professions of medicine and law do not enjoy the exclusive right of self-discipline.
   Another argument, this one supported by J. Edgar Hoover,[11]
is that police review boards inhibit the enforcement of the law,

and this, in turn, encourages those who are eager to take the law into their own hands. This argument continues by stating that violence in the streets can be directly attributed to a breakdown in respect for law and order, precipitated in part by the creation of such review boards. Once the violence has erupted, restoration of law and order is hampered by the restrictive influence of the review board on officers.

For those who disapprove of civilian review boards this is a nice argument, first for its appeal on behalf of law and order, and second for its near immunity to refutation. Until we understand better the causes and developmental paths of destructive demonstrations and riots, we cannot be sure what conditions do encourage violence. Nevertheless, a few skeptical comments apply. As for officers fearing to do their duty by constitutional methods, the principle has already been discussed. Extremely violent situations are admittedly sensitive and dangerous to a high degree, but they still do not warrant either illegal or unjust police actions. The Philadelphia Police Department has, indeed, been complimented for its handling of the 1964 North Philadelphia riots. Is it possible the existence of a civilian review board was an asset to the Department in this instance? Probably the P.A.B. was not either an asset or a liability. Credit belongs to the commanding officers who developed the strategies and to rank-and-file policemen who carried them out. As for the implications that the existence of a review board encourages rioting, one doubts it, considering that riots have broken out in any number of cities having no civilian review.

Part of the criticism of civilian review boards arises from the fear of "coddling criminals." The board, it is claimed, will simply become the pliable tool of those who have committed crimes but seek to thwart the efforts of the police by harassing them in every possible way. The criminal will be able to drag every officer who arrests him before the boards on whatever charge he feels has the greatest chance of embarrassing the officer. The policemen realize, moreover, that boards comprised of civilians unfamiliar with police practices and less wary of known offenders, will be unable to separate truth from falsehood. Consequently, the police will suffer at the hands of the board, and the criminal will be able to thumb his nose at constituted authority. The powers of the police will be unduly undermined, and the *esprit de corps* so necessary to the force destroyed. Above all, the law-abiding citizen will suffer the most, because he will receive decreased police protection.

The fear of wholesale harassment of police officers by professional criminals appears to be unfounded. Fewer than half a dozen complainants of any description have filed more than one complaint with the P.A.B. in eight years. Using the police investigation reports as our source of information, one cannot conclude that the P.A.B. is a haven for criminals. Since some of the complaints never reached the investigation stage, no determination of possible arrest records could be made in about one case in five. But 50% of complainants clearly did not have arrest records of any kind, nor were they known previously to the Philadelphia Police Department for any reason.

Thirty percent of all complainants did have arrest records, which may include any type of offense from serious traffic violations to homicide. It was impossible to single out those who have ever been convicted from those who have not. Nor were the data sufficient to separate such complainants by the severity of the charges on which they had been arrested.

Even in the context of the incidents that led to complainants, over one third of complainants did not behave so as to warrant an arrest. Of those individuals who were arrested, about 40% were cleared by magistrate's court and the charges dismissed.

The final charge against the establishment of civilian review boards claims they are supported by communists to undermine the effectiveness of the police. Norman H. Moore, a sergeant in the Los Angeles Police Department, in an article entitled "Police Review Boards," links the effort to create such boards in our cities with a communist revolutionary conspiracy.[12] A similar allegation has been made in New York City by the president of the Patrolmen's Benevolent Association, although he admitted having no proof that communists were supporting the civilian-dominated board in that city.[13]

Aside from their emotional appeal, those who contend that the civilian review boards are promoted by communists to undermine law enforcement have yet to produce evidence that such boards limit police effectiveness. Furthermore, these charges are naive in their comprehension of revolutionary tactics. In the first place, communist revolutionaries have traditionally fought any kind of accommodation with the bourgeoisie. For example, trade unions which sought to work within the framework of democratic society have been systematically condemned. In the second place, revolutions are much easier to accomplish when political power and police power are concentrated rather than diffused. Any diffusion of power within the society strengthens democratic institutions and weakens the possibility of easy take-over by revolutionaries.

Finally, it is generally agreed that tension and dissension are necessary prerequisites to revolutions. Where review boards are operative, they are an attempt, at least somewhat successful, to reduce and ameliorate community tensions, thus lessening the possibility of frustrations building up to the point where subversives might use them to serve their own goals. One might conclude, then, that communists are willing to exploit any situation that disrupts community stability, but certainly they do not seek to reduce the aggravation if that means restoration of the old order and the maintenance of the community as organized before.

Editor's Postscript

In a state of suspended animation since March, 1967, the eight member Police Advisory Board was dissolved officially on December 27, 1969 by executive order of Mayor James Tate. Previously in March, 1967, Judge Leo Weinrott of the Common Pleas Court sustained a suit brought by the Fraternal Order of Police and ruled that the board was "illegal and void." Though the Pennsylvania Supreme Court overruled Judge Weinrott's decision, Mayor Tate refused to reactivate it. See the final selection in this volume "Models of Police Politics" by Leonard Ruchelman.

Notes

1. *First Annual Report of the Police Review Board of the City of Philadelphia,* September, 1959, p. 1. (Mimeographed.)
2. Spencer Coxe, "Police Advisory Board: The Philadelphia Story," *Connecticut Bar Journal,* XXXV (June, 1961), 139.
3. *Ibid.,* p. 141.
4. *Ibid.,* p. 142.
5. *Ibid.,* p. 145.
6. *Ibid.*
7. We should note here that the Mayor appoints the Executive Secretary independently of the Board, so that the Board has never had any direct means of sanctioning the Secretary should its members be dissatisfied with any of his practices.
8. At a recent hearing of the P.A.B. an Inspector of the Philadelphia Police Department advised the policemen involved in a hearing not to testify because there was an investigation of the same incident being conducted by the F.B.I.
9. See in the matter of *Harrington, et al., v. City of Philadelphia,* Court of Common Pleas, June Term, 1965, petitioning the court for an order restraining the City of Philadelphia from establishing and maintaining a civilian review board.
10. William J. Goode, "Community within a Community: The Professions," *American Sociological Review,* XXII (April, 1957), 194-200, and Harold L. Wilensky, "The Professionalization of Everyone?," *American Journal of Sociology,* LXX (September, 1954), 137-58.
11. Letter from J. Edgar Hoover addressed to all "Law Enforcement Officials" dated January 1, 1966. Reprinted from the *FBI Law Enforcement Bulletin.*
12. Norman H. Moore, "Police Review Boards," *California Peace Officer,* November-December, 1960, p. 5.
13. *New York Times,* September 20, 1966, p. 48.

5. COMMUNITY CONTROL

Alan A. Altshuler

WOULD COMMUNITY CONTROL BE INIMICAL TO GOVERNMENTAL HONESTY, EQUITY, AND PROFESSIONALISM?

The argument that it would has been made most effectively by James Q. Wilson. In his book, *Varieties of Police Behavior,*[1] Wilson maintains that, historically, the local precinct house—oriented more toward the support of ward politicians than of bureaucratic superiors—was the main locus of police bribery, third degree interrogations, and prison shakedowns. The ward-oriented police were indeed tolerant of neighborhood variations from citywide norms (particularly if the neighborhoods were Irish), and they were kind to the friends of ward politicians. But by the same token they were inclined to disregard the rights of friendless minorities (e.g., suspects in cases involving heinous crimes, sexual deviates, political radicals, and Negroes), to protect illicit enterprises, and to conceal official corruption.

The modern professional department, by contrast, tends to be honest and to treat all citizens alike. It does concentrate its surveillance on suspicious-looking individuals (the young, the poor, the black, and especially individuals who combine these characteristics), but it has statistical justification for doing

From *Community Control: The Black Demand for Participation in Large Cities* by Alan A. Altshuler, pp. 37-44. Copyright © 1970 by Western Publishing Co., Inc., reprinted by permission of the Bobbs-Merrill Company, Inc.

so. Most criminals do fall into these categories. It will be zealous
in enforcing the law, and thus make a great many arrests. It
will emphasize that it lacks discretion to overlook "minor"
offenses or to vary its application of the law to suit neighborhood
norms. This zeal will engender a great deal of hostility in the
groups most subject to arrest. But the member of such a group,
once arrested, will benefit as he is charged, booked, and jailed
in an orderly manner without infringement of his legal rights.

The reality, Wilson admits falls somewhat short of the ideal
just stated. The police are poorly educated, poorly paid, and all
too human. They bring the attitudes of their own subcultures
(primarily white, working class, ethnic) with them to the job.
Thus, racism, brutality, and corruption persist. But they are far
less frequent today than in the past; and they are least frequent
in the most highly professionalized departments.

Ghetto residents want more than honesty and equity from
the police, of course. They want these in a context of effective
crime control. This objective as well, the critics of community
control maintain, requires increased centralization. Patrick Murphy, for example, has recently written as follows:

> The crime control system in the United States is not
> working well. It is seriously breaking down in some cities.
> It is a locally controlled "non-system," minimally influ-
> enced by the states and negligibly influenced by the fed-
> eral government. Fragmentation is at its worst in
> policing. . . .
>
> The poor quality of policing in the nation results not
> only from our uniquely fragmented local arrangement
> (40,000 separate, uncoordinated departments) but from
> the underdeveloped state of the police career. The closed
> personnel systems and lack of educational standards have
> resulted in low levels of education among chiefs as well
> as policemen. . . .
>
> Fragmentation of city police departments could
> weaken crime control. . . . More black policemen are

needed. More black police superior officers are needed. Much better relationships between ghetto residents and police are needed. Much more participation by citizens in crime control is needed. Representative citizen advisory committees at department and precinct levels are needed. . . .

[But] the best interests of the ghetto communities, which have the greatest stake in better crime control . . . , would not be served by separation. They could expect less police protection, even if blacker. . . .[2]

Honesty, equity, and effectiveness, then, the critics argue, all tend to be functions of professionalism. And professionalism tends to depend, *inter alia,* upon insulation from politics and upon large scale. The community control model seems antithetical to both.

A further word of explanation is in order here about the relationship of scale to professionalism. In part, the link is that scale permits the support of specialized recruitment and training programs, of highly paid and high-powered top managers, and of interesting career opportunities for ambitious young men. In part it is that larger systems permit the frequent scrambling of personnel, so that tight cliques (able to protect the inefficient and corrupt) have little chance to develop. And in part it is simply that larger systems—perhaps because they are more complex, perhaps because they are more remote from the ordinary citizen in any event, perhaps because they attract elite participants—have always led the way toward public management reform. Adjustments have to be made for historic and constituency characteristics—in particular, older and poorer communities tend to be less amenable to professionalism—but they provide no comfort for the advocates of community control. Within any given city, one can expect a reduction in scale to mean a reduction in professionalism—least severe in high income neighborhoods, more severe in low. The low income neighborhoods, moreover, are the ones in which rackets are most prone to flourish, providing unusual inducements for the police to become corrupt. It is in precisely these neighborhoods that close central supervision and frequent transfers are most needed.[3]

By way of rebuttal, community control advocates contend that the central issue in the ghettos at present is legitimacy, not efficiency. This is particularly true of Wilson's subject, the police. In the 1969 *Newsweek* poll, fully 46 per cent of the national sample thought that local police were harmful to Negro rights. Among northern respondents under thirty, 70 per cent thought that on balance the police were a force for harm in their communities.[4] If a choice had to be made, it would be justifiable in this situation to trade off some efficiency, and even some honesty, for an alleviation of social tension.

As it happens, however, few Negroes believe that enhanced community control would involve reduced efficiency or honesty. With respect to the former, it bears unceasing repetition that effective law enforcement is impossible without community support. It is senseless to justify a system on the basis of its elaborate testing system or its capacity for rapid response to alarms when its substantive product is poor. The police have themselves become a source of tension, a provocation to disorder, in the ghettos. As Burton Levy has noted:

> Virtually every incident of threatened or actual civil disorder in the urban ghetto began with an encounter between a police officer and a Negro citizen. Whatever the factual reality is—as contrasted by the belief systems—clearly the cops serve as the "flash point" for black anger, mob formation, and civil disorder.[5]

In no other field of public activity, moreover, does the colonial analogy strike such a responsive chord. Joseph Lohman took this as the theme of one of his final articles.

> The young, the poor, and the minority groups [he wrote] have frequently viewed the law as not of their making nor to their interest; the law is that of a foreign power and the police is an army of occupation.

This sense of oppression burned most fiercely, he added, among those "thrice defined in their exclusion and deprivation." The current hostility of ghetto communities to the police was having a "disabling effect upon the law enforcement function." Nor was this hostility gratuitous. The police, he had found, did indeed tend to support the racial status quo with greater zeal than seemed necessary. In general, they blamed all demonstrations on "troublemakers" and pursued a racial "double standard" of law enforcement. The main components of this double standard were a number of assumptions, "taken for granted, like the air they breathe, by many police personnel." Central among these assumptions were the following:

1. The inevitability of vice or law violation when there are contacts between persons of differing racial extraction which are not a customary and accepted pattern of that community.
2. The necessity to enforce with police power the social customs and traditions of the community, apart from law (de facto segregation).
3. The necessity to invoke special action against minority groups which is not invoked against members of the majority group. Demonstrations, stop and frisk practices, and confinement of individuals to special districts are instances of the double standard.
4. The necessity to regard all instances of civil disobedience as without any differentiating characteristics . . .[6]

Wilson would say that such abuses have declined, and will disappear in time, with increased professionalism. But Negroes are impatient, and can point to eminent white observers who disagree, if not with Wilson's trend report, at least with his forecast. Burton Levy, for example, writes that until recently he was a champion for the "professionalism" approach. During 1966 and 1967, however, he had an opportunity for intensive observation of police work in all parts of the nation as a consultant to the

U. S. Department of Justice in establishing its police-community relations program. On the basis of this experience, together with his analysis of newly published studies, he has recently (late 1967) "completely reversed" his position. His current judgment is that:

> The problem is not one of a few "bad eggs" in a police department of 1,000 or 10,000 men, but rather of a police system that recruits a significant number of bigots, reinforces the bigotry through the department's value system and socialization with older officers, and then takes the worst of the officers and puts them on duty in the ghetto, where the opportunity to act out the prejudice is always available.[7]

Levy saw no evidence that recruitment, training, or community relations were anywhere having a significant impact on police practice.

In another recent study, Arthur Niederhoffer has noted that "a defeat is looming" for the advocates of professionalism. Only in periods of economic depression have the police ever been able to recruit middle class, college-educated men. It is these who have provided the thrust toward professonalism. In the current period of prosperity, the recruitment base is essentially confined to working class young men who are anxious for security but who have lacked the means or drive to graduate from college. Such men readily become part of the police subculture, but formal training and indoctrination intended to change that subculture have negligible impact on them.[8]

Even where professionalism is most advanced, its veneer has regularly proven too thin to cope with racial tensions. For example, Wilson cites Oakland as one of the most "professional" forces in the nation, but shortly after his book appeared, it was Oakland police who wantonly shot up the local Black Panther headquarters.[9] In the most thorough study that has been made of the Oakland force, Jerome Skolnick concluded that strong anti-Negro prejudice was a norm among its members, and that a white policeman who failed to share it would be resented by his fellows.[10] During the tenure of Chief William H. Parker, the Los Angeles police force was regularly accounted the most "professional" in the country, but it was infused with racism from top to bottom. Reviewing its performance during the Watts riot, Gary Marx concluded that its "refusal to negotiate or use strategies other than a white show of force may have had disastrous consequences." [11]

Turning from the issue of efficiency to that of honesty, Negroes are inclined to say that here, too, professionalism has been overrated. From their vantage points in the ghettos, they claim to observe a great deal of protection of illicit enterprises. When it is argued that the police may lack authority to shut down these enterprises, or that the courts insist on standards of proof that the police cannot meet, they respond that this merely shows where the real problem of corruption in modern America lies: at the top. They take it for granted that the laws themselves are instruments of power, and have been shaped to serve the interests of rich versus poor, seller versus buyer, lender versus borrower, employer versus employee, white versus black. This is why even the "moderates" consider it vital for blacks to become a thoroughly mobilized pressure group in American politics, and why the more extreme look toward establishment of a separate black nation. (If the 1969 *Newsweek* poll can be believed, nearly one-quarter of American Negroes who have an opinion believe that Negroes should have a separate nation within the United States—21 per cent yes, 69 percent no.[12])

Returning to ground level, they argue that, even if corruption is not the explanation, the police do tend to herd "undesirable" activities into special districts, and that these, almost invariably, happen to be occupied by Negroes. Suburban police, by contrast, just drive them out; and Negro communities want authority to do the same. The issue, once again, is equality.

Would actual corruption be greater in community-controlled than in citywide police forces? The supporters of community control are inclined to respond in the negative. Tight central control and frequent transfers may be one way to limit corruption, but another is to conduct frequent outside audits and undercover investigations. It seems most probable that a system of community control would be accompanied by vigorous surveillance along these lines. White journalists and legislators would be waiting to blow every scandal out of proportion, and to use it as a pretext for takeover. Being fully aware of the precariousness of their autonomy, Negro neighborhoods would be especially zealous in their own efforts to avert scandal.

The preceding discussion has focused on the police; but of course they present the hardest case. In other local buraucracies, the threats of brutality, inequity, and corruption are less severe; organization along tight military lines and the systematic use of transfers to prevent clique formation are less common. This is an appropriate place to add, moreover, (a) *that community control should be conceived as a continuum rather than an absolute,* (b) *that its degree will inevitably vary from one field of activity to the next,* and (c) *that its degree may also vary from one dimension of any given policy arena to the next.* Thus, one might reasonably judge that community influence over the police should be less than that over schools, or that supervision of the police from above with respect to fiscal probity should be greater than that with respect to determining tolerable levels of street disorder.

Notes

1. James Q. Wilson, *Varieties of Police Behavior* (Cambridge, Mass.: Harvard University Press), pp. 286-293.
2. Personal communication from Patrick Murphy to the author. Murphy is presently Police Commissioner of New York City.
3. It should be noted that only the last two sentences of this paragraph are based on Wilson.
4. *Newsweek,* June 30, 1969, pp. 19-21.
5. Burton Levy, "Cops in the Ghetto: A Problem of the Police System," in Louis H. Masotti and Don R. Bowen eds., *Riots and Rebellion: Civil Violence in the Urban Community* (Beverly Hills, Cal.: Sage Publications, 1968), pp. 347-358. This quotation is from p. 349.

6. Joseph Lohman, "Law Enforcement and the Police," in Masotti and Bowen, *ibid.*, pp. 359-372. Lohman, a former sheriff of Cook County (Chicago), at the time of his death in 1968 was dean of the University of California (Berkeley) School of Criminology.

7. Levy, in Masotti and Bowen, *op. cit.*, p. 348.

8. Arthur Niederhoffer, *Behind the Shield: The Police in Urban Society* (Doubleday, 1967), chs. 2, 3.

9. New York Times, September 11, 1968, p. 37. They were aggrieved because Huey Newton, a Panther leader accused of killing a policeman, had just been convicted of manslaughter rather than first-degree murder, and thus could not receive the death penalty.

10. Jerome Skolnick, *Jusitce Without Trial* (Wiley, 1966), pp. 80. 81. Skolnick noted, parenthetically, that even on this force the ordinary patrolman's job was mainly keeping the peace rather than enforcing the law.

11. Gary T. Marx, "Civil Disorder and the Agents of Social Control," paper prepared for the annual meeting of the American Sociological Association, August 1968, mimeo, p. 42. See also Paul Jacobs, *Prelude to Riot* (Random House, 1966), pp. 13-60.

12. *Op. cit.*, p. 20.

II. Police Discretion and the Criminal Justice System

Crucial to effective law enforcement is the average police officer who, at just about any time, must be prepared to judge a situation and decide a course of action. Wherever there is the appearance of trouble, he must decide whether to intervene, how to intervene, whether to make an arrest, and whom to arrest. The more ambiguous the circumstances or the more sensitive community conditions, the greater the difficulty in making a decision.

What adds to the pressures of decision-making, is the fact that a patrolman's discretionary capabilities affect the entire criminal justice system; this includes the public prosecutor, the jury, the judge and correction officials, all of whom must act on legal actions initiated by the patrolman. Where he errs, as for example in using incorrect arresting procedures, the patrolman is informed of this soon enough. This, then, is the basis to a great deal of tension between the police and others who compose the legal system. The special dimensions of this process are treated in the readings which follow.

The first selection by Arthur Niederhoffer called "On the Job," poses the problem of the police officer by exploring the fine "art" of deciding when to take action and when not to take action; in either case, the decision will have an important bearing on the quality and tone of law enforcement in the community. The second excerpt by William A. Westley, "The Courts as Enemy," describes the reasons for the policeman's anxieties in his dealings with other components of the legal system and particularly the courts. Though the piece was written in the early 1950's, it helps to explain why the police often appear to be at war with the judiciary in what is termed the "law and order crisis" of the 1960's and 1970's.

Howard Whitcomb builds on this theme from a national perspective in his essay "Constitutional Revolution in Criminal Procedure." Focusing on the United States Supreme Court, he explains how the police on the state and local levels have increasingly become subject to Bill of Rights limitations which originally served to restrict only federal government authorities. As changes are made in Court personnel, an unavoidable question is whether decisions handed down by the controversial "Warren Court" will be modified and to what extent.

In the final selection, "Interrogation and the Criminal Process," Albert J. Reiss, Jr. and Donald J. Black show that though the law enforcement and the judicial parts of the legal system are interdependent, each has its own operating logic and objectives which make cooperation difficult. Drawing on observations of police field interrogations in the three cities of Boston, Chicago, and Washington, the authors demonstrate the extent to which police can exercise their discretion in light of criminal legal procedures as established by the courts. They also try to test whether the famous *Miranda* decision does indeed limit the police in their role of apprehending criminal suspects as is so often alleged.

1. ON THE JOB—NEW YORK CITY

Arthur Niederhoffer

A potent source of cynicism is the new policeman's realization that it is literally impossible to enforce every law "on the book"—the jails would be too small to hold the prisoners—and that one of the important arts he must master is the sense of when to take action and, perhaps more important, when not to. An officer who brings too many trivial cases into the station house is considered incompetent, but an officer who brings in too few is considered a shirker.

The conventional wisdom of the job sets the standard. The old sages of the station house dispense didactic tales to which new members of the force listen avidly, thereby learning that typical incidents to be settled on the street, or occasionally even dodged, are the annoying drunk, the case of disorderly conduct involving adolescents who congregate on street corners, and quarrels between: husband and wife, taxi driver and his fare, neighbor and neighbor, store owner and customer, and landlord and tenants.

When an officer clearly observes a serious violation of law, his discretion is limited; he must arrest. But the average crime is not committed in full view of the policeman. He must con-

From *Behind the Shield: The Police in Urban Society* by Arthur Niederhoffer, pp. 59-63. Copyright © 1967 by Arthur Niederhoffer. Reprinted by permission of Doubleday and Company, Inc.

duct a preliminary investigation which places him in the middle
of a labyrinth, following conflicting reports of witnesses into
blind alleys. Each suspect denies any connection with the crime.
Perpetrators claim to be victims. From time to time progress is
barred by a wall of silence. Shall he make an arrest or not?
Which of the suspects should he arrest? Just when he needs
them most, the usual guideposts are silent. His wisest procedure
is to trust no one. Cynicism improves his technique as an
investigator.[1]

It is the individual policeman's responsibility to decide if
and how the law should be applied, and he searches for the
proper combination of cues on which to base his decision.
These are derived from the typical sociological variables: class,
education, clarity of role prescriptions, reference groups, self-
conception, and visibility. Because the application of the law
depends to a large degree on the definition of the situation and
the decision reached by the patrolman, he, in effect, makes the
law; it is his decision that establishes the boundary between legal
and illegal.

Always searching for this tenuous and blurred dividing line
in the behavior of others, the policeman frequently loses the
ability to distinguish between law and license in himself. As
the result of United States Supreme Court decisions, kaleido-
scopic changes in the practical application of the law have confused the average patrolman until he is often uncertain of the
proper course of action. His ignorance dims the luster of the
law because the policeman learns to manipulate law in the
name of expediency, and this loss of respect, in turn, breeds
more cynicism.

In the administration of justice, the poor, the minorities,
and the deviants need all the protection possible. They suffer
most when the police fail to take proper action. In busy precincts
covering sections inhabited by Negroes or Puerto Ricans, this
sphere of inaction is large. Incidents that would cause commo-
tion and consternation in quiet precincts seem so common in
ghetto neighborhoods that they are often not reported. The
police rationalize this avoidance of duty with theories that the
victim would refuse to prosecute because violence has become

the accepted way of life for his community, and that any other course would result in a great loss of time in court, which would reduce the efficiency of other police functions. These decisions are rarely subjected to review, a particularly disturbing situation to men who are interested in creating a better system of justice.[2]

> Police decisions not to invoke the criminal process largely determine the outer limits of law enforcement. By such decisions, the police define the ambit of discretion throughout the process of other decision-makers—prosecutor, grand and petit jury, judge, probation officer, correction authority, and parole and pardon boards. These police decisions, unlike their decisions to invoke the law, are of extremely low visibility and consequently are seldom the subject of review. Yet an opportunity for review and appraisal of non-enforcement decision is essential to the functioning of the rule of law in our system of criminal justice.[3]

When the professionals attack this non-enforcement of the law, the articulate defender of the status quo has a powerful riposte: he can plead that the social sciences so profusely quoted by the professionals also teach the lesson of cultural relativity. This doctrine encourages an observer from one culture to respect the integrity of another, although its standards of behavior may be different from his own. The implication is that the policeman has some justification for accepting a minority group's way of life on its own terms, and thus for acting the way he does. There is no easy answer to this paradox.

A harsher indictment of the police officer's neglect or refusal to enforce the law has been pronounced by Martin Luther King who holds that nonfeasance amounts to malfeasance:

> The most grievous charge against municipal police is not brutality, although it exists. Permissive crime in

ghettos is the nightmare of the slum family. Permissive
crime is the name for the organized crime that flourishes
in the ghetto—designed, directed, and cultivated by white
national crime syndicates operating numbers, narcotics,
and prostitution rackets freely in the protected sanctuaries
of the ghettos. Because no one, including the police, cares
particularly about ghetto crime, it pervades every area
of life.[4]

Notes

1. Despite his typical mistrust, the average policeman fancies
   himself a keen psychologist, who can by intuition, and/or
   experience, sense when a person being interrogated is lying
   or telling the truth.
2. Joseph Goldstein, "Police Discretion Not to Invoke the
   Criminal Process: Low Visibility Decisions in the Administration of Justice," *The Yale Law Journal,* Vol. 69 (1960),
   pp. 574-575. See also Herman Goldstein, "Police Discretion:
   The Ideal Versus the Real," *Public Administration Review,*
   Vol. 23 (September 1963), pp. 140-148; and Wayne R.
   LaFave, *Arrest: The Decision to Take a Suspect into Custody*
   (Boston: Little Brown and Co., 1965).
3. Joseph Goldstein, *op. cit.,* p. 543.
4. Martin Luther King, "Beyond the Los Angeles Riots: Next
   Stop: The North," *Saturday Review,* Vol. 48 (November
   13, 1965), p. 34.

2. THE COURTS AS ENEMY

William A. Westley

The policeman's experience in the courts represents at once his frustration, his triumph, and his crucifixion. Fundamentally, the appearance in the courts is an unpleasant chore which the policeman has to perform. In City X the policeman frequently has to appear in court on his own time and without remuneration for these services. In fact, if he is diligent, he has to spend a great deal of time in court. The court there is under stern political control. The result for the policeman is that he constantly is forced to battle with the court itself, in addition to the defense attorneys. Should he be persistent in prosecuting a case, the case will be postponed one, two, and maybe up to eleven times. Each time the policeman will be forced to leave home, or bed, to appear in court. When he fails to appear, the case is heard and dismissed for lack of prosecution. This needless waste of time, at his own expense, is one of the most frequent gripes of the policeman in City X. Thus, one man stated:

> Suppose you make five arrests. You come in and make reports. Suppose it is midnight shift. Next day you got to go to court. One case is called, you may have to wait

Reprinted from *Violence and the Police* by William A. Westley, pp. 76-82 by permission of the M.I.T. Press, Cambridge, Massachusetts. Copyright © 1970 by The Massachusetts Institute of Technology. This was first published as a doctoral dissertation in 1951.

three or four hours in court, on your own time, this is, and then the case is continued, which means you have to come back another day. With the vice cases, like as not you will get five continuances, which mean five more days in court. Why, I have been to court up as high as eleven times on one case. Why, if you make from fifty to seventy-five arrests in a month you will spend every day in court and then, even then, lots of times you are not finished with a case. Fifty percent of them will be appealed to the criminal court. And then there will be more continuances and more time in court and for all this you get no overtime pay or time off. You know, when you come down to brass tacks there is not much you can say for police work. Not much good about it. About the only thing you can say of it is it's a good steady position.

Another states:

The worst gripe of the policeman is his long hours of work. He has to spend a lot of extra time in the courts and he is lucky if the court is called during the period when he is on work. Most of the time he is off duty and he has to go to court and he doesn't get paid for it. If a man is a vigorous policeman he has to put in about forty days a year over and above his regular duty just in the courts.

In these cases it is clear that the policeman, who works six days a week anyway, has a real source of irritation in the extra unpaid time he has to spend in the courts.

Additionally irritating is the existence of the "fix." One policeman describes the fix as follows:

The first time it dawned on me that there was such

a thing as a "fix" was in a flea trap in ——— Street. Some
Italian woman caught her husband in bed with a blonde
and she was chasing him down the stairs. My partner got
the husband and I got her. We charged them both with
disorderly conduct. I thought it was a good pinch, but
when we came to court my partner took me aside and
said that somebody had put in a good word for them. That
I could go ahead and prosecute the case if I wanted to,
but it was no use because when the fix was on they would
not be found guilty. That's the way it is all the way
around, now, I have learned. When a policeman considers arresting some local yokel, the first thing they think
about is how much drag the guy has got.

In this case one observes the type of experience that makes
the policeman at once suspicious of the courts and gives him a
feeling of helplessness with respect to them. "I thought it was a
good pinch" . . . "somebody had put in a good word for them"
. . . "they would not be found guilty" . . . "now I have learned."
These thoughts and words signify bitterness and resignation.
The case is without much effect, however, since the policeman
evidently had little stake in making the pinch stick. In the case
that follows, the fix occurred even before it got to court. In this
case the officer felt that the pinch was a way of asserting himself,
a way of punishing the culprit.

Well, yes and no. There was a case where we picked
up a guy who got involved in an automobile accident and
he started asking us lots of questions and then telling us
what to do. And he kept it up for so long that the older
policeman finally pinched him for disorderly conduct. On
the way back in the car he kept abusing us, saying things
like "You guys aren't so big," and "Just put your badges
here and I will knock the s--- out of you." I could just
see the older fellow counting to five but he didn't touch
the guy and then when he got him to the station, he says,

"I am a guy under arrest. I am not going to open the door for you, you open the door for me." I could see the other fellow's pressure was beginning to go up but he opened the door for him and then just as we got inside the station the other guy raised his hand like he was going to strike one of us, but then he looked around the room and saw there were a lot of other policemen there, so he didn't do anything.

Well, he hadn't been out more than a half hour when I had to call in for something else and the sergeant said, "You know that fellow you just brought in?" and I said, "Yeah," and he said, "Well, the mayor just came down and bailed him out." I don't know whether that is the fix or not but I do know that it has been two weeks and the case has not come up in court yet. I learned later that he is one of the city employees.

Some of the officers say that there is not much use in making arrests for minor offenses because the judges do not follow through on it, but that is all I know about it. I don't think they would tell me much, my being a captain's brother and everything.

Here the arresting officer was most conservative in telling of the incident and took great care not to give an expression of his feelings with respect to what he obviously felt to be an injustice. The officers had been insulted, they had used great restraint, had followed the legal rulings, had been deprived of satisfaction. In a sense they had been punished for not punishing the man themselves.

We introduce this case at this point not because it demonstrates anything with respect to the court experience itself, but because it is part of the type of political dealings the policeman involves himself in when he brings a case to court, and it illustrates the types of situations that make him lose faith in the courts and find the experience unpleasant.

Another policeman, when asked whether he got much satisfaction from making a good pinch, replied that he didn't because

Half the time you make a good pinch the case never turns up. You find that the turnkey's sheet is red-pencilled. One time I picked up a man on intoxication. He had no driver's license. The next day when I looked at the turnkey's sheet the name was just scratched off. No word said to the policeman. If they would just call us in and tell us that the guy was a friend of the mayor and had a little dough we wouldn't bitch so much, but it's never telling us anything that makes us mad.

These people with friends. Why, one day I picked up two guys. One of them had a gun that was sticking out of his pocket. The other also had a gun on him. The guy with the gun sticking out of his pocket had sentence suspended. The other guy who wasn't even showing the gun got thirty days and a hundred-dollar fine.

This man felt that if they were going to fix a case they should at least let the policeman in on it and not do it behind his back. He expresses the injustice of the court.

Another policeman gave expression to the more general feeling about the uselessness of bringing cases to the courts when he replied to a question as to whether he ever had a case which was never brought to court. He said:

Well, I got one like that right now. It has been two months and I have never seen the guy. It makes the policeman hate to make any pinches. That's the way it is. I remember in school one of the captains told us that there are two kinds of people you arrest: those who pay the fine and those who don't.

This policeman remembers learning about the fix in school, and in learning about the fix he is absorbing a definition of the courts as an agency to partisan pressures. He learns that the

court is not a dependable institution of punishment, one that
will uphold him in his judgments.

The actual experience of the policemen in the courts tends
to substantiate his feelings about them. Here he finds himself
the supposed expert who does not know his business. The defense attorney at once points to him as an authority on the law
and demonstrates his inadequacy in this respect. One policeman
stated that he disliked lawyers; when asked why, he replied:

> Well, I think you will find that most policemen feel
> the same way about it. You work on a case, you know
> you got a conviction, and then the damned lawyer will
> do anything to get his fee. They accept cases and I know
> they accept cases plenty of times when they know the
> man is guilty. They just set out to confuse you on the
> stand. Why this fellow —— in ——, you probably heard
> about him, famous criminal lawyer. Took the case one
> time where I was testifying about a drunken driver. He
> had driven into another car, broken two people's legs
> and the back of a woman in the process. When we got
> there we found him behind the wheel, stinko. He was out.
> Just sleeping there behind the wheel. Snoring. We hauled
> him in.
>
> Well, this lawyer, he starts out and he asks me, "Did
> you ever work twenty-four hours a day in a shift?" and
> I said, "Yes, I have worked twenty-four hours in a shift."
> He said, "Anybody ever wake you up after being asleep
> like that after you have worked twenty-four hours?" I said
> I didn't recall anything like that, but I have been waked
> up out of a sleep. He said, "Did the telephone ever ring
> while you were asleep?" I said, "Yes," and he said, "And
> when you got up to answer it maybe you didn't know
> exactly what you were doing?" I said "Yes."
>
> He said, "Maybe you didn't walk so straight, you
> staggered a little," and I had to say, "Yes." Well, he never
> did ask me what the man's breath was like, or anything
> like that. Of course not, and I'll be damned if they didn't
> let the guy off.

> Well, now, you can't tell me this lawyer didn't know that the guy was drunk. They are all like that. Boy, that's the last thing in the world I would want my kids to be is a lawyer, and there is not one of them would want to be one.

In the defense attorney the policeman finds a source of irritation, one who manages an interpretation of the law that makes his head swim. Again, the defense attorney often has connections that cause the prosecutor to give at best a futile and weak support to the policeman. The policeman is insecure about his knowledge of the law; he may know that a man is guilty of some transgression but when it comes to a matter of interpeting the law, as the lawyer does, he finds himself the helpless victim of a facile and confident man. The prosecutor is his only protection in this situation, but as we have pointed out, the prosecutor also has his political responsibilities and thus sometimes only offers token aid to the testifying officer. Thus, the testifying officer is likely to emerge embittered, bewildered, and suspicious of the whole court procedure. As in the example cited, he is made the fool and does not enjoy the part.

To protect themselves, the policemen in Department X are carefully instructed by their superior officers before they appear in court. They are told what to say and when to keep their mouths shut. Generally, the idea is to get one good straight story and stick to it through anything. The men themselves appreciate the threat of court and frequently tell of spending the night before with the case on their minds, carefully planning how to outwit the defense attorney.

The policeman's triumph comes when the court vindicates his judgment by a conviction. For the policeman this represents the conclusion of a case he has been working on. If he has defined his relationship with the suspect as one of competition, the conviction represents a victory. At any rate, a conviction reassures him of his own competence and at the same time of the worth of his job. It makes him feel that he is actually achieving something. It thus gives meaning to his life and his work. It provides for him a reassurance as to the correctness of his judgments.

This last point is of more consequence than one might think.

The policeman, being essentially a man of action, must have the confidence to make quick, sure judgments. Frequently, he is in situations where he must judge the guilt or innocence of a particular person. To make such a judgment, he has to be certain of himself. Once he has made such a judgment, he finds it difficult to admit that he is wrong, for this would indicate uncertainty. This fear of uncertainty thus forces him to stick to his initial judgments, in the face of contrary evidence and in spite of the decisions of the court. In this connection the court poses a double threat. On the one hand, the court may not uphold his judgment as to the guilt of the party, and on the other hand, should the court find the man not guilty, the man can then turn around and sue the policeman for false arrest. The policeman, needing the security of past judgments for future judgments, tends to rationalize away the decisions of the court. This is easy to do by saying, "The man was guilty all right, but we just didn't have enough evidence to make it stick," or "The fix was on."

The threat of false-arrest suit is one aspect of the uncertainty for which the policeman has found some recourse. Many of them are taking out insurance from Lloyd's of London. One policeman stated:

> By the way, I am taking out insurance by Lloyd's of London against the false-arrest suits. It's six dollars in the beginning and then three dollars a year and they protect you up to five thousand dollars. That will take a weight off my mind. The only trouble is that they don't protect you against assault charges.

The anxiety that is expressed here with respect to the possibility of false-arrest suits adds to the general unpleasantness that the policeman feels about the courts.

To summarize, the policeman's experience with the courts is one in which he finds an unjust and tiresome chore because of extra time and lack of pay. Because of the defense attorney's interrogations, he often feels that he is being tried rather than the culprit. He is made to play the part of the fool. He is often frustrated in his attempt to make a pinch stick by the political machinations of the courts and the existence of the fix. He tends to lose faith in the courts of justice and in obtaining the support of the courts for his judgments. He may feel that the only way in which the guilty are going to be punished is by the police. He has anxieties about the results of court action, for if the prisoner is declared innocent, he, the policeman, may be subject to a suit for false arrest. He sometimes gets great satisfaction from his court appearances, for when he obtains a conviction he has at once a sense of having accomplished something and a proof of his own competence.

3. CONSTITUTIONAL REVOLUTION IN CRIMINAL PROCEDURE

Howard Whitcomb

Concepts of justice change as society changes and this in turn affects law enforcement. At no time in American history has this been more clearly demonstrated than during the so-called "Warren Court" era, from 1953 to 1969. Legal challenges during this period involved the Supreme Court in a number of sensitive areas including school desegregation, internal security, reapportionment, separation of church and state, obscenity, and freedom of expression. Of the welter of criticism aimed at the Court's pronouncements, however, none has been as intensely and bitterly motivated as that in the area of criminal procedure.

Causing great concern to law enforcement authorities as well as the general public, has been a series of decisions which attempt to establish uniform standards of procedural due process in state and local criminal proceedings; the intention is to make such proceedings comply with federal standards as defined by the Bill of Rights of the United States Constitution. Previous to the Warren Court, the federal judiciary had only shown minimal interest in either the rights of the accused or the tactics used by law enforcement officers in state and local jurisdictions. "Most Americans assumed, without question, that the procedural guarantees of the Bill of Rights would be available to them if they were ever accused of breaking a law; only experts in the

Published for the first time in this book by permission of the author.

field of law realized that this convenient assumption was simply incorrect. Lawyers and others with specialized knowledge of law knew that the procedural rights spelled out in the amendments four through eight of the Constitution would protect citizens from the federal government but not the state (or local) governments." [1]

As the supreme tribunal came to impose an ever more elaborate network of restrictions on traditional and prosecutorial activities, those persons most actively engaged in such activities began to complain. This was to be expected. What was not expected, however, was that the vehemence of their outcry would help generate the "law and order" politics of the present time. Because the constitutional questions at stake have tended to become confused with political rhetoric, this essay attempts to lend some light by tracing the origins and underlying philosophy of such legal development. Was it simply to hamstring law enforcement that the Court so acted or were there other objectives? This essay also attempts to weigh the implications of court imposed limitations for contemporary law enforcement.

Though the ratification of the Bill of Rights occurred in 1791, it was not until 1833 in the case of *Barron v. Baltimore* that the Supreme Court ruled that these amendments to the constitution were designed to serve as protection against federal encroachment alone, and that they did not pertain to state and local governments. Chief Justice Marshall argued that the Bill of Rights "must be understood as restraining the power of the general (federal) government, not as applicable to the States. In their several constitutions they have imposed such restrictions on their respective governments as their own wisdom suggested; such as they deemed most proper for themselves." [2] Marshall's position was to prevail throughout the nineteenth and early twentieth centuries. This was despite the efforts of attorneys who argued that the intent of the framers of the Fourteenth Amendment's due process clause [3] was to extend the protection of all of the provisions of the Bill of Rights to the states and localities as well as to the federal government. In this light, *Gitlow v. New York* in 1925 must be recognized as a case of historical importance: for the first time the Court formally acknowledged that provisions of the Bill of Rights could be held applicable to the states. Speaking for the majority, Mr. Justice Edward T. Sanford stated that "we may and do assume that freedom of speech and of the press—which are protected by the First Amendment from abridgment by Congress—are among the fundamental personal rights and 'liberties' protected by the due process of the Fourteenth Amendment from impairment by the states." [4] The import of the Sanford dictum [5] in *Gitlow* became apparent two years later in *Fiske v. Kansas* when for the first time the Supreme Court upheld a personal liberty claim under the due process clause of the Fourteenth Amendment.[6]

By 1937, a time when the New Deal of Franklin D. Roosevelt was beginning to effect broad national change, the question of the application of the Bill of Rights to state and local jurisdiction had become sufficiently commonplace to warrant a more theoretical discussion of the developments since *Gitlow*. In a landmark decision, *Palko v. Connecticut* (1937), Mr. Justice Benjamin Cardozo provided the needed theoretical framework. Cardozo enumerated the provisions of the original Bill of Rights which had been incorporated to distinguish them from provisions where incorporation arguments had been rejected. Then he stated his rationale: "(t)he line of division may seem to be wavering and broken if there is a hasty catalogue of the cases on the one side and the other. Reflection and analysis will induce a different view. There emerges the perception of a rationalizing principle which gives to discrete instances a proper order and coherence. The right to trial by jury and the immunity from prosecution except as the result of an indictment may have value and importance. Even so, they are not of the very essence of a scheme of ordered liberty. . . . Few would be so narrow or provincial as to maintain that a fair and enlightened system of justice would be impossible without them." [7] According to Cardozo's formula, the protections of the First Amendment [8] and the right of the criminally accused to the benefit of counsel in a capital case [9] were "implicit in the concept of ordered liberty, and thus through the Fourteenth Amendment, became valid as against the states." [10] However, the Fifth Amendment guarantee against double jeopardy, at issue in the *Palko* case, was not held to be essential to an enlightened system of justice and therefore it was not made applicable to the states.

Thus, Cardozo articulated the doctrine that was to become known as "selective incorporation," a doctrine that has continued to command the support of Supreme Court majorities. According to one observer, "what the Cardozo opinion accomplished was to deny or reject any *general* rule of over-all incorporation, while acknowledging that there are, and indeed must be, some rights in a Bill of Rights that are fundamental enough to require 'incorporation' or 'absorption.' " [11]

It wasn't long before another rationale appeared in a dissenting opinion by Mr. Justice Hugo Black in the case *Adamson v. California* (1947). Although Black had joined in the "selective incorporation" rationale of Cardozo in his first term on the Court, he chose to use his *Adamson* dissent as a vehicle for articulating an absolutist position: "My study of the historical events that culminated in the Fourteenth Amendment, and the expressions of those who sponsored and favored, as well as those who opposed its submission and passage, persuades me that one of the chief objects that the provisions of the Amendment's first section, separately and as a whole, were intended to accomplish was to make the Bill of Rights applicable to the states." [12] Black did qualify this position somewhat by noting that if the choice was between the selective process of *Palko* and no incorporation whatsoever, he would prefer the selective process. This was to prove to be a strategic concession since he would eventually lose the jurisprudential battle but win the war.[13] Though Black never persuaded a majority of his colleagues to accept the absolutist position, the Court eventually expanded its concept of what constituted an "enlightened system of justice" during the 1960's so as to include nearly all of the procedural protections of amendments four through eight. In other words, the series of majority opinions based upon a theory of "selective incorporation" would eventually represent the vindication of Justice Black's views in *Adamson*.

Mr. Justice Felix Frankfurter, in his concurring opinion in *Adamson*, further confused matters by advocating a third position on incorporation. He subscribed to neither the Cardozo

selective incorporation nor the Black absolutist position; rather
he argued that the Fourteenth Amendment due process clause
itself, without regard to the more explicit terminology of amendments four through eight, afforded a mechanism for overturning
a state court decision where there had been a clear denial of a
"fair trial." This so-called "case by case" method, makes no
reference to incorporation of the Bill of Rights, wholly or in
part, but turns on considerations such as whether the procedures in question "shock the conscience." For example, in
Rochin v. California, Frankfurter concluded "that the proceedings by which this conviction was obtained do more than offend
some fastidious squeamishness or private sentimentalism about
combatting crime too energetically. This is conduct that shocks
the conscience. Illegally breaking into the privacy of the peti-
tioner (defendant), the struggle to open his mouth and remove
what was there, the forcible extraction of his stomach's contents
—this course of proceeding by agents of government to obtain
evidence is bound to offend even hardened sensibilities. They are
methods too close to the rack and the screw to permit of constitutional differentiation." [14] Furthermore, Frankfurter responded to the critics of this "case by case" approach by noting
that "(w)e are not unmindful that hypothetical situations can be
conjured up, shading imperceptibly from the circumstances of
this case and by gradations producing practical differences despite seemingly logical extension. But the Constitution is 'intended to preserve practical and substantial rights, not to
maintain theories.' " [15] This "fair trial" or "case by case" stance
on the incorpation question was to be carried on during the
1960s by the younger John Marshall Harlan; however, it was not
destined to command support of the Court majority.[16]

By 1961 the "Warren Court" was prepared to actively intervene in the field of state and local criminal procedure. The
emergence of an activist majority is attributable, in part, to
personnel changes on the Court; but it is also likely "that the
Warren Court overthrew the status-quo in the field of criminal
procedure because a majority became committed to a particular
judicial and political philosophy." [17] Specifically, the Court majority became committed to the use of the theory of selective

incorporation as an instrument for established uniform standards of procedural due process in state and local criminal proceedings. In *Mapp v. Ohio,* the Court by the narrowest of margins held that evidence secured by police officers in violation of the Fourth Amendment's "unreasonable searches and seizures" provision was inadmissible in a state criminal proceeding—what is called "the exclusionary rule." Thus the Court eliminated one of the great incongruities in the interpretation of the Fourth Amendment. Previously, in *Wolf v. Colorado* (1949) the Court had held that the "unreasonable searches and seizures" provision was applicable to the states. At the same time, however, it had not been willing to apply the longstanding federal exclusionary rule to the states.[18] In other words, the 1949 incorporation of the Fourth Amendment was an illusory protection to the defendant in a state criminal proceeding, since he still could be convicted on the basis of illegally seized evidence. The *Mapp* decision occasioned a vigorous Harlan dissent. Harlan felt that rather than reaching out to overrule *Wolf* it would behoove the Court to "continue to forbear from fettering the States with an adamant rule which may embarrass them in coping with their own peculiar problems in criminal law enforcement." [19]

The much celebrated *Gideon v. Wainwright* case of 1963 represents another important Warren Court precedent. Here the Court unanimously reversed a decision rendered twenty-one years earlier and ruled that a state must furnish counsel to indigent persons accused of noncapital offenses. Gideon had been sentenced to serve a five-year term in a Florida prison after he had unsuccessfully tried to conduct his own defense in a jury trial on the charge of breaking and entering a poolroom with intent to commit a misdemeanor. Lacking funds, he had been unable to hire a lawyer, and under Florida law only a person charged with a capital offense was entitled to a public defender. The Supreme Court which received Gideon's petition recognized that "in our adversary system of criminal justice, any person haled into court, who is too poor to hire a lawyer, cannot be assured a fair trial unless counsel is provided for him." [20] When tried again with counsel in the Florida courts, Gideon was found not guilty. It is noteworthy that while most of the criminal procedure decisions of the 1960's were widely criticized, the Gideon decision was received with public acclaim. In fact, the states themselves appeared prepared to provide indigents with counsel as evidenced by the fact that twenty-three filed an *amicus curiae* brief [21] on behalf of Gideon thereby urging the Supreme Court to impose a new standard of procedural fairness on the states.

The following year the Court extended the Fifth Amendment's self-incrimination provision to state criminal proceedings in *Malloy v. Hogan,* thus setting the stage for the controversial *Miranda* case. Although *Miranda v. Arizona* (1966) is not technically an "incorporation" case, it nevertheless warrants brief explication because of its notoriety. Here, the plethora of issues relating to constitutional rights during police interrogation were reviewed. Speaking for the majority, Chief Justice Warren ruled on the applicability of the self-incrimination and right-to-counsel provisions of the Fifth and Sixth Amendments respectively:

> (T)he prosecution may not use statements . . . stemming from custodial interrogation of the defendant unless it demonstrates the use of procedural safeguards effective against self-incrimination. By custodial interrogation, we mean questioning initiated by law enforcement officers after a person has been taken into custody or otherwise deprived of his freedom of action in any significant way. As for the procedural safeguards to be employed, unless other fully effective means are devised to inform accused persons of their right of silence and to assure a continuous opportunity to exercise it, the following measures are required. Prior to any questioning, *the person must be warned that he has a right to remain silent, that any statement he does make may be used as evidence against him, and that he has a right to the presence of an attorney, either retained or appointed.* (Emphasis added.)[22]

The derivation of the four-fold procedural warning summarized above, can be traced to the *Gideon and Malloy* decisions. Obviously, if those two decisions had not incorporated the right to counsel and self-incrimination provisions of the Bill of Rights, the Court would have not likely intervened on questions concerning procedural safeguards in police custodial interrogations.

The Supreme Court's agenda in the 1967-1968 term afforded another opportunity to incorporate one of the major procedural protections of the Bill of Rights: the jury trial provision of the Sixth Amendment. However, just as students of the Court were becoming familiar with the mayor's reasoning processes in cases raising issues of "selective" incorporation, the rationale changed. Mr. Justice White described the new approach to the incorporation debate in an extended footnote in *Duncan v. Louisiana:*

> In one sense recent cases applying provisions of the first eight amendments to the States represent a new approach to the "incorporation" debate. Earlier the Court can be seen as having asked, when inquiring into whether some particular procedural safeguard was required of a State, if a civilized system could be imagined that would not accord the particular protection. For example, *Palko v. Connecticut* . . . stated: "The right to trial by jury and the immunity from prosecution except as the result of an indictment may have value and importance. Even so, they are not of the very essence of a scheme of ordered liberty . . . . Few would be so narrow or provincial as to maintain that a fair and enlightened system of justice would be impossible without them." The recent cases, on the other hand, have proceeded upon the valid assumption that state criminal processes are not imaginary and theoretical schemes but actual systems bearing virtually every characteristic of the common-law system that has been developing contemporaneously in England and in this county. The question thus is whether given this kind of system a particular procedure is fundamental— whether, that is, a procedure is necessary to an Anglo-American regime of ordered liberty.[23]

Thus, the focus of the debate shifted to an even more rigorous inquiry than that which had existed since the *Palko* decision of 1937. Since the majority believed that trial by jury in criminal cases was fundamental to the American scheme of justice, it held that the Sixth Amendment's jury trial guarantee was applicable to the states by virtue of the due process clause of the Fourteenth Amendment.

Finally, on the last decision day of the "Warren Court," June 23, 1969, the inevitable occurred. In *Benton v. Maryland,* a six-man majority overruled the Cardozo rationale in *Palko v. Connecticut* while incorporating the Fifth Amendment safeguard against being "twice put in jeopardy of life or limb." Mr. Justice Thurgood Marshall held the double jeopardy provision to represent "a fundamental ideal in our constitutional heritage . . . that . . . should apply to the States through the Fourteenth Amendment." [24] Adding that insofar as it is inconsistent with this holding, *Palko v. Connecticut* cannot be upheld. He explained:

> *Palko* represented an approach to basic constitutional rights which this Court's recent decisions have rejected. . . . Our recent cases have thoroughly rejected the *Palko* notion that basic constitutional rights can be denied by the States as long as the totality of the circumstances do not disclose a denial of "fundamental fairness." Once it is decided that a particular Bill of Rights guarantee is "fundamental to the American scheme of justice," *Duncan v. Louisiana,* the same constitutional standards apply against both the State and Federal Governments. *Palko's* roots had thus been cut away years ago. We today only recognize the inevitable.[25]

It was in the context of this decision that Mr. Justice Harlan stated that "Palko becomes another casualty in the so far unchecked march towards 'incorporating' much, if not all, of the Federal Bill of Rights into the Due Process Clause." [26]

The decisions recounted here—*Mapp v. Ohio, Gideon v. Wainwright, Malloy v. Hogan, Miranda v. Arizona, Duncan v. Louisiana,* and *Benton v. Maryland*—along with a series of less well known incorporation cases [27] represent, for all intents and purposes, the vindication of Justice Black's absolutist position. Virtually all of the major procedural protections of amendments four through eight have been incorporated, save the Fifth's indictment by grand jury provision. Though the Court continues to permit the states to utilize an "information" [28] as an alternative to the grand jury indictment, few would seriously maintain that this procedure undermines due process of law.

The Supreme Court was already in the throes of personnel changes when the *Benton v. Maryland* decision was handed down on June 23, 1969. First, Mr. Justice Abe Fortas, President Johnson's unsuccessful nominee for Chief Justice in the summer of 1968, voluntarily relinquished his seat on the Court in May, 1969 in the face of a series of disclosures regarding financial links with a private foundation. Since he already had the resignation of Chief Justice Earl Warren pending the completion of the 1968-1969 Court term, President Nixon was in the enviable position of having two vacancies to fill. Warren E. Burger's nomination to be Chief Justice was promptly confirmed by the Senate; but one full year elapsed before Harry A. Blackmun filled the seat created by the Fortas resignation. In the interim, two of President Nixon's nominations to fill the Fortas seat, Clement F. Haynsworth, Jr. and G. Harold Carswell, had been rejected by the Senate by narrow margins. Consequently, the first complete term under the new Chief Justice was marred by the absence of a ninth Justice. Whereas the Court operated at full strength during the second term under Chief Justice Burger, the resignations of Justices Black and Harlan in September, 1971 hindered Court operations during the latter months of that year. It was not until January, 1972 that the Court was once again operating in full complement with the additions of Louis F. Powell, Jr. and William H. Rehnquist.

In light of these changes in Court personnel, can we now anticipate a break in the pattern of judicial findings which prevailed during the Warren era? If so, in what direction can we expect the Court to shift? With these important questions in mind, it would be useful to examine several criminal procedure decisions handed down by the Burger Court which might offer some clues.

In *Argersinger v. Hamlin* (1972), the Court unanimously overturned the conviction of an indigent defendant who had been denied the right to counsel in a case involving a misdemeanor. The opinion of the Court, written by Mr. Justice Douglas and expressing the views of six members of the Court, stated "that absent a knowing and intelligent waiver, no person may be imprisoned for any offense, whether classified as petty, misdemeanor, or felony, unless he was represented by counsel at his trial." [29] Clearly this decision represents an important extension of the rationale of *Gideon v. Wainwright* where the requirement of counsel for an indigent defendant had turned on narrower grounds.

An even more striking extension of the tenor of Warren Court criminal procedure decisions can be found in the death penalty case, *Furman v. Georgia* (1972). Here the Court was finally speaking on the capital punishment question which had been pending ever since the seating of Chief Justice Burger. The five-man majority held "that the imposition and carrying out of the death penalty . . . constitutes cruel and unusual punishment in violation of the Eighth and Fourteenth Amendments." [30] In addition to the opinion of the Court, each Justice wrote an opinion expressing his personal views. It should not be overlooked that the five-man majority was made up of the "Warren Court" holdovers while the four dissenters were all Nixon appointees.

Counterbalancing these cases, however, are two criminal procedure decisions which seem to indicate a movement away from the Warren Court precedents of *Duncan v. Louisiana* and *Miranda v. Arizona*. In *Apodaca v. Oregon* (1972),[31] five-members of the Court upheld an Oregon constitutional provision which permits verdicts of 10 of 12 jurors in criminal cases except for those involving first degree murder. Joined by Chief Justice Burger and Justices Blackmun and Rehnquist, Mr. Justice White stated that the Sixth Amendment guarantee of jury trial in criminal cases, made applicable to the states by the Fourteenth Amendment, did not require that the jury verdict be unanimous. The four dissenters' views were well summarized by Mr. Justice Stewart: "In *Duncan v. Louisiana* . . . the Court squarely held that the Sixth Amendment right to trial by jury in a federal criminal case is made wholly applicable to state criminal trials by the Fourteenth Amendment. Unless *Duncan* is to be over-ruled, therefore, the only relevant question here is whether the Sixth Amendment's guarantee of trial by jury embraces a guarantee that the verdict of the jury must be unanimous. The answer to that question is clearly 'yes,' as my Brother Powell has cogently demonstrated in that part of his concurring opinion that reviews almost a century of Sixth Amendment adjudication." [32]

In the other decision, *Harris v. New York* (1971), the Court undercut the famous *Miranda v. Arizona* case by a five to four vote. It ruled that a defendant's credibility could appropriately be impeached by the use of earlier conflicting statements procured without the proper *Miranda* warnings. Speaking for the majority, Chief Justice Burger maintained that "(t)he shield provided by *Miranda* cannot be perverted into a license to use perjury by way of a defense, free from the risk of confrontation with prior inconsistent utterances." [33] Speaking for the dissenters, Brennan responded that "to the extent that *Miranda* was aimed at deterring police practices in disregard of the Constitution, I fear that today's holding will seriously undermine the achievement of that objective. The Court today tells the police that they may freely interrogate an accused incommunicado and without counsel and know that although any statement they obtain in violation of *Miranda* can't be used on the State's direct case, it may be introduced if the defendant has the temerity to testify in his own defense." [34]

Basic to the cases reviewed in this article is the fundamental question: where does a democratic society draw the line between the rights of the individual and those of the community as a whole? In America, it is the Supreme Court which has come to play an ever more crucial role in deciding how the line is to be drawn. But, as we have seen, a happy balance between liberty and order is difficult to achieve. In trying to project the future course of the Burger Court, we can take our cues from history which show that the judiciary rarely undertakes a complete break with the past. As demonstrated even by the "revolutionary" Warren Court, it tries to hold on to the old while searching for the new. Thus, while the balance between the rights of the accused and the needs of law enforcement will be drawn somewhat differently in the years to come—certainly a shift to the right seems to be in the making—sensitivity to due process considerations are not likely to be lost. Consequently, those who enforce the laws will still be obliged to give careful attention to the latest Supreme Court pronouncements.

Notes

1. Alan H. Schechter, *Contemporary Constitutional Issues* (New York: McGraw-Hill, 1972), p. 84. Amendments four through eight of the Bill of Rights can be grouped together since they are designed primarily to provide procedural protections in criminal trials.

2. 7 Peters 243, 247-248 (1833).

3. The first section of the Fourteenth Amendment reads as follows: "All persons born or naturalized in the United States, and subject to the jurisdiction thereof, are citizens of the United States and of the State wherein they reside. No State shall make or enforce any law which shall abridge the privileges or immunities of citizens of the United States; *nor shall any States deprive any person of life, liberty, or property, without due process of law;* nor deny to any person within its jurisdiction the equal protection of the laws." (Emphasis added.)

4. 268 U.S. 652, 666 (1925).

5. Dictum, or more properly *obiter dicta,* is an assertion made in a judicial opinion that is not pertinent to the precise issue involved in the case.

6. 274 US 380 (1927). Whereas Sanford's dictum regarding the incorporation of the speech and press provisions had no

bearing on the Court's decision to affirm Gitlow's conviction, it did become the instrument in the *Fiske* case where the Court unanimously overturned a conviction based upon a Kansas criminal syndicalism statute.

7. 302 US 319, 325 (1937).
8. See Cardozo's majority opinion in *Palko* for a catalog of cases incorporating First Amendment provisions.
9. See, in particular, *Powell v. Alabama,* 287 US 45 (1932).
10. 302 US 319, 325 (1937).
11. Henry J. Abraham, *Freedom and the Court,* 2nd ed. (New York: Oxford University Press, 1972), p. 58.
12. 332 US 46, 71-72 (1947).
13. Schechter, *op. cit.,* p. 88.
14. 342 US 165, 172 (1952).
15. *Ibid.,* at 174.
16. A fourth position on incorporation also surfaced in *Adamson.* The "total incorporation plus" theory of Justices Frank Murphy and Wiley Rutledge was essentially an extension of Justice Black's absolutist position; however, Justice Black rejected this theory as being contrary to his literal construction of the Bill of Rights. More specifically, Murphy and Rutledge were not prepared to say that incorporation was "entirely and necessarily limited by the Bill of Rights. Occasions may arise where a proceeding falls so far short of conforming to fundamental standards of procedure as to warrant constitutional condemnation in terms of a lack of due process despite the absence of a specific provision in the Bill of Rights" (332 US 46, 124). This position surfaced anew in the Connecticut birth control case, *Griswold v. Connecticut* (1965), where Mr. Justice Arthur Goldberg stated that "the Ninth Amendment . . . lends strong support to the view that the 'liberty' protected by the Fifth and Fourteenth Amendments from infringement by the Federal Government or the States is not restricted to rights specifically mentioned in the first eight amendments" (381 US 479, 493).
17. Schechter, *op. cit.,* p. 89.
18. In *Weeks v. United States,* 232 US 383 (1914), the Supreme

Court held that the use of evidence secured through an illegal search and seizure was inadmissible in a federal prosecution.

19. 367 US 643, 681 (1961).
20. 372 US 335, 344 (1963).
21. See discussion of strategies involved in the filing of the *amicus curiae* (friends of the court) briefs in the Gideon case in Anthony Lewis, *Gideon's Trumpet* (New York: Random House, 1964), pp. 141-154.
22. 384 US 436, 444 (1966).
23. 391 US 145, 149-150 (1968).
24. 395 US 784, 794 (1969).
25. *Ibid.*, at 794-795.
26. *Ibid.*, at 808.
27. See, in particular, *Robinson v. California,* 370 US 660 (1962); *Pointer v. Texas,* 380 US 400 (1963); *Klopfer v. North Carolina,* 386 US 213 (1967); and *Washington v. Texas,* 388 US 14 (1967).
28. An accusation in the form of an affidavit of evidence brought by a public prosecutor against a person for some criminal offense. Its form and substance differs in no respect from an indictment by a grand jury.
29. 32 L. Ed 2d 530, 538 (1972).
30. 33 L. Ed 2d 346, 350 (1972).
31. 32 L. Ed 2d 184 (1972). Another case, *Johnson v. Louisiana,* 32 L. Ed 2d 152, decided on the same day, raised a similar question; however, it is not considered here since the defendant's trial occurred before the *Duncan* case was decided.
32. 32 L. Ed 2d 184, 193-194.
33. 401 U.S. 222, 226 (1971).
34. *Ibid.*, at 232.

4. INTERROGATION AND THE CRIMINAL PROCESS—BOSTON, CHICAGO, WASHINGTON

Albert J. Reiss, Jr., and Donald J. Black

The legal system in American society is a loosely articulated set of subsystems. Where the criminal law is concerned, the subsystems are law enforcement, the public prosecutor, legal counsel, the judiciary, and corrections. The legitimacy and administrative responsibility for any of them may derive from different government jurisdictions, giving rise to problems of mutual cooptation and control. Nowhere within the legal system is there formal provision for organizational subordination of one subsystem to the other so that decisions in any one subsystem can be directly and effectively enforced in others by administrative or other organizational sanctions. The law itself, rather than organizational implementation, generally governs such relationships.

Though each subsystem is highly dependent upon the others and they are hierarchically organized so that the outputs of one become the inputs of another, each is more highly integrated around its focal orientation than around an orientation that is common to the legal system. This paper focuses on conflict over legitimacy of means that arises between the police in the law enforcement system and the appellate courts in the judicial system. It examines a current controversy over the legality of means

From "Interrogation and the Criminal Process" by Albert J. Reiss, Jr., and Donald J. Black, *The Annals,* 374 (November, 1967), 47 to 57. Reprinted by permission.

of interrogation. The conduct of interrogation by the police has received much attention since the *Escobedo* and *Miranda* decisions of the United States Supreme Court.[1]

All subsystems within the legal system may be regarded in organizational terms as primarily information- and people-processing systems. The law-enforcement system is the major originating point for both people and information about them as they are processed in the legal system. Given the loose articulation of units in the system and their divergent ends, conflict arises as to the means which each organization may use to achieve its immediate organizational ends vis-à-vis those of the legal system qua legal system.

Procedural Conflict in the Legal System

Conflict between the judicial and the law-enforcement subsystems is, in a broad sense, endemic in the legal system, particularly conflict between the appellate courts and the police. The judicial system, especially its higher courts, is organized to articulate a moral order—a system of values and norms—rather than an order of behavior in public and private places. By contrast, the police are organized to articulate a behavior system—to maintain law and order. Theirs is a system of organizational control. Nowhere is this more apparent than in their processing of people and information.

Indeed, the justices of our highest courts and the police officer on patrol represent almost opposite poles in their processing of people and information. The officer in routine patrol is principally oriented toward maintenance of behavior systems and is least likely to interpret the law as he exercises discretion in making decisions. By contrast, a justice of the Supreme Court is least likely to see organizational and behavioral consequences of his decisions and most likely to interpret the law in terms of a moral order.

The police organization bears the major responsibility for implicating persons in the criminal legal system and for gathering information that the public prosecutor may effectively process in the courts. While the information for a case that may be prosecuted effectively in the courts is governed by rules of evidence and procedure, the organizational emphasis of the police is upon generating information that links a person with a criminal event or helps to maintain public order. The appellate courts, however, control the criteria for admissibility of evidence including the legitimacy (legality) of the means for securing it. Their criteria are established by the moral system of the law rather than in terms of organizational criteria of effective enforcement of the law.

To be sure, the appellate courts are enmeshed in the balancing of interests and in the pursuit of such abstract ends as the protection of society and the maintenance of justice. Both ends and interests, however, get defined in terms of a moral order. Where judicial interpretation is concerned, the courts may respond to behavioral and organizational changes, but within the confines of articulating a moral order that is the law. Where law enforcement is concerned, the police may respond to behavioral and organizational changes, but within the confines of organizational control of behavior.

There is an important sense in which the relevance of information to law enforcement differs from its relevance to the courts. Again, this arises from the variation in their functions within the legal system. For the police, the end of securing information is to increase their knowledge of crimes and the solution of crimes by the arrest of persons. Along with the public prosecutor, they have an investment in "making it stick," but their organizational concern is less for the legitimacy of means than for the rather immediate end of enforcing behavior standards. For the appellate courts, information is relevant to the body of the law; it is an issue of law rather than of organizational effectiveness.

Despite a spate of scientific criminology for developing laboratory evidence by police organizations and despite a spate of rules regarding such evidence, the core of information for both systems remains that secured and presented by oral statement. For the police, as for the courts, the oral interview is crucial in supplying information. Whether dignified by names such as interrogation or testimony, it is a structure of question and answer in social encounters, be it the private or public setting, the station house or court room, the office or chambers. Until recently, however, the procedures for eliciting such oral information, whether by the police, lawyers, or judicial officers, have received relatively little formal attention.

Admittedly, there is a considerable body of rules governing the admissibility of evidence in trial proceedings. Such rules generally relate to the conduct of matters *within* the immediate jurisdiction of the court, such as the admissibility of hearsay during the trial. Given the loose articulation of subsystems within the legal system and the absence of any formal central authority to enforce conformity across subsystems, the major means any subsystem has for controlling others in the legal system is through its own operating organization. For the police, control of other subsystems is exercised through the discretionary decision to arrest. For the courts, it is exercised through the control of the admissibility of evidence, particularly by means of the exclusionary rule. *Miranda* is a case in point.

When the court establishes criteria for admissibility, however, it does so within the context of a specific legal issue rather than in terms of a generic legal or organizational problem. Thus, *Miranda* does not come to terms with the general issue of the interview as a mode of gaining information, nor of the role of interrogation, for that matter. Rather, the decision states criteria for the admissibility of admissions or confessions, criteria that relate to the rights of persons with respect to self-incrimination.

Like the police, the behavioral scientist is oriented toward behavior in organizational systems. In designing behavioral research that has relevance to legal issues, not unlike the police he confronts problems of operationalizing legal concepts. This becomes apparent when one attempts to undertake research with respect to the legal issues relating to interrogation, particularly if one regards recent decisions as early cases in a potential series of decisions that may have relevance to information gained through questioning of suspects.

The *Miranda v. Arizona* decision of the United States Supreme Court makes it obligatory for police officers, *inter alia*, to apprise suspects of their constitutional rights before "in-custody interrogation" if the admission gained from the interrogation is to be admissible as evidence. It is far from clear when an "in-custody" situation legally begins, when questioning becomes interrogation, or when information becomes an admission. Furthermore, from an organizational point of view, the limiting of police practices by controlling admissibility of evidence secured through "in-custody interrogation" within an interrogation room of a station-house logically opens the way to greater use of interrogation in field settings. Moreover, for the behavioral scientist, there is a general question of the kinds of information available for processing in the system apart from interrogation. Would the elimination of all questioning within in-custody situations eliminate a major source of information? These are difficult matters for operationalization if they are to have relevance to questions at issue in the legal system.

This paper reports selected findings pertaining to interrogations in encounters between police officers and suspects in patrol settings. For purposes of the field study, an interrogation was defined operationally as any questioning of a probing nature that went beyond mere identification of the person and that led to defining the person as a suspect or offender. The field patrol officer, unlike the detective or officer who interrogates in the now stereotyped setting of the interrogation room at the station, must use an interview or questioning to define the situation and the participants in it. Both the assertion of some authority and the development of facts are essential elements in such a process.[2]

Furthermore, in field patrol work, the officer usually encounters suspects in the situation where an event is presumed to have occurred and generally at a point relatively immediate to the event itself. By way of contrast, the detective usually encounters a suspect at a time and place removed from the occurrence of the event—either at the station where the suspect has been brought for questioning or in a public or private place where he seeks information from the suspected person. Interrogation or questioning thus may play a somewhat different role for the two types of officers. Yet in both cases, a central question is how much is gained by questioning or admission that would aid in conviction over and above that already gained from other sources of evidence. If there is a witness to a criminal event prior to the questioning of the arrested person by detectives at the station, what is added through interrogation?

The Observation Study

The data for this paper were gathered through direct observation by thirty-six observers in high-crime-rate police precincts of Boston, Chicago, and Washington, D.C., during the summer of 1966.[3] It should be emphasized that the information pertains only to questioning of suspects by uniformed police officers in encounters of field patrol. To the degree that *Miranda* is strictly interpreted as applying to in-custody interrogations in a station house, the data are not immediately relevant to the frontal issue raised in that decision; rather, they relate more to questions concerning the extension of the *Miranda* rule to field settings.[4]

Patrolmen are the first police to enter most crime situations and hence the first to have contact with any suspects available in the immediate setting. Typically, the police are mobilized to handle incidents in one of two major ways. The great majority of incidents handled by patrolmen arise subsequent to a citizen complaint by telephone followed by a *"dispatch"* to the patrol car. The second major way in which the police become involved in incidents is through *"on-view"* work—police intervention in a field situation that occurs at the officer's discretion rather than in response to a radioed command. The "stop-and-frisk" is an example of an on-view incident. The two types of mobilization carry with them differential opportunities for discretionary action and differential limiting conditions on how the officer exercises his discretion.

Moreover, the way the police are mobilized to deal with incidents affects the kind of evidence they secure, and hence the relative importance of questioning of suspects. The police must link evidence to crimes *and* to violators. Specifically, they must demonstrate that a criminal or other violation has occurred (evidence of a crime) and that a particular person is liable for it (evidence of guilt). Broadly speaking, there are two major kinds of evidence that can be offered in each case—oral and physical. Most oral testimony is by way of witnessing an event or acknowledging participation in it.

Evidence of guilt is differentially available depending upon the type of mobilization in field settings. In on-view encounters with suspects, the major evidence of guilt lies in the testimony of the officer as complainant and witness. Physical evidence such as a weapon in the suspect's possession, stolen property, and the like usually depends as well upon the officer's testimony that it was found in the crime setting or on the suspect. Questioning of the suspect and an admission from him may add little to what is available from the officer in on-view encounters.

Evidence of guilt in dispatched encounters of the police with suspects usually rests upon the testimony of others who are witnesses to the event. This arises from the simple fact that the officer usually arrives after the offense has occurred. Even when there is some physical evidence lending weight to the belief that a crime has occurred, the officer has to rely on testimonial evidence as to who is suspect. Without a sworn complaint in such situations, "probable cause" may not be satisfied. Questioning of suspects and admission thus may loom large as factors in whether or not an officer arrests in dispatched situations, particularly when conflicting statements are made by complainants and suspects. The role that questioning plays in police work then may depend to a great extent on how the officer enters a situation and on what kind of oral testimony is available to him.

Characteristics of Field Interrogations

Patrolmen conduct interrogations in only about one-third of their encounters with suspects. The proportion is roughly the same in dispatched situations and on-view situations. The frequency with which patrol officers interrogate is greater than that with which they conduct personal and property searches, as only one-fifth of the police-suspect transactions included a search. However, in almost one-third of the encounters where an interrogation took place, a search of person, property, or both also was conducted.

One characteristic of field interrogations distinguishing them from those conducted in an interrogation room at a police station is that, not uncommonly, more than one suspect is questioned at the same time. In over one-third of the interrogations observed, two or more persons were questioned, and in about one-fifth, three or more were questioned. That the field interrogation is so often a confrontation between group and group places it somewhat at odds with popular stereotypes of the interrogation as an encounter between one or more officers and a lone suspect. In the absence of other patrol units to lend assistance, the classic technique of separating suspects for interrogation is often unavailable to officers in a field setting. The support and surveillance given by his fellows may well mitigate some of the suspect's vulnerability in such field confrontations.

Most field interrogations—about three-fourths—took place only in a field setting, usually on the street or in a private place such as a dwelling. Nine in ten included interrogation at the field setting, some also involving questioning during transportation to the police station or at the station itself. Less than 5 per cent of the suspects were interrogated only at the station.

Not only did most occur far from an interrogation room, but a substantial majority involved temporary field detention before the suspect was either formally arrested or released. About one-half of the suspects were detained for less than ten minutes and three-fourths for less than twenty minutes. Nearly all of these persons were released in the field setting. Over nine-tenths of the suspects were detained less than forty minutes; nevertheless, about 5 per cent were detained an hour or more before the police made a decision to book or release.

There was a good deal of variety in the content of the questions asked. Field interrogations often have more to do with ascertaining whether or not someone *might* be criminally liable than with extracting a self-incriminating statement from a person already suspected. Mere information-gathering aimed at structuring the facts in the situation is perhaps the major concern of a patrolman entering a possible crime situation. Detectives,

by contrast, ordinarily begin their investigation after the preliminary structuring of the situation by patrol officers. Consequently, about three-fourths of the interrogations had as a
manifest aim something other than obtaining an oral admission
of guilt from the suspect. The questions frequently concerned
such matters as what specifically occurred; the discrepancies in
the versions of the parties involved; whether or not, indeed, the
alleged incident occurred at all; and the like. This is not to say,
however, that such seemingly innocuous probes rarely elicit admissions or incriminating statements. It is during this process
that suspects quite often make admissions voluntarily.

Interrogation of Adult Suspects

There were 248 encounters in which an adult suspect was
interrogated in a field setting by the police. The type of evidence available to the officer on guilt of the suspect is clearly a
function of how the officer entered the setting. Of the 248 encounters where an adult suspect was questioned, 116 (47 per
cent) eventuated in an arrest; exactly one-fourth of the arrests
were made in on-view settings. In 93 per cent of the on-view
arrests as contrasted with 42 per cent of the dispatched arrests,
the officer would have been able to offer some testimony that a
crime event took place in his presence or that he had both evidence and observation that the suspect was definitely linked to
the crime, for example, the suspect had a stolen car in his possession. The differences are even greater considering the fact that
in 66 per cent of all on-view, as compared with 24 per cent of
all dispatched arrests, the *only* evidence available was the on-view
testimony of the officer that the offense occurred in his presence.

Considering the interrogation situations where the officer
did not make an arrest, a similar pattern with sharper contrast
prevails. For 94 per cent of the on-view encounters, the only
evidence available to the officer that the suspect committed the
crime would have been his own testimony, while that was true
for only 11 per cent of all dispatched situations. Put another
way, in dispatched encounters, the officer more often must rely

upon evidence from others to satisfy the criteria of a legal arrest. Indeed, considering the arrests for Part I offenses, when the officer was dispatched, he had to rely upon other evidence in 22 of 29 arrests that were booked, whereas the officer witnessed the three Part I on-view offenses where there was an arrest and booking.

While officers need to rely on other evidence less often in Part II offenses that are booked, the same pattern is evident. Of 42 dispatched Part II offenses booked, 15 had to be made solely on other evidence while for only one of the 23 on-view bookings did the officer have to rely upon other evidence.

Clearly, too, an officer is much less likely to make an on-view arrest for a felony than for a misdemeanor. But three of the 32 bookings for Part I offenses were on-view, whereas 23 of the 65 Part II bookings were on-views. This difference undoubtedly arises from the fact that felonies typically occur in private, as contrasted with public, places; hence felonies in progress are not generally visible to the officer on patrol. The police usually are mobilized to a felony situation by a complainant. Here is a case where the law of arrest complements the empirical pattern of the organization of crime. In felony situations, the law requires only "reasonable grounds" or "probable cause" before a legal arrest is made, whereas in misdemeanor situations there generally is the "in-presence" or "warrant" requirement for an arrest to be made.

The Productivity of Field Interrogations

Recall that a rather broad definition of interrogation was used in the field observation study such that it was considered an interrogation when the officer was directing his questioning toward identifying elements of the crime and assurances that it constituted a bona fide arrest situation. Often he may not have been attempting to elicit a self-incriminating statement as an admission of guilt or a confession *per se*. The officer interrogated in 31 per cent of the 801 nontraffic encounters with adult suspects. That interrogation was not integral to making a field arrest and booking is apparent from the fact that in 54 per cent of the 198 Part I and Part II bookings of adults there was no interrogation. Correlatively, the officer interrogated in 25 per cent of 603 nontraffic encounters with adult suspects where he did not eventually book a suspect. Indeed, only 39 per cent of all 248 interrogations for Part I and Part II offenses led to a booking.

On the whole, the kind of interrogation that the officer conducts in field settings is relatively unproductive of admissions. Of the 116 *arrests* (including suspects never booked) that included interrogation by officers, 91 (78 per cent) did not eventuate in admission. Of the 132 encounters where persons were interrogated and not arrested, 121 (92 per cent) did not involve an admission. About 86 per cent of all encounters involving interrogation did not result in an admission. This is substantially below the figure reported for in-station interrogations where about 50 per cent of all interrogated suspects are reported to make an admission.[5]

Considering only Part I crimes classified as felonies, the situation is not substantially different. Among adult suspects interrogated, there were 27 arrests for felonies and 17 felonies where there was no arrest. Somewhat more than 80 per cent of the encounters with felons did not result in an admission when interrogation took place. Since 78 per cent of all interrogations of arrested persons did not lead to an admission, there is almost no difference in admissions among arrested persons depending upon the seriousness of the criminal charge. In encounters with nonarrested persons, however, a somewhat greater per cent of encounters with nonarrested (15 per cent) than of *all* encounters with nonarrested persons (8 per cent) resulted in an admission. In any case, admission on interrogation in field settings did not make suspects substantially more liable to arrest.

The kind of interrogation conducted in field settings seems remarkably unproductive of admissions of guilt. Of all admissions in field situations, more were made voluntarily prior to questioning than were made after questioning. Among encounters with arrested persons, there were 25 admissions out of 116 interrogations; 68 per cent of these were voluntary admissions before questioning, and the questioning served only to provide the officer with additional information or evidence. Among those not arrested, there were only 11 admissions in 132 interrogations. Of these, 45 per cent were voluntary. Assuming that *Miranda* admits of voluntary confessions under nearly all circumstances, questioning in field settings is at least modestly productive of admissions that clearly would be allowed as evidence in court.[6]

A surprising fact is that admissions after questioning are less productive of arrest than are voluntary admissions in field settings. Of the 22 voluntary admissions before interrogation, 77 per cent eventuated in arrest; of the 14 admissions after questioning, 57 per cent resulted in arrest.

Among the 58 encounters with suspected felons, six resulted in voluntary admissions and three included admissions after questioning. Five of the six, including voluntary admissions, led to an arrest, compared with one of the three admissions after questioning. Though the numbers are so small as to render the comparison of doubtful value, voluntary admission seems more linked to arrest than does admission following interrogation.

Interrogations and Evidence

It is difficult to determine how important interrogation is in producing evidence that eventuates in conviction. Given the fact that evidence is evaluated at each step of a criminal proceeding and not all of it enters the trial proceeding nor judicial determination, there is no *a priori* way of assessing outcomes validly on the basis of evidence. Indeed, given the high proportion of pleas of guilt entered by the defendant, the role of evidence itself is moot in many proceedings. These and other factors make it difficult to determine how important interrogation is in a pattern of evidence.

Nonetheless, certain questions can be asked of the data that are relevant to the general problem of the role of interrogation in a pattern of evidence. One such question concerns how often an admission would be the only form of evidence available. Each interrogation involving a suspect was examined to determine what evidence was available to the patrol officer making the investigation. While detailed information was available on the kind of evidence, a simple distinction was made as to whether the evidence was available to the officer by dint of his personal observation of the alleged offense or through acquisition of physical evidence or testimony by others. In some situations, of course, both, or even all three kinds, were available to the officer.

The striking pattern is that of the fifty felonies committed by adults who were subsequently interrogated, there were only three instances where the officer needed to rely upon interrogation to secure evidence. None of these three cases involved an arrest, however. Further, the three interrogations where there was no evidence failed to yield admissions. All admissions therefore were made when there was other evidence or officer testimony as to occurrence of the event and the implication of the suspect. This suggests that people admit or confess when they are aware that "the evidence is against them."

In three of the thirty felonies where there was an arrest and booking, the officer's only evidence was his own observation. For six of the bookings, the offense was observed by the officer and there also was other evidence; in 21 bookings his case rested upon witnesses or other evidence. In those eight arrests for felonies where the suspect was released without booking, all involved reliance upon other evidence, including witnesses or complainants. Generally, these are situations in which the complainant refuses to sign a complaint that could lead to effective prosecution of the felony. *For every felony arrest, then, whether the suspect was booked or not, the officer would not have needed to interrogate to offer evidence in support of the arrest.* While it could be argued that, for the eight felony suspects released without booking, an admission could have substituted for the failure of the complainant to sign a complaint, none of these suspects made an admission to the officer.

For the twenty felony situations where no arrest was made, the officer could have relied on his own testimony in two cases and evidence from others in fifteen cases. In only three cases was he left essentially without evidence in the field setting, and in each of these the interrogation failed to yield an admission.

It should be clear, then, that in the large majority of cases where an officer interrogates in a field setting following an allegation about a felony, he does have some basis for proceeding, apart from any admission from the suspect, whether or not he actually makes an arrest.

Conclusion

The relative absence of formal provision for the resolution of conflict in the American legal system results in each organization's controlling others in the system through constraints on the processing of people and information as inputs to their own organization. This paper has focused on the specific case where the courts attempt to control the behavior of law-enforcement officers through the exclusionary rule, particularly as set forth in the *Miranda* decision. The data presented relate to arrest and interrogation of suspects in field patrol settings, situations to which *Miranda* potentially may be extended. Furthermore, the data from field settings are of relevance in that they relate to the question of how necessary in-custody interrogation is, given prior processing of suspects in the field patrol setting.

Unfortunately, no study has been undertaken that views suspects in process from the field setting where arrest takes place, through processing in custody, public prosecution, and trial proceedings. In the absence of such general processing studies, the relevance of data on interrogations in field settings for legal issues is debatable. Nonetheless, a few observations are offered, addressed to the specific issues of whether the liability of suspects to criminal charges is substantially reduced by *Miranda* warnings and whether the rate of arrest, in turn, would be substantially affected by their introduction into field settings.

The data for this paper on interrogations of suspects in field patrol settings show that arresting officers always had evidence apart from the interrogation itself as a basis for arrest. Indeed, voluntary admissions were substantially more frequent than were admissions following interrogation. For the most part, however,

interrogation was unproductive of admissions in the field setting. It would appear then that the introduction of *Miranda*-
type warnings into field settings would have relatively little effect
on the liability of suspects to criminal charges, particularly in
felony cases—assuming current police behavior with respect to
arrest.

Nonetheless, it is difficult to define the point at which
Miranda-type warnings should be given in field settings. Quite
clearly, the officer in field patrol must process information by
questioning in field settings in order to define the situation and
the roles of participants in it. At the very least, he must often
use questioning to define the roles of complainant and suspected
offender. Conceivably, the introduction of such warnings very
early in the process of contact with citizens could affect the
liability of suspects to criminal charges adversely from the perspective of the legal system.

The extension of warnings against self-incrimination to field
settings is presumed to affect the rate of arrest adversely. The
general profile of police work that emerges from this investigation, however, suggests that this argument is less forceful than
many presume. The extent to which patrolmen exercise their
discretion not to invoke the criminal process—even in felony
situations—when there is adequate evidence for an arrest, raises
a serious question of whether this effect of the discretionary
decision on liability for criminal charges is not greater than any
potential effect of *Miranda* warnings.

The extent to which the police exercise discretion to arrest
bears on the issue of the consequences of procedural restrictions
in two ways. First, it makes clear the fact that the volume of
cases which police generate as inputs for the prosecutor and the
courts is far from a maximum, given temporary police practice.
Second, their practices throw into relief the degree to which
the law-enforcement system deviates from a prosecution-oriented
model to a community-oriented or behavioral-system-oriented
model of "justice." The release of offenders at police discretion,
for whatever reason, renders ineffective any control system based
on limitation of their outputs as inputs, as is the case with the
exclusionary rule.

A great deal of the conflict between the police and the courts over interrogation procedures may have less impact on the police system than is generally believed. Nevertheless, within the police system, its consequences may be greater for detectives than for routine patrol officers. This difference in consequences may be directly related to the greater organizational distance from criminal violators at which detectives do investigative work. In-station interrogation, unlike routine patrol interrogation, is more prosecution-oriented; hence, existing procedural restrictions in interrogation may be more consequential than would be an extension of those restrictions.

Notes

1. *Escobedo v. Illinois,* 378 U.S. 478 (1964); *Miranda v. Arizona,* 384 U.S. 436 (1966).
2. David J. Bordua and Albert J. Reiss, Jr., "Sociology in Law Enforcement," in Paul F. Lazarsfeld, William Sewell, and Harold Wilensky (eds.), *Uses of Sociology* (New York: Basic Books, 1967).
3. See Donald J. Black and Albert J. Reiss, Jr., "Patterns of Behavior in Police and Cititzen Transactions," in Albert J. Reiss, Jr. (ed.), *Studies in Crime and Law Enforcement in Major Metropolitan Areas,* U.S. President's Commission on Law Enforcement and Administration of Justice Field Survey III (Washington, D.C.: U.S. Government Printing Office, 1967).
4. *State v. Intogna,* 419 P. 2d 59 (Arizona, 1966). The court explained "custodial interrogation" to mean questioning when a person "has been taken into custody or otherwise deprived of his freedom in any significant way." This definition was then applied to an interrogation that occurred in a field setting, with the conclusion that "a defendant questioned by an officer with a drawn gun within three feet of him was deprived of his freedom in a significant way." This case was tried before *Miranda,* but the court followed the interpretation of *Escobedo* given in *Miranda* to rule on the

admissibility of the defendant's admission. *Intogna*, then, represents an early extension of *Miranda* to field settings.

5. A study by the Georgetown University Law Center's Institute of Criminal Law and Procedure found that of the defendants questioned by the police, 34 per cent were interrogated only at the time and place of arrest, 35 per cent at the police precinct, and 25 per cent at both places. Of the suspects interrogated, 45 per cent were reported by their attorneys to have given statements. See "Miranda Impact," *Georgetown University News Service,* July 9, 1967.

6. During the observation period, the *Miranda* warning rarely was given to suspects in field settings. A citizen was apprised of at least one of the rights specified in the *Miranda* decision in 3 per cent of the police encounters with suspects. In only three cases were all four rights mentioned in *Miranda* used in the warning. Even when suspects were apprised of their rights, there is no evidence that they were less likely to make admissions. See Black and Reiss, *op. cit.,* pp. 102-109.

III. POLICE ABUSE

Police misconduct may be defined as the unauthorized exercise of police discretion where the policeman acts without the formal capacity to impose legal sanctions. There are essentially two kinds of police misconduct. One kind occurs in situations where emotions run high such as during mass demonstrations or riots—incidents of police beatings and sometimes killings are examples of what can happen. The other kind of police misconduct is carried out systematically and regularly as revealed in persistent patterns of police brutality or corruption. Both types pose major burdens to society though it can be argued that the latter, i.e., abuse which is deliberate and calculating, is potentially more insidious to the social system.

The various factors which contribute to such forms of behavior are examined in the readings which follow. The first two selections focus on the problem of racial hostility among policemen as measured by its pervasiveness and by the quality of violence that it can generate. "Police in the Ghetto" was initiated by the Kerner Commission and is based on a survey of respondents in fifteen large northern cities. It documents the contention that blacks and whites view their police departments in quite a different light, particularly as to frequency with which police use harassment and abuse. "The Algiers Motel Incident" is much more descriptive in its treatment of an incident which took place during the Detroit riot of 1967. As analyzed by John Hersey, the episode divulges many of the raw ingredients of police-minority tensions: policemen taking the law into their own hands; racist thinking by men who do not believe they are racist; interracial sex.

The third piece called "Police Riot," is an excerpt from the report of a task force study group (the Walker Study Team) for the President's Commission on the Causes and Prevention of Violence. It is based on a 53-day investigation of the battle which took place between Chicago police and demonstrators during the Democratic National Convention of August, 1968. In this blow-by-blow account of events leading to violence, we see how the police, who are supposed to contain riots, actually caused one. But we also see how lack of citizen civility can goad the police into irresponsible action.

In the last selection which treats police corruption, we rely on the testimony of New York City policemen speaking for themselves before a special board of inquiry. The Knapp Commission, named after its chairman Whitman Knapp, was appointed by Mayor John Lindsay in the Spring of 1970 to investigate charges of widespread police graft. Here we get a revealing picture of the ease with which corruption becomes rooted in a police organization and the ways in which average citizens as well as underworld elements contribute to such profligacy. What is perhaps even more significant, we see how difficult it is to reform a system once it goes bad.

1. POLICE IN THE GHETTO

Angus Campbell and Howard Schuman

In view of the importance of the police in the complicated social problems of the cities, our survey invested a considerable segment of the questionnaire in exploring the experiences of our Negro and white respondents with the police of their community. Our data make it clear that this is an area of urban life which looks quite different to white and Negro citizens.

We began this series with a question dealing with what we thought would be the most common complaint that might be offered concerning the police: they do not come quickly when they are called. We asked our respondents first whether they thought this happened to people in their neighborhood, then whether it had ever happened to them personally, and finally whether it had happened to anyone they knew. As Table 1 demonstrates, Negroes are far more likely than whites to feel that people in their neighborhood do not receive prompt police service, one in four of them report they have experienced poor service themselves (compared to about three-fifths as many whites) and they are twice as likely as whites to say they know people to whom this has happened.

From *Supplemental Studies for the National Advisory Commission on Civil Disorder,* The National Advisory Commission on Civil Disorders, pp. 42-43. Published by the United States Government Printing Office, 1968.

Table 1

"Now I want to talk about some complaints people have made about the (Central City) police. First, some people say the police don't come quickly when you call them for help. Do you think this happens to people in this neighborhood?" [In percent]

| | Negro | | | White | | |
	Men	Women	Total	Men	Women	Total
Yes	51	52	51	29	24	27
No	36	31	34	58	62	60
Don't know	13	17	15	13	14	13
	100	100	100	100	100	100

Has it ever happened to you?" [In percent]

| | Negro | | | White | | |
	Men	Women	Total	Men	Women	Total
Yes	24	26	25	16	13	15
No	39	42	40	25	24	24
Don't know	1	0	1	1	1	1
Don't think it happens in their neighborhood	36	31	34	58	62	60
	100	100	100	100	100	100

"Has it happened to anyone you know?" [In percent]

| | Negro | | | White | | |
	Men	Women	Total	Men	Women	Total
Yes	31	35	33	18	15	17
No	27	30	28	20	20	20
Don't know	6	4	5	4	3	3
Don't think it happens in their neighborhood	36	31	34	58	62	60
	100	100	100	100	100	100

The second question dealt with the incidence of the show of disrespect or use of insulting language by the police. The racial differences in response to this inquiry are even more pronounced (Table 2). While relatively few white people felt this sort of thing happened in their neighborhood and even fewer reported it had happened to them or to people they know, substantial numbers of Negroes, especially men, thought it happened in their neighborhoods and many of these reported that they had experienced such treatment themselves.

The third question asked if the police "frisk or search people without a good reason" and the same pattern of racial differences emerges (Table 3). This is not an experience which occurs

Table 2

"Some people say the police don't show respect for people and use insulting language. Do you think this happens to people in this neighborhood?"
[In percent]

	Negro			White		
	Men	*Women*	*Total*	*Men*	*Women*	*Total*
Yes	43	33	38	17	14	16
No	38	41	39	75	75	75
Don't know	19	26	23	8	11	9
	100	100	100	100	100	100

"Has it ever happened to you?" [In percent]

	Negro			White		
	Men	*Women*	*Total*	*Men*	*Women*	*Total*
Yes	20	10	15	9	5	7
No	40	49	45	15	19	17
Don't know	2	0	1	1	1	1
Don't think it happens in their neighborhood	38	41	39	75	75	75
	100	100	100	100	100	100

"Has it happened to anyone you know?" [In percent]

	Negro			White		
	Men	*Women*	*Total*	*Men*	*Women*	*Total*
Yes	28	23	26	12	9	11
No	29	34	32	11	13	12
Don't know	5	2	3	2	3	2
Don't think it happens in their neighborhood	38	41	39	75	75	75
	100	100	100	100	100	100

Table 3

"Some people say the police frisk or search people without good reason. Do you think this happens to people in this neighborhood?" [In percent]

	Negro			White		
	Men	*Women*	*Total*	*Men*	*Women*	*Total*
Yes	42	30	36	12	9	11
No	41	40	41	78	75	76
Don't know	17	30	23	10	16	13
	100	100	100	100	100	100

"Has it ever happened to you?" [In percent]

	Negro			White		
	Men	*Women*	*Total*	*Men*	*Women*	*Total*
Yes	22	3	13	6	1	4
No	36	55	45	16	24	20
Don't know	1	2	1	0	0	0
Don't think it happens in their neighborhood	41	40	41	78	75	76
	100	100	100	100	100	100

"Has it happened to anyone you know?" [In percent]

	Negro			White		
	Men	*Women*	*Total*	*Men*	*Women*	*Total*
Yes	28	20	24	8	6	7
No	28	36	32	12	17	14
Don't know	3	4	3	2	2	2
Don't think it happens in their neighborhood	41	40	41	78	75	75
	100	100	100	100	100	100

to many white people and they do not think it happens in their neighborhoods. Three times as many Negroes do believe it happens in their neighborhoods and report that it has happened to them personally.

Finally, we asked a direct question about "police brutality" —do the police rough up people unnecessarily when they are arresting them or afterwards? Over a third of the Negro respondents reported this happened in their neighborhoods, while 10 percent of the whites so reported (Table 4). Much smaller numbers of both races reported that they had experienced unnecessary roughness themselves but Negroes were four times more likely to report such treatment. Far more Negroes than whites

Table 4

"Some people say the police rough up people unnecessarily when they are arresting them or afterwards. Do you think this happens to people in this neighborhood?"

| | Negro | | | White | | |
	Men	Women	Total	Men	Women	Total
Yes	37	32	35	10	9	10
No	42	41	41	80	76	78
Don't know	21	27	24	10	15	12
	100	100	100	100	100	100

"Has it ever happened to you?" [In percent]

| | Negro | | | White | | |
	Men	Women	Total	Men	Women	Total
Yes	7	1	4	2	0	1
No	50	56	53	18	23	20
Don't know	1	2	2	0	1	1
Don't think it happens in their neighborhood	42	41	41	80	76	78
	100	100	100	100	100	100

"Has it happened to anyone you know?" [In percent]

| | Negro | | | White | | |
	Men	Women	Total	Men	Women	Total
Yes	27	20	24	7	6	7
No	28	35	32	11	15	13
Don't know	3	4	3	2	3	2
Don't think it happens in their neighborhood	42	41	41	80	76	78
	100	100	100	100	100	100

report knowing someone who had been roughed up by the police. The great discrepancy which we find between the numbers of Negroes who say they were themselves unnecessarily frisked or roughed up and the numbers who testify that they know someone to whom this has happened reflects the manner in which reports of such incidents travel through the Negro community.

Reports of unfavorable experiences with the police are clearly more numerous among the younger members of both racial groups than among their elders. . . . Younger people are more likely to think police offenses occur in their neighborhoods, to report that offenses have been committed against them personally, and to know other people against whom they have been committed. . . . [A]brasive relations with the police are not only a racial problem in these northern cities, they are also a problem of youth. Negro young people are much more likely to complain of police offenses than the older generations of their race, especially of those police actions which involve bodily contact. However, the same age trend, about equally pronounced, is found in the white population. These findings are consistent, of course, with police records of the age characteristics of arrestees of both races.

2. THE ALGIERS MOTEL INCIDENT—
DETROIT
John Hersey

"Before we went into the hall, we heard some other shots which sounded like to our right or the back of the building. . . ." One line of speculation followed by the investigators associates these shots with the death of Fred Temple in room A-3; the timing of this death is not agreed upon by various witnesses. "We went into the hall. There was a few people out in the hall going back and forth in the rooms and coming out. They were dressed in light-blue shirts, dark-blue pants, and were wearing helmets"—uniform, during the uprising, of the Detroit police.

"At this time," Fonger * wrote in his report, "a Detroit Officer came out of the room followed by another unloading a nickel covered pistol and saying, 'That one tried for my gun.' It is not clear to this officer if these men were City Policemen, or private policemen, as they were not wearing a badge or other identifying items." It had, however, been clear to Fonger, in the darkness at the back door, that Detroit policemen preceded him into the building.

From *The Algiers Motel Incident* by John Hersey, pp. 248-249, 251-252, 271-272, 281. Copyright © 1968 by John Hersey. Reprinted by permission of Alfred A. Knopf, Inc.
* John M. Fonger is a Michigan state policeman.

"There were two officers that came out," Fonger testified, "and one of them had a nickel-plated revolver and he was taking the shells out of the gun and he said, 'That one tried for my gun,' . . . or, 'That one had a gun.' We then went into the room and there was a Negro male lying against the bed with numerous holes in him—or should I say—I'll have to clarify that also. He was bleeding from the front in numerous spots. His eyes were open."

"It appeared to this officer," Fonger wrote, "that this subject was still alive, as it appeared as he was breathing. . . .

"This officer then went back into the hall and observed two officers dressed as those described above, drag a Negro male with black pants and a black piece of material over his hair out of a room, and put him against a wall of the hall. Another Negro male, with only his under shorts, was then dragged out and also placed against the wall. . . . A remark was made that they should pray."

"We checked the room which would be to the front," Fonger testified, "to the west, which would be probably the southwest corner. . . . We checked this room for snipers. We checked the closet, we checked the bathroom. We came out of the room."

"Shortly after this," he wrote, "two white females were thrown down the stairs, one with a large cut on her cheek. They were told to get against the wall and pray. Other Negroes were also brought down from upstairs and placed against the wall."

*   *   *   *   *

How had Ronald August, Robert Paille, David Senak, and the other Detroit police officers at the Algiers during the incident been trained to behave in these circumstances?

The *Riot Control Plan* of the Detroit Police Department, in a chapter entitled "Guide Lines for the Individual Officer," gives these instructions:

"Maximum effectiveness will result if the officers at the scene are able to gain and hold the respect of the rioting element. This respect will be attained by a thoroughly professional approach to the problem. . . .

"Conduct: Courteous but firm. Policemen must maintain a completely neutral attitude at the scene of a disorder and completely avoid fraternization with either element. He should strenuously avoid the use of insulting terms and names. Expressions which may be used casually without thought of offending are nevertheless offensive to members of minority groups and invariably antagonize the person or group to whom they are addressed. . . .

"Listen to and take command from your superior officers. . . .

" 'Hand-to-hand' fighting or individual combat must be avoided as far as possible. . . .

"Never at any time should a single officer attempt to handle one rioter. The idea of individual heroic police action is not only unnecessary, it may be positively damaging and foolhardy. . . .

"Don't be prejudicial or guilty of unnecessary or rough handling of persons involved. Use only that force which is necessary to maintain order, effect the arrest, and protect oneself from bodily harm.

"The officer assigned to crowd control must always act in such a manner as to insure impartial enforcement of the law, and afford to all citizens the rights guaranteed to them by the Constitution and the legislative statutes."

* * * * *

"One of the officers," Lee * told me, "he said, 'We're going to get rid of all you pimps and whores.' They asked the girls did they want to die first or watch us die."

"Questioned them up against the wall," Early's ** notes said, "& ripped all K's *** clothes off & half of Juli's *** Policeman said, 'Hey, you broads, do you want to die first or see the others & then go?' "

* A witness to the incident, a black man.
** S. Allen Early, Jr., an attorney who took the girls to the authorities.
*** The two white girls.

"One of the policmen," Roderick * said to me, "told the girls to take off their clothes. Senak pulled them out to the center of the room. Tore one of them's dress off—hooked it with the thing on the end of his gun—and made the other one pull her dress off. He said, 'Why you got to fuck them? What's wrong with us, you nigger lovers?'"

Sortor * testified in court that both girls had their dresses torn. "I seen one, had her clothes—uh—off. . . . I seen the officers pull them off. . . . the policemen . . . and some Army mens. . . . All of them pulled, pulled her clothes off her." The girl, Sortor testified, wound up naked except "just her panties."

"The officers," the police synopsis on Sortor said, "had pulled their clothes off and all they had on were their panties."

The girls were returned to the wall. "The girls' dresses were torn from behind. Dismukes ** told me. "The dress had fallen off one and was lying around her feet. The other was holding hers up in front."

A handful of airborne troops, "men in green uniforms," Juli testified, "came in as a group after they had ripped our clothes off." "The soldiers came in," Karen told Early, "and everyone stood around as if they were waiting for something."

The police synopsis of the statement of Wayne Henson,*** who had entered with Thomas *** and never advanced beyond the front doorway, said "Henson observed . . . 4-5 airborne police watching."

"When they'd stripped the girls down," Sortor said to me, "they told me and Lee and them to look at them. Said, 'Ain't you ashamed?'"

The men in uniform who were not hitting people at the wall, Sortor testified, were "just standing back. Just standing there laughing, you know, all like that."

*   *   *   *   *

Warrant Officer Thomas was not alone in his impulse to flee after the murder of Auburey Pollard in the game that he, Thomas,

* Black witnesses.
** A private guard.
*** National guardsmen.

had so blithely joined. The hallway was virtually clear of uniformed men in a very short time. Convenient firing was heard not far away; all but a handful ran to do their duty.

"And then some more shooting started down the block there," Green * told Eggleton.** All of them rushed out of the Manor house there and ran down the block. Two policemen were left there."

"And then I heard some more shooting from outside," Michael,* who was still lying on the floor in A-4 at the time of which he was speaking, testified: "And then some of the officers and all of them went outside because I heard—let's see, the soldier told me, he say, 'That's another one of your friends out there shooting at us.'"

"I remember," Sortor testified, "that I heard officers say they were shooting down the street, and some of them ran out—ran out of there, and that's when the officer—when they left, this officer went into this room and got Michael and them up, and they told us we could leave."

* Black witnesses.
** The Prosecutor.

3. POLICE RIOT—CHICAGO

The Walker Study Team

By about 5 p.m. Wednesday the U.S. Attorney's report says about 2000 persons, "mostly normally dressed," had already assembled at the [Conrad] Hilton [Hotel]. Many of these were demonstrators who had tired of waiting out the negotiations and had broken off from the marchers and made their way to the hotel. It appears that police already were having some difficulty keeping order at that location. Says the U.S. Attorney's report: "A large crowd had assembled behind the police line along the east wall of the Hilton. This crowd was heavily infiltrated with 'Yippie' types and was spitting and screaming obscene insults at the police."

A policeman on duty in front of the hotel later said that it seemed to him that the obscene abuses shouted by "women hippies" outnumbered those called out by male demonstrators "four to one." A common epithet shouted by the females, he said, was "Fuck you, pig." Others included references to policemen as "cock suckers" and "mother fuckers."

A short time later a reporter noticed a lot of debris being hurled from one of the upper floors of the Hilton. He climbed into a police squad car parked in the area and with the aid of police binoculars saw that rolls of toilet paper were coming from

From *Rights in Conflict*, A Report Submitted to the National Commission on the Causes and Prevention of Violence, pp. 235-285. Reprinted in Bantam Books, Inc. Published originally by the United States Government Printing Office.

the 15th floor, a location he pinpointed by counting down from the top of the building. He then went to the 15th floor and found that the section the paper was coming from was rented by Senator McCarthy campaigners. He was not admitted to the suite.

If Dellinger's marchers in Grant Park now moved to the Hilton area, an additional 5000 demonstrators would be added to the number the police there would have to control. . . . . .

The Crossing

At about 6 or 6:30 p.m., one of the march leaders announced by loudspeaker that the demonstrators would not be allowed to march to the Amphitheatre. He told the crowd to disperse and to re-group in front of the Conrad Hilton Hotel in Grant Park. . . . .

Police in the area were in a far from cheerful mood. A neatly dressed sociology student from Minnesota says he stepped off the sidewalk onto the grass and two policemen pulled their billy clubs back as though ready to swing. One of them said, "You'd better get your fucking ass off that grass or I'll put a beautiful goddam crease in your fucking queer head." The student overheard another policeman say to a "hippie-looking girl of 14 or 15, 'You better get your fucking dirty cunt out of here.' " The growing feeling of entrapment was intensified and some witnesses noticed that police were letting people into the park but not out. The marshal referred to the situation as a "trap."

As the crowd moved north, an Assistant U.S. Attorney saw one demonstrator with long sideburns and hippie garb pause to break up a large piece of concrete, wrapping the pieces in a striped T-shirt.

Before the march formally disbanded, an early contingent of demonstrators, numbering about 30 to 50, arrived at the spot where Congress Plaza bridges the Illinois Central tracks at approximately the same time as a squad of 40 National Guardsmen. The Guard hurriedly spread out about three feet apart across Congress with rifles at the ready, gas masks on, bayonets fixed.

Now as the bulk of the disappointed marchers sought a way out of the park, the crowd began to build up in front of the Guard. "I saw one woman driving a new red late-model car approach the bridge," a news correspondent says: "Two demonstrators, apparently badly gassed, jumped into the back seat and hoped to get through the Guard lines. Guardsmen refused to permit the car through, going so far as to threaten to bayonet her tires and the hood of her car if she did not turn around. One Guardsman fired tear gas point blank beside the car." . . . . .

The crowd's basic strategy, a medic recalled, was "to mass a sizeable group at one end of the line," as if preparing to charge. Then, when Guardsmen shifted to protect that area, a comparatively small group of demonstrators would push through the weak end of the line. Once the small group had penetrated the line, the medic says, members would "come up behind the Guardsmen and taunt them, as well as push and shove them from the rear." A Guard official said later that his men were attacked with oven cleaner and containers filled with excrement. . . . . .

As the crowd swelled, it surged periodically towards the Guard line, sometimes yelling, "Freedom, freedom." On one of these surges a Guardsman hurled two tear gas canisters. Some of the tear gas was fired directly into the faces of demonstrators. "We came across a guy really badly gassed," a college coed says. "We were choking, but we could still see. But this guy we saw was standing there helpless with mucous-type stuff on his face, obviously in pain."

An Assistant U.S. Attorney says he saw "hundreds of people running, crying, coughing, vomiting, screaming." Some women ran blindly to Buckingham Fountain and leaped into the water to bathe their faces. The Guard medic quoted earlier says he was again assaulted by demonstrators when he went into the crowd to treat a man felled by "a particularly heavy dose of tear gas."

"In Grant Park, the gassed crowd was angered . . . more aggressive," says the history professor. Shortly after the gassing, says the Guard medic quoted earlier, "two forces of police arrived. They immediately waded into the crowd with clubs swinging indiscriminately, driving them off the bridge and away from the area." Once more, the Guardsman said, he was assaulted by demonstrators—this time when he tried "to treat an individual who received a severe head injury from the police."

Surging north from Congress Plaza to a footbridge leading from the park, the crowd encountered more Guardsmen. More tear gas was dispensed. Surging north from the site of the gassings, the crowd found the Jackson Boulevard bridge unguarded. Word was quickly passed back by loudspeaker, "Two blocks north, there's an open bridge; no gas." As dusk was settling, hundreds poured from the park into Michgian Avenue.

The Crowd on Michigan Avenue

At 7:14 p.m., as the first groups of demonstrators crossed the bridge toward Michigan Avenue, they noticed that the mule train of the Poor People's Campaign was just entering the intersection of Michigan and Jackson, headed south. The wagons were painted, "Jobs & Food for All."

The train was accompanied by 24 policemen on foot, five on three-wheelers, and four in two squadrols. A police official was in front with the caravan's leaders. The sight of the train seemed to galvanize the disorganized Grant Park crowd and those streaming over the bridge broke into cheers and shouts. "Peace now!" bellowed the demonstrators. "Dump the Hump!" This unexpected enthusiastic horde in turn stimulated the mule train marchers. Drivers of the wagons stood and waved to the crowd, shouting: "Join us! Join us!" To a young man watching from the 23rd floor of the Hilton Hotel, "the caravan seemed like a magnet to demonstrators leaving the park."

The Balbo-Michigan Crowd Builds Up

When the crowd's first rank reached the intersection of Balbo and Michigan, the northeast corner of the Hilton, it was

close to approximately 2000 to 3000 demonstrators and spectators. The police were armed with riot helmets, batons, mace,
an aerosol tear gas can and their service revolvers (which they
always carry). Behind the police lines, parked in front of the
Hilton, was a fire department high pressure pumper truck hooked
up to a hydrant. Pairs of uniformed firemen were also in the
vicinity. The growing crowds, according to the U.S. Attorney's
report, were a blend of "young and old, hippies, Yippies, straights,
newsmen and cameramen," even two mobile TV units. . . . . .

From within the crowd were rising the usual shouts from
some of the demonstrators: "Hell no, we won't go!" . . . "Fuck
these Nazis!" . . . "Fuck you, L.B.J.!" . . . "No more war!" . . .
"Pigs, pigs, pigs." . . . "The streets belong to the people!" "Let's
go to the Amphitheatre!" "Move on, Move on!" . . . "You
can't stop us." . . . "From the hotel," recalls a student, "people
who sympathized were throwing confetti and pieces of paper out
of the windows and they were blinking their room lights." . . . . .

Isolated Incidents

Occasionally during the early evening, groups of demonstrators would flank the police lines or find a soft spot and
punch through, heading off on their own for the Amphitheatre.
On the periphery of the Hilton and on thoroughfares and side
streets further southwest, a series of brief but sometimes violent
encounters occurred.

For example, says the manager of a private club on Michigan Avenue, "a large band of long-haired demonstrators . . .
tore down the American flag" overhanging the entrance to the
club "and took it into Michigan Avenue attempting to tear it."

At about 7 p.m. from the window of a motel room in the
1100 block of South Michigan, a senator's driver noticed a group
of demonstrators walking south, chanting: "Hell no, we won't
go!" and "Fuck the draft." They were hurling insults at passing
pedestrians and when one answered back, the witness says, "five
demonstrators charged out of Michigan Avenue onto the sidewalk, knocked the pedestrian down, formed a circle around his

fallen body, locked their arms together and commenced kicking him in a vicious manner. When they had finished kicking their victim, they unlocked their arms and immediately melted back into the crowd. . . ." . . . . .

Back at the Conrad Hilton

Vice President Humphrey was now inside the Conrad Hilton Hotel and the police commanders were afraid that the crowd might either attempt to storm the hotel or march south on Michigan Avenue, ultimately to the Amphitheatre. The Secret Service had received an anonymous phone call that the Amphitheatre was to be blown up. A line of police was established at 8th and Michigan at the south end of the hotel and the squads of police stationed at the hotel doors began restricting access to those who could display room keys. Some hotel guests, including delegates and Senator McCarthy's wife, were turned away.

By 7:30 p.m. a rumor was passing around that the Blackstone Rangers and the East Side Disciples, two of Chicago's most troublesome street gangs, were on their way to the scene. (This was later proven to be untrue; neither of these South Side gangs was present in any numbers in either Lincoln Park or Grant Park.) At this point, a Negro male was led through the police line by a police officer. He spoke to the police officer, a city official and a deputy superintendent of police. He told them that he was in charge of the mule train and that his people wanted no part of this mob. He said he had 80 people with him, that they included old people and children, and he wanted to get them out of the mob. The police officer later stated the group wanted to go past the Hilton, circle it, and return to the front of the hotel where Reverend Ralph Abernathy could address the crowd. . . . . .

In a few minutes, Reverend Ralph Abernathy appeared and, according to the police officer's statement, "said he wanted to be taken out of the area as he feared for the safety of his group." The police officer directed that the train be moved south on Michigan to 11th Street and then, through a series of turns through the Loop, to the West Side. . . . .

A policeman on Michigan later said that at about this time a "female hippie" came up to him, pulled up her skirt and said, "You haven't had a piece in a long time." A policeman standing in front of the Hilton remembers seeing a blonde female who was dressed in a short red minidress make lewd, sexual motions in front of a police line. Whenever this happened, he says, the policemen moved back to prevent any incident. The crowd, however, egged her on, the patrolman says. He thought that "she and the crowd wanted an arrest to create a riot." Earlier in the same general area a male youth had stripped bare and walked around carrying his clothes on a stick. . . . . .

The intersection at Balbo and Michigan was in total chaos at this point. The street was filled with people. Darkness had fallen but the scene was lit by both police and television lights. As the mule train left, part of the group tried to follow the wagons through the police line and were stopped. According to the deputy superintendent of police, there was much pushing back and forth between the policemen and the demonstrators.

Continual announcements were made at this time over a police amplifier for the crowd to "clear the street and go up on the sidewalk or into the park area for their demonstrations." The broadcast said, "Please gather in the park on the east side of the street. You may have your peaceful demonstration and speechmaking there." The demonstrators were also advised that if they did not heed these orders they would face arrest. The response from many in the crowd, according to a police observer, was to scream and shout obscenities. A Chicago attorney who was watching the scene recalls that when the announcements were broadcast, "No one moved." The deputy superintendent then made another announcement: "Will any non-demonstrators, anyone who is not a part of this group, any newsmen, please leave the group." Despite the crowd noise, the loud-speaker announcements were "loud and plainly heard," according to an officer. . . . . .

While this was happening on Michigan Avenue, a separate police line had begun to move east toward the crowd from the block of Balbo that lies between Michigan and Wabash along the north side of the Hilton.

Just as the police in front of the Hilton were confronted with some sit-downs on the south side of the intersection of Balbo and Michigan, the police unit coming into the intersection on Balbo met the sitting demonstrators. What happened then is subject to dispute between the police and some other witnesses.

The Balbo police unit commander asserts that he informed the sit-downs and surrounding demonstrators that if they did not leave, they would be arrested. He repeated the order and was met with a chant of "Hell no, we won't go." Quickly a police van swung into the intersection immediately behind the police line, the officers opened the door at the rear of the wagon. The deputy chief "ordered the arrest process to start."

"Immediately upon giving this order," the deputy chief later informed his superiors, "we were pelted with rocks, bottles, cans filled with unknown liquids and other debris, which forced the officers to defend themselves from injury. . . . My communications officer was slugged from behind by one of these persons, receiving injuries to his right eye and cheekbone." . . . . .

The many films and video tapes of this time period present a picture which does not correspond completely with the police view. First, the films do not show a mob moving west on Balbo; they show the street as rather clean of the demonstrators and bystanders, although the sidewalks themselves on both sides of the street are crowded. Second, they show the police walking east on Balbo, stopping in formation, awaiting the arrival of the van and starting to make arrests on order. A total of 25 seconds elapses between their coming to a halt and the first arrests.

Also, a St. Louis reporter who was watching from inside the Haymarket lounge agrees that the police began making arrests "in formation," apparently as "the result of an order to clear the intersection." Then, the reporter adds, "from this apparently controlled beginning the police began beating people indiscriminately. They grabbed and beat anyone they could get hold of." . . . . .

"The crowd tried to reverse gears," the reporter says. "People began falling over each other. I was in the first rank between police and the crowd and was caught in the first surge. I went down as I tried to retreat. I covered my head, tried to protect my glasses which had fallen partially off, and hoped that I would not be clubbed. I tried to dig into the humanity that had fallen with me. You could hear shouting and screaming. As soon as I could, I scrambled to my feet and tried to move away from the police. I saw a youth running by me also trying to flee. A policeman clubbed him as he passed, but he kept running.

"The cops were saying, 'Move! I said, move, god dammit! Move, you bastards!' " A representative of the ACLU who was positioned among the demonstrators says the police "were cussing a lot" and were shouting, "Kill, kill, kill, kill, kill!" A reporter for the *Chicago Daily News* said after the melee that he, too, heard this cry. A demonstrator remembers the police swinging their clubs and screaming, "Get the hell out of here." . . . "Get the fuck out of here." . . . "Move your fucking ass!" . . . . .

The crowd frantically eddied in a halfmoon shape in an effort to escape the officers coming in from the west. A UPI reporter who was on the southern edge of the crowd on Michigan Avenue, said that the advancing police "began pushing the crowd south." A cherry bomb burst overhead. The demonstrators strained against the deputy superintendent of police's line south of the Balbo-Michigan intersection. "When I reached that line," says the UPI reporter, "I heard a voice from behind it say, 'Push them back, move them back!' I was then prodded and shoved with nightsticks back in a northerly direction, toward the still advancing line of police."

"Police were marching this way and that," a correspondent from a St. Louis paper says. "They obviously had instructions to clear the street, but apparently contradicting one another in the directions the crowd was supposed to be sent."

The deputy superintendent of police recalls that he ordered his men to "hold your line there" . . . "stand fast" . . . "Lieutenant, hold your men steady there!" These orders, he said, were not obeyed by all. He said that police disregarded his order to return to the police lines—the beginning of what he says was the only instance in which he personally saw police discipline collapse. He estimates that ten to 15 officers moved off on individual forays against demonstrators. . . . . .

Thus, at 7:57 p.m., with two groups of club-wielding police converging simultaneously and independently, the battle was joined. The portions of the throng out of the immediate area of conflict largely stayed put and took up the chant. "The whole world is watching," but the intersection fragmented into a collage of violence.

Re-creating the precise chronology of the next few moments is impossible. But there is no question that a violent street battle ensued.

People ran for cover and were struck by police as they passed. Clubs were swung indiscriminately. . . . . .

"I saw squadrons of policemen coming from everywhere," a secretary said. "The crowd around me suddenly began to run. Some of us, including myself, were pushed back onto the sidewalk and then all the way up against . . . the Blackstone Hotel along Michigan Avenue. I thought the crowd had panicked. . . . . .

"Fearing that I would be crushed against the wall of the building . . . I somehow managed to work my way . . . to the edge of the street . . . and saw police everywhere.

"As I looked up I was hit for the first time on the head from behind by what must have been a billy club. I was then knocked down and while on my hands and knees, I was hit around the shoulders. I got up again, stumbling and was hit again. As I was falling, I heard words to the effect of 'move, move' and the horrible sound of cracking billy clubs.

"After my second fall, I remember being kicked in the back, and I looked up and noticed that many policemen around me had no badges on. The police kept hitting me on the head."

Eventually she made her way to an alley behind the Blackstone and finally, "bleeding badly from my head wound," was driven by a friend to a hospital emergency room. Her treatment included the placing of 12 stitches. . . . . .

A lawyer says that he was in a group of demonstrators in the park just south of Balbo when he heard a police officer shout, "Let's get 'em!" Three policemen ran up, "singled out one girl and as she was running away from them, beat her on the back of the head. As she fell to the ground, she was struck by the nightsticks of these officers." A male friend of hers then came up yelling at the police. The witness said, "He was arrested. The girl was left in the area lying on the ground." . . . . .

A *Milwaukee Journal* reporter says in his statement, "when the police managed to break up groups of protesters they pursued individuals and beat them with clubs. Some police pursued individual demonstrators as far as a block . . . and beat them. . . . In many cases it appeared to me that when police had finished beating the protesters they were pursuing, they then attacked, indiscriminately, any civilian who happened to be standing nearby. Many of these were not involved in the demonstrations."

In balance, there is no doubt that police discipline broke during the melee. The deputy superintendent of police states that—although this was the only time he saw discipline collapse —when he ordered his men to stand fast, some did not respond and began to sally through the crowd, clubbing people they came upon. An inspector-observer from the Los Angeles Police Department, stated that during this week, "The restraint of the police both as individual members and as an organization, was beyond reason." However, he said that on this occasion:

> There is no question but that many officers acted without restraint and exerted force beyond that necessary under the circumstances. The leadership at the point of conflict did little to prevent such conduct and the direct control of officers by first-line supervisors was virtually non-existent.

The deputy superintendent of police has been described by several observers as being very upset by individual policemen who beat demonstrators. He pulled his men off the demonstrators, shouting "Stop, damn it, stop. For Christ's sake, stop it."

"It seemed to me," an observer says, "that only a saint could have swallowed the vile remarks to the officers. However, they went to extremes in clubbing the Yippies. I saw them move into the park, swatting away with clubs at girls and boys lying in the grass. More than once I witnessed two officers pulling at the arms of a Yippie until the arms almost left their sockets, then, as the officers put the Yippie in a police van, a third jabbed a riot stick into the groin of the youth being arrested. It was evident that the Yippie was not resisting arrest." . . . . .

"In one incident, a young man, who apparently had been maced, staggered across Michigan . . . helped by a companion. The man collapsed. . . . Medical people from the volunteer medical organization rushed out to help him. A police officer (a sergeant, I think) came rushing forward, followed by the two other nightstick-brandishing policemen and yelled, 'Get him out of here; this ain't a hospital.' The medical people fled, half dragging and half carrying the young man with them. . . ." . . . . .

During the course of arrests, one girl lost her skirt. Although there have been unverified reports of police ripping the clothes from female demonstrators, this is the only incident on news film of any woman being disrobed in the course of arrest.

While violence was exploding in the street, the crowd wedged, behind the police sawhorses along the northeast edge of the Hilton, was experiencing a terror all its own. Early in the evening, this group had consisted in large part of curious bystanders. But following the police surges into the demonstrators clogging the intersection, protesters had crowded the ranks behind the horses in their flight from the police.

From force of numbers, this sidewalk crowd of 150 to 200 persons was pushing down toward the Hilton's front entrance. Policemen whose orders were to keep the entrance clear were pushing with sawhorses. Other police and fleeing demonstrators were pushed from the north in the effort to clear the intersection. Thus, the crowd was wedged against the hotel, with the hotel itself on the west, sawhorses on the southeast and police on the northeast.

Films show that one policeman elbowed his way where he could rescue a girl of about ten years of age from the vise-like press of the crowd. He cradled her in his arms and carried her to a point of relative safety 20 feet away. The crowd itself "passed up" an elderly woman to a low ledge.

"I was crowded in with the group of screaming, frightened

people," an onlooker states, "We jammed against each other, trying to press into the brick wall of the hotel. As we stood there breathing hard . . . a policeman calmly walked the length of the barricade with a can of chemical spray [evidently mace] in his hand. Unbelievably, he was spraying at us." Photos reveal several policemen using mace against the crowd. . . . . . "Some of the police then turned and attacked the crowd," a Chicago reporter says. A young cook caught in the crowd relates that:

"The police began picking people off. They would pull individuals to the ground and begin beating them. A medic wearing a white coat and an armband with a red cross was grabbed, beaten and knocked to the ground. His whole face was covered with blood." . . . . .

As a result, a part of the crowd was trapped in front of the Conrad Hilton and pressed hard against a big plate glass window of the Haymarket Lounge. A reporter who was sitting inside said, "Frightened men and women banged . . . against the window. A captain of the fire department inside told us to get back from the window, that it might get knocked in. As I backed away a few feet I could see a smudge of blood on the glass outside."

With a sickening crack, the window shattered, and screaming men and women tumbled through, some cut badly by jagged glass. The police came after them. "A patrolman ran up to where I was sitting," said a man with a cut leg. "I protested that I was injured and could not walk, attempting to show him my leg. He screamed that he would show me I could walk. He grabbed me by the shoulder and literally hurled me through the door of the bar into the lobby. . . .

"I stumbled out into what seemed to be a main lobby. The young lady I was with and I were both immediately set upon by what I can only presume were plainclothes police. . . . We were cursed by these individuals and thrown through another door into an outer lobby." Eventually a McCarthy aide took him to the 15th floor.

In the heat of all this, probably few were aware of the Haymarket's advertising slogan: "A place where good guys take good girls to dine in the lusty, rollicking atmosphere of fabulous

Old Chicago. . . ." . . . . . There is little doubt that during this whole period, beginning at 7:57 p.m. and lasting for nearly 20 minutes, the preponderance of violence came from the police. It was not entirely a one-way battle, however.

Firecrackers were thrown at police. Trash baskets were set on fire and rolled and thrown at them. In one case, a gun was taken from a policeman by a demonstrator.

"Some hippies," said a patrolman in his statement, "were hit by other hippies who were throwing rocks at the police." Films reveal that when police were chasing demonstrators into Grant Park, one young man upended a sawhorse and heaved it at advancing officers. At one point the deputy superintendent of police was knocked down by a thrown sawhorse. At least one police three-wheeler was tipped over. One of the demonstrators says that "people in the park were prying up cobblestones and breaking them. One person piled up cobblestones in his arms and headed toward the police." Witnesses reported that people were throwing "anything they could lay their hands on. From the windows of the Hilton and Blackstone hotels, toilet paper, wet towels, even ash trays came raining down." A police lieutenant stated that he saw policemen bombarded with "rocks, cherry bombs, jars of vasoline, jars of mayonnaise and pieces of wood torn from the yellow barricades falling in the street." He, too, noticed debris falling from the hotel windows. . . . . .

A number of police officers were injured, either by flying missiles or in personal attacks. One, for example, was helping a fellow officer "pick up a hippie when another hippie gave [me] a heavy kick, aiming for my groin." The blow struck the officer partly on the leg and partly in the testicles. He went down, and the "hippie" who kicked him escaped.

In another instance, a Chicago police reporter said in his statement, "a police officer reached down and grabbed a person who dove forward and bit the officer on the leg. . . . Three or four fellow policemen came to his aid. They had to club the demonstrator to make him break his clamp on the officer's leg." In another case, the witness saw a demonstrator "with a big mop of hair hit a police officer with an old British Army type metal helmet." The reporter said he also heard "hissing sounds from

the demonstrators as they were spraying the police." Later he
found empty lacquer spray and hair spray cans on the street.
Also he heard policemen cry out, "They're kicking us with knives
in their shoes." Later, he said, he found that demonstrators "had
actually inserted razor blades in their shoes." . . . . .

Wild in the Streets

By 8:15 p.m., the intersection was in police control. One
group of police proceeded east on Balbo, clearing the street
and splitting the crowd into two. Because National Guard lines
still barred passage over the Balbo Street bridge, most of the
demonstrators fled into Grant Park. A Guardsman estimates
that 5,000 remained in the park across from the Hilton. Some
clubbing by police occurred; a demonstrator says he saw a brick
hurled at police; but few arrests were made.

Now, with police lines beginning to reform, the deputy
superintendent directed the police units to advance north on
Michigan. He says announcements were again made to clear the
area and warnings given that those refusing to do so would be
arrested. To this, according to a patrolman who was present,
"The hippie group yelled 'fuck you' in unison."

Police units formed up. National Guard intelligence officers
on the site called for Guard assistance. At 8:30 the Secret Service
reported trucks full of Guard troops from Soldier Field moving
north on Michigan Avenue to the Conrad Hilton and additional
units arrived about 20 minutes later. The troops included the
same units that had seen action earlier in the day after the
bandshell rally and had later been moved to 22nd Street.

By 8:55 p.m., the Guard had taken up positions in a U-
shaped formation, blocking Balbo at Michigan and paralleling
the Hilton and Grant Park—a position that was kept until
4 a.m. Thursday. Although bayonets were affixed when the
troops first hit the street, they were quickly removed. Explains
a Guardsman who was there: "The bayonets had gotten in our
way when we were on the Congress Street bridge." At one point,
a demonstrator tried to "take the muzzle off" one of the Guards-

men's rifle. "All the time the demonstrators were trying to talk to us. They said 'join us' or 'fuck the draft.' We were told not to talk to anyone in the crowd." One Guard unit followed behind the police as a backup group.

With the police and Guard at its rear, the crowd fractured in several directions as it moved away from Balbo and Michigan. Near Michigan and Monroe another casualty center had been set up in the headquarters of the Church Federation of Greater Chicago. This, plus the melding of the crowds northbound on Michigan and east-bound on Monroe, brought about 1,000 persons to the west side of Michigan between Adams and Monroe, facing the Art Institute. There were few demonstrators on the east side of Michigan.

At 9:25 p.m., the police commander ordered a sweep of Michigan Avenue south from Monroe. At about this same time the police still had lines on both the west and east sides of Michigan in front of the Hilton and additional National Guard troops had arrived at 8th Street.

At 9:57 p.m., the demonstrators still on Michigan Avenue, prodded along by the southward sweep of the police, began marching back to Grant Park, chanting "Back to the park." By 10:10 p.m., an estimated 800 to 1,000 demonstrators had gathered in front of the Hilton.

By then, two city street sweeping trucks had rumbled up and down the street in front of the hotel, cleaning up the residue of violence—shoes, bottles, rocks, tear gas handkerchiefs. A police captain said the debris included: "Bases and pieces of broken bottles, a piece of board (1″ x 4″ x 14″), an 18-inch length of metal pipe, a 24-inch stick with a protruding sharpened nail, a 12-inch length of ½-inch diameter pipe, pieces of building bricks, an 18-inch stick with a razor blade protruding . . . several plastic balls somewhat smaller than tennis balls containing approximately 15 to 20 sharpened nails driven into the ball from various angles." When the delegates returned to the Hilton, they saw none of the litter of the battle.

As the crowd had dispersed from the Hilton the big war of Michigan and Balbo was, of course, over. But for those in the streets, as the rivulets of the crowd forked through the areas north of the hotel, there were still battles to be fought. Police violence and police baiting were some time in abating. Indeed, some of the most vicious incidents occurred in this "post-war" period. . . . . .

The U.S. Attorney states that as the crowd moved north on Michigan Avenue, "they pelted the police with missiles of all sorts, rocks, bottles, firecrackers. When a policeman was struck, the crowd would cheer. The policemen in the line were dodging and jumping to avoid being hit." A police sergeant told the FBI that even a telephone was hurled from the crowd at the police. . . . . .

In the first block north of the Hilton, recalls a man who was standing outside a Michigan Avenue restaurant, demonstrators "menaced limousines, calling the occupants 'scum,' telling them they didn't belong in Chicago and to go home."

As the police skirmish line moved north, and drew nearer to the squad cars, the lieutenant said, he saw several persons shoving paper through the cars' broken windows—in his opinion, a prelude to setting the cars on fire. A theology student who was in the crowd states that "a demonstrator took a fire extinguisher and sprayed inside the car. Then he put paper on the ground under the gas tank. . . . People shouted at him to stop." To break up the crowd, the lieutenant said, he squirted tear gas from an aerosol container and forced the demonstrators back. . . . . .

"Two or three policemen, one with a white shirt, advanced on the crowd," one witness said, "The white-shirted one squirted mace in arcs back and forth before him."

A cameraman for the *Chicago Daily News* photographed a woman cowering after she had been sprayed with mace. A *News* representative states that the officer administering the mace, whom the photographers identified as a police lieutenant, then turned and directed the spray at the cameraman. The cameraman shot a photograph of this. The police lieutenant states that he does not remember this incident.

A priest who was in the crowd says he saw a "boy, about 14 or 15 white, standing on top of an automobile yelling something which was unidentifiable. Suddenly a policeman forced him down from the car and beat him to the ground by striking him three or four times with a nightstick. Other police joined in . . . and they eventually shoved him to a police van."

A well-dressed woman saw this incident and spoke angrily to a nearby police captain. As she spoke, another policeman came up from behind her and sprayed something in her face with an aerosol can. He then clubbed her to the ground. He and two other policemen then dragged her along the ground to the same paddy wagon and threw her in.

"At the corner of Congress Plaza and Michigan," states a doctor, "was gathered a group of people, numbering between 30 and 40. They were trapped against a railing by several policemen on motorcycles. The police charged the people on motorcycles and struck about a dozen of them, knocking several of them down. About 20 standing there jumped over the railing. On the other side of the railing was a three-to-four-foot drop. None of the people who were struck by the motorcycles appeared to be seriously injured. However, several of them were limping as if they had been run over on their feet."

A UPI reporter witnessed these attacks, too. He relates in his statement that one officer, "with a smile on his face and a fanatical look in his eyes, was standing on the three-wheel cycle, shouting, 'Wahoo, wahoo,' and trying to run down people on the sidewalk." The reporter says he was chased 30 feet by the cycle.

A few seconds later he "turned around and saw a policeman with a raised billy stick." As he swung around, the police stick grazed his head and struck his shoulders. As he was on his knees, he says someone stepped on his back.

A Negro policeman helped him to his feet, the reporter says. The policeman told him, "You know, man I didn't do this. One of the white cops did it." Then, the reporter quotes the officer as saying, "You know what? After this is all over, I'm quitting the force."

An instant later, the shouting officer on the motorcycle swung by again, and the reporter dove into a doorway for safety.

Near this same intersection, a Democratic delegate from Oklahoma was surrounded in front of his hotel by about ten persons, two of them with long hair and beards. He states that they encircled him for several minutes and subjected him to verbal abuse because they felt he "represented the establishment" and was "somewhat responsible for the alleged police brutality." The delegate stood mute and was eventually rescued by a policeman.

At Van Buren, a college girl states, "demonstrators were throwing things at passing police cars, and I saw one policeman hit in the face with a rock. A small paddy wagon drove up with only one policeman in it, and the crowd began rocking the wagon. The cop fell out and was surrounded by the crowd, but no effort was made to hurt him."

At Jackson, says the graduate student quoted earlier, "People got into the street on their knees and prayed, including several ministers who were dressed in clerical garb. These people, eight or ten of them, were arrested. This started a new wave of dissent among the demonstrators, who got angry. Many went forward to be arrested voluntarily; others were taken forcibly and some were beaten. . . . Objects were being thrown directly at police, including cans, bottles and paper."

"I was in the street," a witness who was near the intersection states, "when a fire in a trash basket appeared. . . . In a few minutes, two fire engines passed south through the crowd, turned west on Van Buren and stopped. They were followed by two police wagons which stopped in the middle of the block. As I walked north past the smaller of the two wagons, it began to rock." (The wagon also was being pelted by missiles, the U.S. Attorney states, and "PIGS" was painted on its sides.)

"I retreated onto the east sidewalk," the witness continued. "Two policemen jumped out of the smaller wagon and one was knocked down by a few demonstrators, while other demonstrators tried to get these demonstrators away. The two policemen got back to the wagon, the crowd having drawn well back around them." The U.S. Attorney's report states that one of the policemen was "stomped" by a small group of the mob.

A young woman who was there and who had attended the bandshell rally earlier in the afternoon states that the crowd rocked the wagon for some time, while its officers stayed inside.

"Then," she says, "the driver came out wildly swinging his club and shouting. About ten people jumped on him. He was kicked pretty severely and was downed. When he got up he was missing his club and his hat."

A police commander says that at about this moment he received "an urgent radio message" from an officer inside the van. He radioed that "demonstrators were standing on the hood of his wagon . . . and were preparing to smash the windshield with a baseball bat," the commander recalled. The officer also told him that the demonstrators were attempting to overturn the squadrol and that the driver "was hanging on the door in a state of shock." The commander told the officer that assistance was on the way.

"I heard a '10-1' call on either my radio or one of the other hand sets being carried by other men with me," the U.S. Attorney states, "and then heard, 'Car 100-sweep!' [Car 100 was assigned to the police commander.] With a roar of motors, squads, vans and three-wheelers came from east, west and north into the block north of Jackson."

"Almost immediately a CTA bus filled with police came over the Jackson Drive bridge and the police formed a line in the middle of the street," says a witness. "I heard shouts that the police had rifles and that they had cocked and pumped them. Demonstrators began to run." . . . . .

"I ran north of Jackson . . . just as police were clearing the intersection and forming a line across Michigan," says the witness quoted above. "The police who had formed a line facing east in the middle of Michigan charged, yelling and clubbing into the crowd, running at individuals and groups who did not run before them." . . . . .

"As the fray intensified around the intersection of Michigan and Jackson, a big group ran west on Jackson, with a group of blue-shirted policemen in pursuit, beating at them with clubs," says the U.S. Attorney's report. Some of the crowd ran up the alleys; some north on Wabash; and some west on Jackson to State with the police in pursuit." . . . . .

An Assistant U.S. Attorney later reported that "the demonstrators were running as fast as they could but were unable to get out of the way because of the crowds in front of them. I observed the police striking numerous individuals, perhaps 20 or 30. I saw three fall down and then be overrun by the police. I observed two demonstrators who had multiple cuts on their heads. We assisted one who was in shock into a passer-by's car.

"A TV mobile truck appeared . . . and the police became noticeably more restrained, holding their clubs at waist level rather than in the air," a witness relates. "As the truck disappeared . . . the head-clubbing tactics were resumed." . . . . .

One demonstrator states that he ran off Michigan Avenue on to Jackson. He says he and his wife ran down Jackson and were admitted, hesitantly, into a restaurant. They seated themselves at a table by the window facing onto Jackson and, while sitting at the table, observed a group of people running down Jackson with policemen following them and striking generally at the crowd with their batons. At one instance, he saw a policeman strike a priest in the head with a baton.

At the intersection of Jackson and Wabash, said a student whose wife was beaten in the race from Michigan, "the police came from all four directions and attacked the crowd. Demonstrators were beaten and run to the paddy wagons. I saw a black policeman go berserk. He charged blindly at the group of demonstrators and made two circles through the crowd, swinging wildly at anything." . . . . .

An Assistant U.S. Attorney watching the action on various side streets reported, "I observed police officers clearing people westward . . . using their clubs to strike people on the back of the head and body on several occasions. Once a policeman ran alongside a young girl. He held her by the shoulder of her jacket and struck at her a few times as they were both running down the sidewalk." . . . . .

A traffic policeman on duty on Michigan Avenue says that the demonstrators who had continued north often surrounded cars and buses attempting to move south along Michigan Avenue. Many males, in the crowd, he says, exposed their penises to passers-by and other members of the crowd. They would run up to cars clogged by the crowd and show their private parts to the passengers.

To men, the officer says, they shouted such questions as, "How would you like me to fuck your wife?" and "How would you like to fuck a man?" Many of the demonstrators also rocked the automobiles in an effort to tip them over. A policeman states that bags of feces and urine were dropped on the police from the building. . . . . .

As the crowd moved south again on Michigan, a traffic policeman, who was in the vicinity of Adams Street, recalls, "They first took control of the lions in front of the Art Institute. They climbed them and shouted things like, "Let's fuck" and "Fuck, fuck, fuck!" . . . . . At this same intersection, an officer rescued two Loop secretaries from being molested by demonstrators. He asked them. "What are you doing here?" They replied, "We wanted to see what the hippies were like." His response: "How do you like what you saw?"

Old Town: The Mixture as Before

While all that was going on in and around Grant Park, Lincoln Park on Wednesday was quiet and uncrowded; but there was sporadic violence in Old Town again that night. Two University of Minnesota students who wandered through the park in the morning say they heard small groups of demonstrators saying things like "Fuck the pigs," and "Kill them all," but by this time that was not unusual. They also heard a black man addressing a group of demonstrators. He outlined plans for the afternoon, and discussed techniques for forming skirmish lines, disarming police officers, and self defense.

Also during the morning Abbie Hoffman was arrested at the Lincoln Hotel Coffee Shop, 1800 North Clark, and charged with resisting arrest and disorderly conduct. According to Hoffman's wife, Anita, she and her husband and a friend were eating breakfast when three policemen entered the coffee shop and told Hoffman they had received three complaints about an obscene word written on Hoffman's forehead. The word was "Fuck." Hoffman says he printed the word on his forehead to keep cameramen from taking his picture. . . . . .

Who Rules the Police?

Most of the violence against police, from all reports, was the work of gang-type youths called "greasers." They dismantled police barricades to lure squad cars down Stockton Drive, where one observer says "punks engaged in some of the most savage attacks on police that had been seen." Ministers and hippies in the area were directing traffic around the barricades and keeping people from wandering into the danger area. Two ministers in particular were trying to "keep the cool." . . . . .

Back at the Hilton

By 10:30 p.m., most of the action was centered once more in Grant Park across from the Hilton, where several hundred demonstrators and an estimated 1,500 spectators gathered to listen to what one observer describes as "unexciting speeches." There was the usual singing and shouting. Twice during the evening police and Hilton security officers went into the hotel and went to quarters occupied by McCarthy personnel—once to protest the ripping of sheets to bandage persons who had been injured and a second time to try to locate persons said to be lobbing ashtrays out of the windows. But compared to the earlier hours of the evening, the rest of the night was quiet.

In Grant Park, the sullen crowd sat facing the hotel. Someone with a transistor radio was listening to the roll call vote of states on the nomination and broadcasting the count to the rest of the throng over a bullhorn. There were loud cheers for Ted Kennedy, McCarthy, McGovern and Phillips ("He's a black man," said the youth with the bullhorn.) Boos and cries of "Dump the Hump" arose whenever Humphrey received votes. "When Illinois was called," says the trained observer, "no one could hear totals because of booing and the chant, 'To Hell with Daley.' "

During this time the police line was subject to considerable verbal abuse from within the crowd and a witness says that both black and white agitators at the edge of the crowd tried to kick policemen with razor blades embedded in their shoes, Periodically several policemen would make forays into the crowd, punishing demonstrators they thought were involved.

At about "Louisiana," as the roll call vote moved with quickening pace toward the climax of Humphrey's nomination, the crowd grew restless, recalls a trained observer. About this same time, according to the Log, the police skirmish line began pushing the demonstrators farther east into the park. A report of an officer being struck by a nail ball was received by police. Film taken at about this time shows an officer being hit by a thrown missile, later identified as a chunk of concrete with a steel reinforcement rod in it. The blow knocked him down and, as he fell, the crowd cheered and yelled "More!" The chant, "Kill the pigs," filled the air.

"At 'Oklahoma,' " recalls an observer, "the Yippie on the bullhorn said, 'Marshals ready. Don't move. Stay seated.' "

The front lines rose [facing the police] and locked arms, and the others stayed seated. Humphrey was over the top with Pennsylvania, and someone in the Hilton rang a cow bell at the demonstrators. Boos went up, as did tension. A bus load of police arrived. Others standing in front of the Hilton crossed Michigan and lined up behind those in front of the demonstrators.

The chant of "Sit down, sit down" went out. An American flag was raised on a pole upside down. Wandering began among demonstrators and the chant continued.

Shortly before midnight, while Benjamin Ortiz was speaking, National Guard troops of the 2/129 Inf. came west on Balbo to Michigan to replace the police in front of the Hilton. "For the first time," says an observer, "machine guns mounted on trucks were pulled up directly in front of the demonstrators, just behind the police lines. The machine guns, and the Guard's mesh-covered jeeps with barbed wire fronts made the demonstrators angry and nervous. Bayonets were readied. In films of this period the word 'pig' can be seen written on the street.

"Ortiz continued, 'Dig this man, just 'cause you see some different pigs coming here, don't get excited. We're going to sleep here, sing here, sex here, live here!' "

As the police moved off, one of the first Guard maneuvers was to clear demonstrators from Michigan's east sidewalk. This was done to allow pedestrian traffic. The crowd reacted somewhat hostilely to the maneuver, but by and large, the demonstrators seemed to view the Guard as helpless men who had been caught up in the events and did not treat them as badly as they had the police. Having secured the sidewalk, the guards shortly retired to the east curb of Michigan Avenue. A line of "marshals" sat down at the edge of the grass at the feet of the guards. Access to the hotel was restored and people began to move from the hotel to the park and vice versa. By now, there were an estimated 4,000 persons assembled across from the Hilton. Most of the crowd sat down in a mass and became more orderly, singing "America" and "God Bless America." McCarthy supporters joined the crowd and were welcomed.

By 12:20 a.m., Thursday, the crowd had declined to 1,500 and was considered under control. By 12:33 a.m., the police department had retired from the streets and the Guard took over the responsibility of holding Michigan from Balbo to 8th Street. At 12:47 a.m., another contingent of Guard troops arrived at the Hilton. Delegates were returning and were being booed unless they could be identified as McCarthy or McGovern supporters. Those delegates were cheered and asked to join the group.

The crowd grew in number. By 1:07 a.m., the Secret Service estimated 2,000 persons in the park across from the hotel. Ten minutes later the crowd had grown by another 500. Those in the park were "listening to speeches—orderly" according to the log.

January 1969

4. POLICE CORRUPTION—NEW YORK CITY

The Knapp Commission

Testimony of Patrolman William R. Phillips

The witness is Patrolman William R. Phillips of the New York City Police Department. At the outset of his testimony, Patrolman Phillips identified himself as a policeman who had accepted money in connection with the protection of a house of prostitution and the fixing of some court cases. He said he had been a member of the police force for more than 14 years and added: "I've worked in every precinct in Manhattan from the 32d to the First, East and West, in one capacity or another—as a detective, uniformed patrolman, plainclothesman, youth squad and a detective in a district cruiser car."

The questions in the testimony were posed by Michael F. Armstrong, chief counsel to the Knapp Commission, unless otherwise indicated.

Q. In your class in the academy how many or what per cent would you say of those men were dedicated and had no idea of becoming involved in any kind of corrupt activity?

A. At that time?

Q. Right.

From public hearings of the Knapp Commission in New York City as reported by *The New York Times,* October 20, October 27, October 30, December 15, December 29, 1971. Copyright © 1971 by the New York Times Company and reprinted by permission.

A. 90 per cent—85, 90 per cent.

Q. How were you treated as a rookie coming into the precinct?

A. First you arrive at a station house, you're not considered one of the people who they talk to. Like you're off in a corner, with your own little group. I came into the 19th Precinct with about five or six, possibly seven other rookies at the time. And we had our own little group, and the other fellows who had been in the precinct for a while, they had their own group. You were not accepted into this group right away. As a matter of fact, no one even spoke to you at that time.

Q. What was the first contact you had in the 19th Precinct with anything that you could characterize as corrupt activity in any way?

A. Well, I was working on a foot post, and the fellow who had been working the post behind me said to me, "Listen, if you want to have something to eat at the restaurant around the corner, he takes care of the man on post."

So I wandered into the restaurant, and I sat down and I ate. And not knowing what to do, I got up and I naturally offered the man to pay. And he said: "Oh, no, you have a post. Well, we'll take care of you whenever you want to eat." And I left a tip, and then I walked out.

Q. Did your understanding and contact with the money that was available in the precinct increase as you became more experienced?

A. Yes. You might say the doors open up, and as you'd be involved with these other people who are older police officers, and they see how you work, how you operate, they would take you into their confidence a little at a time.

Q. And what kind of activities did you engage in and did you observe as a foot patrolman in the 19th Precinct?

"Contracts" With Businesses

A. As a foot patrolman there was contracts with dance halls and bars and grills, construction sites and that nature.

Q. How much was paid?

A. On most of these contracts at that time it was like $5 or $10 a night on a weekend.

Q. Per night per man?

A. Right.

Q. How about construction sites, how did that work?

A. The construction was a little bit different. If you had a foot post the foreman of the construction site would pay you probably once a week $5 or $10. He would also have a contract with the sector car, which would be anywhere from $40 to $80 per month plus the sergeant would have his own individual contract and plus, if the captain was on the pad, he'd have his own contract, too.

Q. How much do you think you estimate you got in money above your salary in these fashions while on foot patrol in the 19th Precinct?

A. At that time maybe about $40 a month.

Q. And was that about average?

A. Well, no, not really. You had to have the right post to make any money. There was some posts there was just no money on at all.

Q. How many men did you work with at that time?

A. Oh, there was—in my particular area, with people I was involved in—maybe 30, 40 men.

Most Took Money

Q. Aside from the officers who participate in the Christmas pad and took free meals, how many of the others, or how many officers accepted the kind of monies that you've been talking about from bars and construction, to your knowledge?

A. Everyone but one.

Q. How much money did you make when you were in the sector car?

A. Between $75 and $100 a month.

Q. Where did you make that money?

A. From most of the same places—dance halls, cabarets, and most of it was construction.

Q. While you were in the 19th Precinct, was money paid inside the precinct between police officers to get services done?

A. Yes, it was.

Q. Did you pay the clerical man?

A. Not in the 19th Precinct. There was—on these citations that I received (for exceptional work in the line of duty), they have to be written up in special form, and it was customary for the officer who was seeking departmental recognition to pay the clerical man who did the typing $5 if he typed the thing up. The first one I was involved in, I was told that this is the right thing to do by an old-timer in the precinct.

He said, "Did you take care of the clerical man for the writeup of your recognition?"

I said, "Gee, no, I didn't."

He said, "You should go down and do that."

Christmas Gifts

I approached the individual and I said, "I want to give you something for writing it up," and he said, "No, I don't do that."

And this individual never did. But subsequent to that I had paid other police officers for this service.

Q. How much did you pick up around Christmas time?

A. The 19th, I guess about $400, plus a lot of whiskey.

Q. And does your reputation follow you as you go through the department? Do you know who the pople are who will take money and who won't take money?

A. In this particular department you can make a phone call and find out in five minutes who the individual is, what his hobbies are, what his habits are and whether or not he takes money.

Q. What happened with respect to the police officer who is straight?

A. Well, he's in his own little group. He's not accepted into the group of people who engage in this type of activity, because they are afraid they can't trust him, to begin with, and they are not going to tell him what they are doing on the street.

COMMISSIONER SPRIZZO: What happens to the construction sites that don't pay?

THE WITNESS: You never found one that didn't. The people involved in the construction business—when you come onto a construction site and you ask for the permits, or you say you have a violation or, "Can I see the papers involved in this particular construction site"—by this terminology, you say, "Listen, you know, what can I do for you guys?"

Praise for Colleagues

Q. In describing these operations, Officer, in your estimation, were the police officers who served with you in the 19th good police officers?

A. They were the best cops I've ever seen since I've been on the job.

Q. What do you mean by that?

A. Arrests, responding to assignments, a spirit of closeness between one another.

Q. Did you receive any money in the 19th Precinct from diplomats you were assigned to protect?

A. I didn't receive any money from them, but in these different embassies they would send large amounts of whiskey into the station house.

I've seen cases of champagne picked up. And there was fellows at the time assigned to these dignitaries, but the dignitaries weren't in this country, and they received different gifts—gold watches, money, stuff like that, which were unsolicited by them. These were gifts given by the dignitaries to the officers.

CHAIRMAN KNAPP: But not money?

THE WITNESS: In some cases, yes, sir, there was money.

CHAIRMAN KNAPP: Always unsolicited?

THE WITNESS: Those were unsolicited, yes, sir.

Q. When you say "runners coming in and dropping off work," maybe you could explain a little bit what that means?

A. In one specific location that we were assigned in—as a matter of fact, it was the first day that we had been assigned to the Sixth Division—my partner and myself got in our own private automobile and we proceeded to a location on 120th Street and Eighth Avenue. We were to suppress a gambling operation there. The individual's name was Eggy.

Q. Eggy?

A. Eggy. He was a colored man. We pulled our automobile up at 120th Street and Eighth Avenue. And this fellow who was a known gambler was waiting for us to arrive. He knew that there would be new men coming up in the area that day. It was on a Monday morning.

He walked over to the car and he says, "Are you the new COBS men?" Never seen him before, never seen us. He says— we said, "Yes, we are."

He says, "You gets 20 a day. Is that all right?"

I look at my partner, he looks at me, we don't know what is going on. My experience with the policy was very limited.

He says, "Don't worry, everything is O.K. Division is taking care of the bureau, we take care of the men who were here before you, we take care of you."

Q. And speaking not about your own group but about your knowledge of the division plainclothes who have the primary responsibility in the area, what percentage of the plainclothes men assigned to the division, to the Sixth Division at that time, do you feel participated in the pad?

A. Everyone, to my knowledge.

Q. Everyone?

A. Everyone.

*   *   *   *   *

Testimony of Waverly B. Logan, former policeman

The witness is Waverly B. Logan, a former New York City policeman. Mr. Logan testified that he was appointed to the Police Department in June, 1968, and served his two and a half years on the force at the Police Academy, with the tactical patrol force, in the 80th Precinct, in the 73d Precinct and with the preventative enforcement patrol. For the last year he has been a cab driver.

The questions were asked by Michael F. Armstrong, chief counsel of the Knapp Commission.

Q. During that period of time, did you come in contact with any activities involving the taking by police officers of benefits in exchange for services or anything else of that sort?

A. When I was in T.P.F.* I was sort of young, taken right from the academy, and there's very little corruption I experienced in the T.P.F. unit. They know about corruption in the precinct from talking with them. They tell—all the guys in T.P.F. tell me about contracts, when the T.P.F. unit comes in that they would give out summonses and break contracts and that's why they wasn't liked. . . . They wasn't liked by the precinct because they would break contracts.

Q. So that in T.P.F. there was no corrupt activities as far as you were concerned?

A. There was no corrupt activities as far as money was concerned.

Q. I see. They occasionally get free meals and soft drinks and things like that?

A. Free meals they would occasionally give. If you was walking the foot post, the guy on the foot post, if he ever had that foot post before, he would tell you what places to go to eat, who would give you half prices, who would give it to you on the arm.

Q. What would (a policeman in the 73d Precinct do) if he were assigned to a foot post?

A. If he was assigned to a foot post and if it was on a 12 o'clock to 8 o'clock, he would come in the station house and go down to the basement and drink coffee. Or if he knew a place to coop, a girlfriend's house, he would go up to his girlfriend's house in the precinct. If he lived close enough, he would even go home.

Q. And leave a telephone number where he could be reached.

* Tactical Patrol Force, an elite police unit.

A. Yes. You would always leave your telephone number at the switchboard, so that the switchboard operator can always get in touch with you if there was a front break or something on your post and you need a man to send, they would always need a foot man.

Q. Do you recall incidents happening when burglaries were reported, your being introduced to a particular kind of behavior in connection with burglary?

A. Usually when a burglary occurred in the precinct, more than one car, if a car responds, regardless of whose sector they are in, as many cars as possible respond for backup. So this particular burglary was on Pitkin Avenue around Saratoga, in a men's clothing store. So I responded to this burglary. Me and my partner went into the back of the building where a door was open. We went in.

There was about six or seven radio cars out in front. A lot of cops was inside. Everybody was stuffing clothes down their pants, in their shirt, up their sleeve. Everybody looking fat because they were stuffing so much clothes in their pants. And my partner was telling me that the owners usually take it out on their income tax. Usually declare—say more was stolen than was actually taken or they would take it out on their insurance.

So he say this way you just getting a little back. He said, "Go ahead and take some, it's all right if you do."

So I took a shirt. And I was kind of afraid. I don't think I even wore the shirt.

Q. How long were you on the PEP squad? *

A. Eleven months.

Q. What was the attitude of the men when the squad was formed?

A. The men felt that they was in a new Police Department. They was in a Police Department all by itself. It was going to be a good squad, have good bosses. That there was no holds barred. That they see violations of the law, they was going to make an arrest. Everybody was anxious to work. Wanted to really do a good job, like being born again.

Q. And how long do you think this attitude lasted?

* Preventive Enforcement Patrol, a special squad of black and Puerto Rican policemen operating in the ghetto areas of New York City.

A. A month, maybe two.

Q. And then do you recall hearing about a particular incident?

A. Yes, I did.

Q. Tell us what that incident was.

A. Two patrolmen that was in my unit was patroling in the 32d Precinct. They came across one of those policy spots. They had a bell alarm on the door. So they rung the bell. The guy opened the door. He went inside and they arrested the policy bank. Took him to the 32d Precinct. Booked him, I understand 32d Precinct said that they knew where it was all the time and they were just waiting to get it.

Then we left there and went back to the squad room. And the squad room seemed like our sergeant was very excited about it because we had made a felony police arrest while in uniform.

And he called up one of the assistant chief inspectors right away at his home, tell him that we had just made a policy collar in uniform, and he felt it was great. And when he got off the phone he said. "The chief inspector said, 'We wasn't up in Harlem to make policy arrests.' "

Q. Do you recall an incident involving a raid on a large crap game in December of 1969?

A. Two patrolmen and myself was on foot patrol on Lenox Avenue when we saw two plainclothesmen cops. They was assigned to the 32d Precinct to watch out for taxi stickups. They was fairly new. One of them, as I recall, they had been to the academy with me. They told us about a big crap game on 139th Street in a basement. There was a big contract for that 32d Precinct and that they couldn't hit it.

They weren't allowed to make an arrest on it. So we told them that we don't have contracts and we will go and take that game. So they gave us the address and we went up there. As a matter of fact, we walked up there. It was quite a few blocks. Went down in the basement. Kicked the door open there. Took the game. Had everybody up the side of the wall, about 30 guys. Then we called on the radio for the sergeant. One was a radio patrol and one of them was the sergeant's car, with the sergeant in it.

The sergeant stayed outside. He called me out in the hallway

then and asked me what did I have? So I told him what had
happened. And I told him that our boss was on the way and he
should be here shortly. And when my boss came one of the
older patrolmen was there, from the 32nd. He seemed to know
my sergeant and he seemed to shake his hand and called the
sergeant by his first name, his arms around him, they had been
friends for years.

So I observed this same patrolman, he took one of the guys
that was in the dice game. He said he knew him for a long time.
He walked him all the way down this long hallway to the front.
And he had his arms around him and he came. And then he let
him go.

So when he came back he told me as a friend of mine, he'd
been giving me narcotics arrests.

I said "I'm no fool."

So he didn't say no more. So a little while later this—we
were still waiting for the patrol wagon to respond to take all
these prisoners. It happened two or three more times. It kept
happening.

Then they started letting guys go because he was on the
Sanitation Department. Letting guys go because he was working
this place, that place. And it got down to but we didn't have but
12 prisoners.

Q. Twelve out of originally 30 or 40?

A. Thirty people, 30 or more. So we put them in the wagon
and everybody was in there. The other prisoners was in there.
They saw what had happened, they was trying to force $10 in
my hand, saying: "I'll give you $10. Let me go, let me go."

*   *   *   *   *

Testimony of Captain Daniel McGowan

The witness is Captain Daniel McGowan of the Police Department. He testified that he had been a member of the city's
police force for 23 years and had served as a patrolman, sergeant
and lieutenant before becoming a captain in 1966.

Unless otherwise indicated, the questions were posed by Michael F. Armstrong, chief counsel to the commission.

Q. With respect to the feeling of cooperation within the Police Department, it is in the area of rooting out corruption, do you find in your work that it is easy to get information from police officers with respect to corruption?

A. No, it's very difficult. The police do not volunteer this information generally.

CHAIRMAN KNAPP: Do they go further than that and refuse to give it?

THE WITNESS: Well, I don't know of any specific instances where you could pin somebody down that they refused to give it. I think the attitude is not get involved unless you have to.

Q. Can you give us some idea of what your understanding and experience has been as to the feeling of police officers and why they feel this way?

A. Well, the mentality of the policeman is an insular one. They are surrounded by a hostile city. He has to be defensive. There are many forces that would like to destroy the department and its effectiveness. And so they are subject to insularity.

This is one of the big problems that we face.

Q. And they develop a sense of loyalty to each other; is that the idea?

A. That's correct, yes.

Q. Does this sense of loyalty, in your view, carry over to the point where it makes it difficult to uncover someone who is genuinely corrupt?

A. Well, I think policemen have been aware of some horrible examples of other police officers who have come forward, with all good intentions, to uncover a corrupted situation.

I remember in Denver, I think 1961, the Police Department was relatively free of corruption. It developed a burglary ring amongst some of the patrolmen there, and another patrolman became aware of it, reported his findings to the chief, and the chief sent him to a psychiatrist for examination.

When the psychiatrist sent him back to the chief, saying he

was perfectly sane and telling the truth, the chief reluctantly acted on the accusation. There were indictments and a substantial portion of the department was found to be involved.

But the chief had to leave, had to resign, and the officer who uncovered it had to resign and leave the city.

So this is a problem—that policemen know that if they expose corruption, that they are taking a substantial risk of alienating themselves from their fellow officers.

Q. And you say this attitude exists in the New York City Police Department, within your experience.

A. Yes. It's been well documented.

CHAIRMAN KNAPP: Captain McGowan, is there a term called "stand-up cop"?

THE WITNESS: Yes.

CHAIRMAN KNAPP: What does it mean?

THE WITNESS: Well, it means he wouldn't inform on his fellow officers.

CHAIRMAN KNAPP: Does it mean particularly that he will lie if necessary to protect his fellow officers from corrupt charges?

THE WITNESS: If necessary, yes.

Q. How about the supervisors? How about their role with respect to this attitude in the department?

A. Well, they were all patrolmen themselves at one time, and they have the same police attitude toward it. It is still defensive.

Q. Have you found that the supervisors are reluctant to—I don't mean this as a general thing, but that there is a tendency among supervisors to protect themselves by not exposing corruption under them which might reflect upon them?

A. Yes, as in the instance of the Denver police chief, the fact that he moved strongly and did act upon the information once he was convinced that it was true, and he was removed, he had to resign.

And I think there was a general reluctance on all of us not to show our weaknesses, that we have not been able to control our subordinates. And it is very unrealistic to expect that the subordinate is going to show up his own ineptitude.

Q. Are there sometime credibility gaps between the superior officers and the men working under them, where the superior officer, himself, may have a bad reputation in the corruption area?

A. Yes, I think if he had a bad reputation and it is known and he's issuing stock orders that corruption will cease and desist, then everybody will say, "Well, he's saying it for the record but he doesn't really mean it."

Q. Do you have in mind specific instances within the department where this kind of a situation apparently exists?

A. Oh, I think, you know, over the 23 years that has happened, where the Police Commissioner or the inspector will issue these orders, and the captain will say, "Oh, I've seen this thing before," and adopt a cynical attitude towards it.

Q. And at a lower supervisory level, right up to today, there are supervisors who are in this position, where their men feel that they, themselves, are involved and, therefore, don't take seriously what they say about corruption?

A. I suppose there are some few, I don't know. I can't give you any specific examples, but I'm sure there are some few examples.

Q. Now, there are superior officers involved in actively trying to combat corruption within their own commands; is that right?

A. Yes. Yes.

Q. What are the difficulties that they run into when they try to make an effort in this direction?

A. Well, one of the difficulties is, they have too great a span of control; there are not enough subordinate superiors to assist them in the supervision of their men.

Then again, the unrealistic goals that are set for them, the enforcement goals. This is particularly true in, I think, plainclothes, gambling enforcement and narcotics enforcement, that they are saddled with a tremendous amount of paper work, a volume of paper work that is constantly increasing.

And that, in addition to taking away from their primary responsibilities by being assigned to other duties temporarily because of some duty or strike duty or U.N. situations—they spend so little time sometimes in their offices that when they get back to them they are just signing papers and have little opportunity to fulfill their primary responsibility—supervision.

Q. In your view, what has been the department's response to the problem of corruption, historically? How have they gone about it and how, in your view, has this been effective or ineffective?

A. Well, this has been mostly from the case method; that is, responding to specific complaints and allegations rather than going out and trying to uncover the basic problems and trying to correct them at that level.

Q. Do you think that this approach has been successful?

A. Quite obviously the Knapp Commission wouldn't be in existence if it were.

Q. In your view, in the past, in other words, the reaction of the department to the corruption problem has been a defense one, just handling the cases that are brought in by way of allegation; is that right?

A. Yes, for several reasons. One is the sheer volume. The volume is a tremendous amount and I think, you know, somewhere along the line decisions were made—well, you know, if we really go all out for this, are we going to unalterably destroy the efficiency and the morale of the department?

I take the opposite view. I think that you have to—in order to get good efficiency and good morale, you have to root out the widespread corruption problem.

Q. Do you have a view about the so-called rotten-apple theory as it applies to corruption, Captain McGowan?

A. Well, the Knapp Commission hearings, I think . . . have shown the range if not the depth of police corruption. I would say that we should point out the vast difference between gratuities and corruption itself; one as different as between morals and ethics. But it's all there for us to see. And we can quibble about the amount of personnel involved, it's 5 per cent or 50 per cent, but it's unacceptable levels.

And I think the few rotten apples in the barrel is a rationalization, a dilution, so many of us do not want to face up to the fact that we can be associated with an organization that has so many aberrant members.

Q. How about the attitude of the public?

A. I think this is the single most important thing. If the public is aroused, if they want a better Police Department, if they want a more honest Police Department, they will have it. And if they don't concern themselves with this matter, then we won't have it.

*   *   *   *   *

Testimony of Detective Frank Serpico

The witness is Detective Frank Serpico. He testified that he joined the Police Department on Sept. 11, 1959, and has been assigned to the 81st Precinct in Brooklyn, the Bureau of Criminal Identification, the 90th Precinct in Brooklyn for plainclothes duty, the Seventh Division in the Bronx, Patrol Borough Manhattan North and the Narcotics Division in Brooklyn.

Unless otherwise indicated the questions were asked by Michael F. Armstrong, chief counsel to the commission.

Q. I'd like to direct your attention to April or May of 1967, and specifically to your acquaintance with Detective Durk. Had you had any conversations with Durk about his relationship with any people in the Mayor's office?

A. Yes.

Q. Specifically who?

A. Well, he had discussed with me the possibilities of arranging a meeting with the Mayor. Later he stated that he was going to arrange a meeting with the Mayor's aide, Jay Kriegel. And that we could go and tell him all the facts that I had observed.

Q. Was a meeting in fact arranged?

A. Yes.

Q. And who was present at the meeting?

A. Myself, Detective Durk and Jay Kriegel.

Q. In other words, you told him all of the incidents that you have testified to here today, plus any other incidents that may have occurred to you then and do not occur to you now? You gave him the full experience that you had had to date in plainclothes insofar as it related to corruption?

A. Yes.

Q. And did you discuss it in terms of names and places and specifications?

A. Whenever I was aware of them, yes.

Q. And what was Mr. Kriegel's reaction to the events that you told him about?

A. Well, he was quite shocked. He was more surprised that —he stated that he had heard rumors to this effect, but he had never heard it from a policeman before.

Kriegel's Reply

Q. And what did Mr. Kriegel say that would be done about what you were telling him?

A. Well, I had informed him of the part I was supposedly playing for the Police Department, and he said that he would check to see if, in fact, an investigation was on the way or not.

Q. And what you were supposed to be doing about this matter?

A. Yes. And I told him that to date I had not been contacted.

CHAIRMAN WHITMAN KNAPP: In other words, Inspector Behan had said that you would have a meeting with first the deputy, but that never transpired; is that right?

A. That is correct.

Q. Did Mr. Kriegel say anything to you about taking care that the investigation not be—that if there were an investigation going on, that it not be hurt?

A. Yes.

Q. What did he say about that, in what context?

A. He said that is why he would have to check to see if in fact an investigation was or wasn't being conducted, because if it was, his investigation might blow the other investigation.

Q. And what did he say he would do?

A. He said he would discuss it with the Mayor and ascertain what was happening and what was to be done.

Q. Do you recall having a conversation with Detective Durk about this time relative to meeting with someone else in order to enlist his aid in combating the corruption that you saw?

A. There came a time when Detective Durk stated that he would arrange or was in the process of arranging a meeting with the Commissioner of Investigations.

The Fraiman Aspect

Q. And who was the Commissioner of Investigation at that time?

A. Arnold Guy Fraiman.

Q. And Detective Durk was working at the time in the squad attached to the Commissioner of Investigation?

A. That's correct.

Q. And did he in fact arrange a meeting?

A. Yes.

Q. What was the purpose of it as he stated it to you and as you discussed?

A. Well, he thought that we now had the opportunity to speak directly to the Commissioner of Investigations, and inform him of the facts about corruption.

Q. To what end?

A. That he might take appropriate action in resolving it.

Q. Who was present at the meeting?

A. Myself, Detective Durk and Commissioner Fraiman.

Q. To the best of your recollection, what was said in the meeting?

A. Well, at the meeting I again informed the Commissioner of all the facts that I had related to the other people, and if in fact any additional incidents that had occurred to that time, I related them to him.

Q. Did you give names and places and amounts to the best of your recollection?

A. Yes, I did.

Q. What was Commissioner Fraiman's reaction to this information?

A. Well, after hearing all that I said, he said. "Well, what do you want me to do about it?" At which time I stated I was only a patrolman and I was merely apprising him of the facts, and that he was the Commissioner and should have more knowledge as to what to do than myself.

Q. Was any suggestion made that you carry an electronic device yourself in investigating the corruption?

A. Yes.

About the Wire

Q. And what was your reaction to the suggestion that you carry a wire?

A. I stated that if I personally wore a wire the only thing that—the only information I could get was from patrolmen on a patrolmen level, and I was not interested in just locking up patrolmen; that I wanted to take it on a much higher level where the problem lied.

Q. What was Commissioner Fraiman's reaction to the suggestion that a bug be placed in the surveillance truck, to the best of your recollection?

A. When I left there that day I was under the impression that a bug was in fact to be placed in the surveillance truck.

Q. Did you express any views about the way you felt the investigation should be handled?

A. Yes.

Q. What were those views?

A. Well, my views were they should be conducted on a high level, and I felt that the Commissioner was in a better position than myself to offer suggestions as to how it was to be resolved.

Q. To your knowledge, was any investigation carried out by the Department of Investigation of the facts that you brought to them?

A. To my knowledge, no.

CHAIRMAN KNAPP: You mean no as far as you know?
A. That's correct.
Q. Did you tell Commissioner Fraiman that you had been to see Mr. Kriegel?
A. No. Detective Durk suggested that we not tell him of the meeting with Kriegel.
COMMISSIONER JOHN E. SPRIZZO: Was there any reason for that, why you were not going to tell Fraiman about the meeting with Kriegel?
A. Well, Durk at this time had informed me that Kriegel was not going to pursue the investigation, and I guess he didn't want Kriegel to know that he had gone elsewhere.
Q. I have no further questions. If you have anything that you'd like to say that you think hasn't been covered—
A. Yes. I have a statement that I prepared and would like to read.

Serpico's Statement

CHAIRMAN KNAPP: Please go ahead.
A. Through my appearances here today I hope that police officers in the future will not experience the same frustration and anxiety that I was subjected to for the past five years at the hands of my superiors because of my attempt to report corruption.

I was made to feel that I had burdened them with an unwanted task. The problem is that the atmosphere does not yet exist in which an honest police officer can act without fear of ridicule or reprisal from fellow officers.

We create an atmosphere in which the dishonest officer appears the honest one and not the other way around. I hope that this investigation and any future ones will deal with corruption at all levels within the department and not limit themselves to cases involving individual patrolmen.

Police corruption cannot exist unless it is at least tolerated at higher levels in the department. Therefore, the most important result that can come from these hearings is a conviction by police officers, even more than the public, that the department will change.

I also believe that it is most important for superior officers in the Police Department to develop an attitude of respect for the average patrolman. Every patrolman is an officer and should be treated as such by his superiors.

Importance of Attitude

A policeman's attitude about himself reflects in large measure the attitude of his superiors toward him. If they feel his job is important and his stature, so will he.

It is just as important for policemen to change their attitudes toward the public. A policeman's first obligation is to be responsible to the needs of the community he serves.

The department must realize that an effective continuing relationship between the police and the public is more important than an impressive arrest record.

The system of rewards within the Police Department should be based on a policeman's over-all performance with the public rather than on his ability to meet arrest quotas. Merely uncovering widespread patterns of corruption will not resolve the problem.

Basic changes in attitude and approach are vital. In order to insure this, an independent permanent public investigative body dealing with police corruption, like this commission, is essential.

*   *   *   *   *

Testimony of Detective Sergeant David Durk

The following statement is excerpted from testimony before the Knapp Commission by David Durk, a police officer.

I'm here because I'm a policeman, and it is just very hard to say it, but these have been a lonely five years for Frank Serpico,

Paul DeLees and me. I've had a lot of time to think about what being a cop means to me, and maybe you can understand better some of the things I've said.

At the very beginning, the most important fact to understand is that I had and have no special knowledge of police corruption. We knew nothing . . . that wasn't known to every man and officer in (the police) divisions. We knew nothing about the police traffic in narcotics that wasn't known and testified to here by Paul Curran of the State Investigations Commission. We knew these things because we were involved in law enforcement in New York City, and anyone else who says he didn't know had to be blind, either by choice or by incompetence.

The facts have been exposed. This commission, to its enormous credit, has exposed them in a period of six months.

We simply cannot believe, as we do not believe today, that those with authority and responsibility in the area, whether the District Attorneys, the police commanders or those in power in City Hall, couldn't also have exposed them in six months, or at least in six years; that is, if they wanted to do it.

We were met with suspicion and hostility, inattention and laziness.

I am not saying that all those who ignored the corruption were themselves corrupt. Whether or not they were is almost immaterial in any case. The fact is that the corruption was ignored. . . . The fact is that almost wherever we turned in the Police Department, wherever we turned in the city administration, and almost wherever we went in the rest of the city, we were met not with cooperation, not with appreciation, not with an eagerness to seek out the truth, but with suspicion and hostility and laziness and inattention, and with our fear that at any moment our efforts might be betrayed.

To me, being a cop means believing in the rule of law. It means believing in a system of government that makes fair and just rules and then enforces them.

Being a cop also means serving, helping others. If it is not too corny, a cop is to help an old lady walk the streets safely, to help a 12-year-old reach her next birthday without being gang-raped, to help a storekeeper make a living without keeping a shotgun under his cash register, to help a boy grow up without having needles in his arms.

To me it is not a job, but a way of life.

Some people say that the cops live in the midst of inhumanity, amidst all the violence and cheating, violence and hate, and I guess to some extent it is true. But being a cop means also to be engaged with life. It means that our concern for others is not abstract, that we don't just write letters to The Times or give $10 once a year. We hit the street every day of our lives.

In this sense police corruption is not about money at all, because there is no amount of money that you can pay a cop to risk his life 365 days a year. Being a cop is a vocation or it is nothing at all, and that's what I saw being destroyed by the corruption of the New York City Police Department, destroyed for me and for thousands of others like me.

We wanted to believe in the rule of law. We wanted to believe in a system of responsibility. But those in high places everywhere, in the Department, in the DA's office, in City Hall, were determined not to enforce the law, they turned their heads away when law and justice were being sold on every street corner.

We wanted to serve others, but the Department was a home for the drug dealers and thieves. The force that was supposed to be protecting people was selling poison to their children, and there could be no life, no real life for me or anyone else on that force when, every day, we had to face the facts of our own terrible corruption.

I saw that happening to men all around me; men who could have been good officers, men of decent impulse, men of ideals, but men who were without decent leadership, men who were told in a hundred ways every day, go along, forget about the law, don't make waves and shut up.

They did go along. They did learn the unwritten code of the Department. They went along and they lost something very precious. They were a long way toward not being men anymore. And all the time I saw the other victims, too, especially the children—children of 14 and 15 and 16, wasted by heroin, turn into street corner thugs and whores, willing to rape their own mother for the price of a fix.

That was the price of going along, the real price of police corruption—not free meals, but broken homes in dying neighborhoods, and a whole generation of people being lost.

They went along and they lost something very precious.

That's what I joined the Department to stop. So that is why I went to The New York Times, because attention had to be paid. And in a last desperate hope that if the facts were known, someone must respond. Now it is up to you. I speak to you now as nothing more and nothing less than a cop.

We need you to fix responsibility for the rottenness that was allowed to fester. It must be fixed both inside and outside the Department. Inside the Department, responsibility has to be fixed against those top commanders who allowed the situation to develop.

Responsibility has to be fixed because no patrolman can believe he should care about corruption if his superiors can get away without caring. Also because commanders, themselves, have to be told again and again, and not only by the Police Commissioner, that the entire state of the Department is up to them, and most of all, responsibility has to be fixed because it is the first step toward recovering our simple but necessary conviction that right will be rewarded and wrong-doing punished.

Responsibility must also be fixed outside the Police Department, against all the men and agencies that have helped bring us to our present pass, against all those who could have helped expose the corruption but never did.

Like it or not, the policeman is convinced that he lives and works in the middle of a corrupt society, that everybody is getting theirs and why shouldn't he, and that if somebody cared about corruption, something would have been done about it a long time ago.

So your report has to tell us about the District Attorneys

and the courts and the Bar, and the Mayor and the Governor and what they have done, and what they have failed to do, and how great a measure of responsibility they also bear. Otherwise, if you suggest or allow others to suggest that the responsibility belongs only to the police, then for the patrolmen on the beat and in the radio cars, this commission will be just another part of the swindle.

The policeman is convinced he lives in a corrupt society.

You have to speak to the conscience of this city, speak for all of those without a voice, all those who are not here to be heard today, although they know the price of police corruption more intimately than anyone here.

The people of the ghetto and all the other victims, those broken in mind and spirit and hope, perhaps more than any other people in this city, they depend upon the police and the law to defend not just their pocket-books but their very lives and the lives and welfare of their children.

Tow-truck operators can write off bribes on their income tax. The expense-account executive can afford a prostitute. But nobody can repay a mother for the pain of seeing her children hooked on heroin.

Of course, all corruption is bad, but we cannot fall into the trap of pretending that all corruption is equally bad. There is a difference between selling free meals and selling narcotics. If we are unable to make that distinction, then we are saying to the police that the life of a child in the South Bronx has the same moral value as a cup of coffee, and this could not be true for this society or for the police force. You must show us the difference.

Finally, you must speak for the policemen of this city, for the best that is in them, for what most of them want to be, for what most of them will be, if we try.

Once I arrested a landlord's agent who offered to bribe me if I would not lock up a tenant who was bothering other tenants in the building. I put the cuffs on him. A crowd of people actually were around and actually said, "Viva policia!"

Of course, it was not just me or even the police that they were cheering. They were cheering because they had glimpsed in that one arrest the possibility of a system of justice that could work to protect them, too. They were cheering because if that agent could get arrested, maybe they had rights, that they were citizens and maybe one day life would really be different for their children. For me, that moment was what police work is all about.

It took five years of Frank Serpico's life and five years of mine to help bring this commission about. It has taken the lives and dedication of thousands of others to preserve as much of a police force as we have. It has taken many months of effort by all of you to help show this city the truth.

What I ask of you now is to help make us clean again, to help give us some leadership to look to the force, to walk at ease with their fellow citizens and perhaps one day on a warm summer night, hear again the shout. "Viva policia!"

IV. The Police versus Civil Authority

Max Weber, the noted German scholar, states that "Under normal conditions, the power position of a fully developed bureaucracy is always overtowering." With great persistence and using a variety of methods, he explains, it strives for greater and greater independence in the sociopolitical system.

So this would appear to be the case in the nation's largest urban centers where the police organizations, among other bureaucratic groups, have become militantly active in behalf of their own special interests. Now, as never before, the police are prepared to engage in political combat, challenging civil authority on a wide range of social and political issues. In our biggest cities, as the readings will show, they have had surprising success. The articles which appear in the succeeding pages were selected for the insights they give into the following questions: How do police effect themselves in politics, with what resources and strategies? How are other groups and institutions responding? What are the consequences of this for the communities in which this is happening?

The first selection called "Law and Disorder" is derived from a staff report to the National Commission on the Causes and Prevention of Violence. Of special interest is the confrontation of a black mayor with white policemen during a period of racial violence in Cleveland. Where such confrontation continues unchecked, as is shown here, racial tensions are likely to be exacerbated rather than moderated.

In the next two articles, " 'No' Says the P.B.A." and "Blue Power," we get a detailed view of police power at work in the cities of New York and Detroit. Policemen circulating petitions, lobbying for legislation, running controversial advertisements, endorsing candidates and even campaigning for candidates are evidence of the full development of a new kind of political mechanism—what can be called the police machine. How this affects the traditional patterns of political organization, and particularly the old party machine, is analyzed in the last article called "Models of Police Politics." Assessing the impact of the police on the political environments of New York, Chicago and Philadelphia, the author poses three basic models of police politics.

1. LAW AND DISORDER—CLEVELAND

Louis H. Massotti and Jerome E. Corsi

From the history of racial disturbances in Cleveland and other American cities, Clevelanders, on the morning of July 24, 1968, had every reason to expect that more trouble lay ahead. If past patterns were repeated, more violence would flare at nightfall. The authorities had to devise a strategy to cope with it.

More than 100 leaders of the black community gathered at City Hall about 8:30 a.m. to meet with Mayor Stokes. The attendance at this meeting was entirely black; not even the white members of the mayor's staff were permitted to take part. Many at the meeting had been up all night, assisting in City Hall or walking the streets, attempting to quell the violence.

Stokes opened the meeting with his assessment of the situation, then called for discussion on how best to handle it. A number of options were available to the mayor: He could impose a curfew, strengthen police and National Guard units in the troubled area, or use various combinations of force such as placing National Guard in the area and not police. Many at the meeting were concerned that if police were allowed to remain in the area, there would be further shooting. They feared that

From *Shoot-Out in Cleveland* by Louis H. Masotti and Jerome R. Corsi, A Report to the National Commission on the Causes and Prevention of Violence, pp. 67-77, 81, 82, 85-91. Published by the United States Government Printing Office, May, 1969.

black nationalists would be made fidgety by the continued presence of the police and would begin shooting, or that if police
were allowed to remain in the area, they would seek revenge for
their three comrades who were killed the night before. Several
spoke in opposition to a curfew, noting that if it were applied to
just one area it would be resented by the citizens of that area
and would not prevent outsiders from coming into the area and
beginning violence again.

The meeting at City Hall produced no real consensus, and
Mayor Stokes revealed no plans of his own. When the meeting
broke up about 10 a.m., he retired to his office to discuss strategies with his staff, while about 20 of the participants in the meeting, most of them militants, adjourned to the Auditorium Hotel
to continue discussions.

An hour later Stokes addressed a press conference originally
scheduled for 9:30 a.m. He attributed Tuesday night's violence
to "a gang who will meet the full measure of the law" and described the present situation on the East Side as "quiet."

> Security measures are being maintained with a minimum
> number of National Guardsmen on our streets and a siz-
> able force in ready reserve should they be needed. I have
> met with Negro leadership at City Hall and they have
> joined me in an all-out effort to make sure that Cleveland's
> night of terror will not turn into a riot. We are constantly
> re-evaluating the situation and assure that this city will not
> be governed by hoodlums.

The mayor indicated that he had not yet decided upon a strategy
for Wednesday evening.

Early in the afternoon the group of militants returned from
the Auditorium Hotel to City Hall. Now they presented a definite
proposal to the mayor: They would go back into the community
and try to bring it under control themselves, preventing looting,
burning, and additional loss of life. They wanted a period of
time to attempt this; if it did not work, Stokes could choose a

different strategy. Stokes listened. He still made no commitment.

This was not the first time such a proposal had been suggested to Stokes. Bertram Gardner, who had spent the night on the streets, proposed such a course to the Mayor in a conversation about 7:30 a.m. Gardner wanted Stokes to take the police and Guard out of the area, while Gardner sent about 200 or 250 blacks into the community to try to calm feelings. He wanted only about 6 hours: from about 11 a.m. to about 5 p.m. At the 8:30 a.m. meeting, others had proposed a similar course.

About midafternoon, Stokes discussed the idea with others in a small meeting in his office. Richard Greene, director of the Community Development Department, endorsed the proposal. He felt that the black community ought to be given a chance to "pull itself together." Councilman George Forbes expressed confidence that the strategy would work. Not all were convinced. General Del Corso expressed serious reservations about the wisdom of the proposal.

When the mayor made his decision, he did not make it rashly. He had had the benefit of numerous opinions and arguments for and against competing strategies. Some options, like the curfew, had been seen as fraught with difficulties. Stokes had heard compelling arguments about the volatile situation that would be created by the continuing presence of white law enforcement officers in the black community. The "all black" strategy appeared to be the only rational policy to reduce bloodshed. In accepting it, Stokes knew he was taking a calculated risk. There would be safeguards, however. He accepted the suggestion by Richard Greene that Negro policemen function in the area as well as the black leaders. He would also station police and the National Guard around the perimeter of the area, so that they could respond quickly if trouble did arise.

Though the decision was not his alone, Stokes had to assume full responsibility for it. It was a novel strategy, one that a white mayor would have had greater difficulty in instrumenting. It was Stokes' rapport with the Negro community that brought forth the proposal in the first place and that now gave hope that it would work.

At 4:15 p.m., Mayor Stokes released a detailed plan for

Wednesday night. About 6 square miles of the city were to be cordoned off until 7 a.m., Thursday morning. The southern boundary would be Euclid Avenue, eastward from East 55th Street. The northern boundary would be Superior Avenue, from East 55th to Rockefeller Park, then along the park's eastern edge up to St. Clair, eastward along St. Clair (with a small section north of it) to the city line adjoining East Cleveland. This perimeter was to be patrolled by units of three National Guardsmen and one police officer, beginning at 7 p.m. The National Guard was to retain a mobile reserve to deploy within the cordoned area should serious trouble arise.

"Normal patrol within the cordoned-off area," said the memo, "will be restricted to regular Cleveland police as directed by the Safety Director. National Guard troops will be committed to the area only if needed."

Though the memorandum did not mention that only Negro policemen would be allowed in the area, Mayor Stokes spelled out this provision in a press conference at 4:45 p.m.

> There will only be Negro policemen and possibly a Negro sheriff in the area guarding the people. . . . There will be 109 [individuals] who will represent the groups themselves and about five hundred persons who are familiar with this situation will be in the area.

All white nonresidents, including newsmen, were to be kept from the area. The mayor repeated that it was important for people to stay home and off the streets. He made two further announcements: that the sale of liquor in Cuyahoga County (embracing Cleveland) had been stopped for 72 hours beginning at 11 a.m., Wednesday; that four emergency centers had been set up in East Side churches and community centers to provide food and shelter for those displaced by Tuesday night's disturbances.

The Reverend DeForest Brown, director of the Hough Area Development Corporation, was named spokesman for the Mayor's

Committee which was to patrol the streets that night. Said Brown:

> We, out of our concern, have accepted the responsibility to restore law and order out of a chaotic situation. Leaders will be out talking to the black community about its responsibility to itself.

The mayor had made his decision. On Wednesday evening black control was established for the black community.

*   *   *

Wednesday, July 24, passed in heat and mugginess, the mugginess fed by light rainshowers that swept over the city at noontime. Through the day the police responded to sporadic calls of looting and of looters hawking stolen goods on street corners. They closed bars that were violating the liquor ban and investigated rumors of looting and violence planned for Wednesday evening. Here and there merchants boarded up the windows of their stores or carted away valuable merchandise. (Later there were claims that some merchants took what they could, then encouraged looters to take the rest, figuring they would get adequate recompense from their insurance companies.) As 7 p.m. approached, the roving patrols of police and Guardsmen retreated to the perimeter of the cordoned area. There was a thunderstorm early in the evening, but at dusk the sky was clearing and the heat and mugginess lingered.

The Negro leaders carried the message from City Hall back to their communities, meeting with small groups to explain the evening's strategy and to organize for effective peacekeeping. At the office of Pride, Inc., on St. Clair, Wilbur Grattan, a black nationalist associated with the New Republic of Africa, addressed a group of about 30, most of whom were members of the Circle of African Unity. Grattan had spent much of the previous night in peacekeeping and most of the day in the meetings that led to Mayor Stokes' decision to exercise black control in the black community. He described what had been discussed during those meetings, praised the bold policy that had been adopted, then turned to matters of organization for the evening. After being told by Grattan that they would receive orange arm bands labeled "The Mayor's Commitee," the group worked out the problems of geographic assignments for each of them. Baxter Hill, director of Pride, Inc., closed the meeting in his office with a reminder of the significance of the responsibilities they were about to undertake.

Hill stayed on for awhile at the Pride office, which was to be the headquarters for the peacekeeping operation through the night. (A Negro radio station broadcast the telephone number of Pride frequently during the evening, urging listeners to report crowds, looting, or other indications of trouble.) The expected 500 peace patrols were to be divided into four "companies," headed by Harllel Jones, William (Sonny) Denton of the United Youth Council, and two from Baxter Hill's organization: Benjamin Lloyd and Ronald Turner.

While the Negro leaders were hastily organizing their peacekeeping force, the Cleveland Police Department was preparing for its role in the troubled area. White policemen were assigned to work with National Guardsmen patrolling the perimeter of the cordoned area. At Fifth District headquarters, situated within the area, police climbed aboard military trucks and joked about being back in the Army. American Legionnaires served them coffee. About 100 Negro policemen (out of a total of 165 Negro officers in the 2,200-man police force) were assigned to patrol the cordoned area, using 21 patrol cars. Negroes on the county sheriff's staff were assigned to help them. White police, it was understood, would enter the area only if the Negro officers needed additional assistance.

*   *   *

The sky had not yet darkened when firetrucks were called to East 105th and Superior to extinguish fires that were rekindles (accidental or intentional) of burned-out stores. A crowd gathered to watch. Nearby, some Negro businessmen were removing merchandise from their stores and, when the owner of a record store left, some who had stood watching walked in and helped themselves to odds and ends he had left behind.

The crowd at the intersection had swelled to several hundred when members of the Mayor's Committee arrived to disperse them. A few of the peace patrols talked to the crowd in front of the record store. Most stood in the middle of the intersection, imploring the crowd to go home. A rumor was afloat that a child was trapped in the basement of a burning pawnshop. Firemen said they had searched the basement and no child was there. Noting that such a thing could happen, the Mayor's Committee pleaded with parents to take their children home.

Children stayed on. Some of them found clothing in the back of a store that had been nearly gutted the night before, and soon a crowd was surging toward the rear of the store. After considerable cajoling, the Mayor's Committee managed to discourage the looting. But the technique of talking to the crowd from the middle of the intersection was not dispersing the people. Walter Beach, Ron Lucas, Baxter Hill, and Harllel Jones decided that if they were going to be effective, they had to walk among the crowd and talk to the people, two or three at a time. Though it took more than an hour to disperse the crowd, the technique worked.

Through the night, teams of peace patrols drove up and down the commercial streets of the area, stopping wherever four or more people were standing around, pleading with them to disperse. Occasionally members of the Mayor's Committee stood in front of stores where windows had been broken or iron gates torn down, directly confronting the potential looters. This technique could not be wholly effective, for the Mayor's Committee lacked the manpower for permanent guards at every commercial establishment. Potential looters, some of them professionals, lurked in the shadows, sometimes for hours, waiting for the peace patrols to leave the scene. Days later they would be seen hawking stolen goods on street corners. Occasionally a looter broke into a store, setting off the burglar alarm, then hid nearby until someone came to investigate, turned off the alarm, and walked away. Most looters made off with what they could carry, but some filled automobiles with merchandise.

The Mayor's Committee observed adults, including women, among the potential and actual looters, but teenagers gave them the most trouble. Roving bands of teenagers usually were the first to break into a store, then proved unresponsive to the appeals of the peace patrols. "We couldn't control the kids," Walter Burks, executive assistant to the Mayor, recalls. "We would tell them to stop and they would walk away and you would get into your car to drive someplace else and you would drive back and they were right back with their hands in [the windows of a looted store]." Some of the troublesome youths, says Burks, were not more than 10 years old. The next day Mayor Stokes ascribed most of the trouble Wednesday night to "roving bands of young people generally between the ages of fourteen and seventeen."

An observer who accompanied members of the Mayor's Committee on their patrols recalls that some were particularly effective in their work. Harllel Jones, a young militant, wiry and ordinarily soft-spoken, dispersed a crowd at 123d and St. Clair that had gathered in front of a furniture store that had been broken into. "At 105th and Massey," the observer adds, "Harllel dispersed perhaps the potentially most dangerous crowd of about two hundred people. It took him about twenty to twenty-five minutes." Like the other militants who were particularly effective Wednesday night, Harllel Jones succeeded by making eloquent pleas to the pride of the black community. "If there was one man who stands out as having done the most effective job possible of maintaining peace," said the observer, "it was Harllel Jones."

Noticeable by their absence were the clergymen and other moderate and middle-class Negro leaders. Though a number of them had participated in the meetings at City Hall, few were on the streets Wednesday night and their effectiveness was limited. Had more moderates helped out, the members of the peace patrol felt, the sporadic looting might have been prevented entirely.

White policemen appeared in the cordoned area over the protests of the Mayor's Committee. When a pawnbroker's window was broken at East 101st and St. Clair, white policemen responded to the call. They ignored requests of the peace patrol to leave. Similar incidents occurred elsewhere. At East 123d and St. Clair, an observer recalls, an alarm went off in a furniture store.

> All of a sudden National Guardsmen and white policemen, who apparently had been stationed in East Cleveland, appeared on the scene. They started backing up toward the buildings as if they were actually in a state of emergency. Nothing had occurred and, fortunately, the Law Director arrived on the scene.

Law Director James talked to the white officers, and they left.

*   *   *

The reaction of some white policemen to Mayor Stokes' strategy of black control was made clear to those monitoring the police radio Wednesday night.

This came in response to a report of a heart-attack case within the cordoned area: "White or nigger? Send the Mayor's Committee."

When a report was broadcast that a child had fallen off a second-floor porch, the return call came: "Tell the Mayor's Committee to handle it."

When the police dispatcher requested cars to respond to a fire call, an anonymous voice suggested that Mayor Stokes "go p . . . on it." Responses to other calls included "F . . . that nigger Mayor!"

At the Fifth District headquarters, the heavily guarded bastion within the troubled area, police responded in a fury of curses and epithets, directed toward Stokes and Safety Director McManamon, when told they could not carry rifles while patrolling the perimeter of the cordoned area. A policeman there, delivering a monolog to a bystander on what is "wrong" with Negroes gave this assessment of Mayor Stokes: "You need a sheepdog to lead sheep; you don't have a sheep lead other sheep."

The tension at Fifth District headquarters lasted through the evening. Two television newsmen who entered the building were grabbed from behind by a commanding officer, pushed through the building, and thrown out into the parking lot where other policemen shouted at them abusively. After appealing to another commanding officer they were let back in, and ultimately the first officer apologized for ejecting them.

*   *   *

At a press conference late the next morning, Mayor Stokes pronounced the strategy for Wednesday night a qualified success.

> It is our considered opinion that we made significant head-way last night in bringing to an end the violence and lawlessness that has occurred on our East Side. No one was killed or shot or seriously injured during the night.

Stokes admitted that there had been trouble; he reported that 3 fires had been set, 36 stores looted, and 13 persons arrested in the troubled area. "Most of the trouble," he said, "was caused by young teenagers, roving in small bands." He expressed thanks to the National Guard patrolling the perimeter, the Negro policemen working within the area, and especially the 300 members of the Mayor's Committee "who patrolled the troubled areas until dawn to keep things cool." He announced that bus service and garbage pickup had resumed in the cordoned area and that city workers had begun to tear down dangerously damaged buildings. He emphasized, however, that more trouble could be expected.

Earlier in the morning, Stokes had met with Negro leaders at City Hall. During that meeting the resentment over the limited participation of moderate Negro leaders in the peacekeeping was brought into the open. It was generally agreed that the peace patrols had been only partially effective; the arson and looting had been only partially curbed. Changes were needed: A curfew now might help remove the gangs from the streets; more cars equipped with radios were needed; more sound trucks would help; and broken windows should be boarded before nightfall.

While the Negro leaders continued their discussion in the City Council chamber, the mayor addressed the press conference. There he announced a change in strategy: The National Guard, he said, was being brought into the area to protect stores against looting. This change in strategy, like others he made that Thursday, was to haunt Carl Stokes for weeks to come, for it provided an indication to his critics that he had given in to pressure from others or conceded the failure of his Wednesday-night strategy. Throughout the ensuing controversy, Stokes would maintain that the strategy had succeeded because it had prevented bloodshed, and he valued life over property. Changes in the strategy, he argued, became appropriate after tempers had cooled in the black community and the protection of property could be safely entrusted to white law enforcement officers.

One of the first to criticize the mayor was Councilman Leo Jackson, whose district includes part of Glenville and who is said to represent the views of older, established Negro residents. "If you want to say what happened last night—no shootings, no sniping—was a success, then it was," Jackson told a reporter. "But if you consider the looting, the destruction, the breaking of windows, the wholesale gutting of buildings, last night's activities were a total failure."

Businessmen whose stores were victimized Wednesday night were bitterly critical of the mayor's policy. The white owner of a looted clothing store drove to the scene about 1 a.m. and could not get out of his car because of an attacking mob. A Negro policeman ordered him out of the area for his own safety. At the perimeter he pleaded with National Guardsmen and police for help, but was told there was nothing they could do. The owner of a looted furniture store got the same response from police at Fifth District headquarters. A partner in a drycleaning chain, two of whose stores had been looted the previous night, had his main plant looted of clothing Wednesday night—half a

million dollars' worth, he estimated. "We're wiped out," he said
bitterly. "We couldn't get help. That means 70 people out of
work—70 families without incomes."

White policemen were openly critical of the mayor's Wednesday-night strategy. A 30-year-old patrolman angrily submitted
his resignation. When Police Chief Michael Blackwell called the
mayor's strategy "a brilliant idea," there were murmurings that
Blackwell, a 42-year veteran of the force, was a traitor to his
department and a politician protecting himself.

Gen. Del Corso, who had argued for much stronger measures
Wednesday night, declined to criticize the mayor.

> I made my suggestions but the Mayor made the decision
> and I am sure he did a lot of soul-searching all day. We're
> here to assist and cooperate with the Mayor. He wanted
> to use this means [citizen-patrols] and it is beginning to
> be productive. It is proving successful.

It came as a shock to City Hall when, on August 9, Gen. Del
Corso told the Ohio Crime Commission that Stokes had "sur-
rendered to black revolutionaries."

That same day, after the Stokes administration presented a
summary of events to city councilmen and to the press, Council
President James V. Stanton, considered by many to be a leading
contender for the office occupied by Carl Stokes, joined in the
criticism. "I find no moral grounds," he said, "for taking duly
constituted law enforcement away from the families and property
of that area regardless of any justification by the Administration
that there was no loss of life." Stanton's charge brought a re-
joinder from Safety Director Joseph McManamon. "He can't say
that," McManamon retorted, "unless he means that Negro policemen aren't duly constituted officers." He added that the concen-
tration of Negro policemen on Wednesday evening added up to
the normal number of police in the area.

In the days following the Wednesday-night disturbances, support for the mayor's strategy, sometimes in the form of newspaper

advertisements, came from civil rights groups, religious and charitable organizations, liberal political groups, and from Cleveland educators, industrial leaders, and other prominent citizens. A professional polling organization found that 59 percent of its respondents supported the mayor's strategy; 14 percent criticized it; the rest were uncertain.

*   *   *

Four hundred National Guardsmen moved into the cordoned area on Thursday morning to help Cleveland police control the sporadic but persistent looting. Police were also kept busy through the day enforcing the liquor ban and tracking down rumors of violence threatened for Thursday night. Teenagers employed by Pride, Inc., carted away debris from damaged buildings.

Meanwhile, Mayor Stokes pondered a strategy for Thursday night, questioning whether to impose a curfew and whether to allow National Guardsmen and white policemen in the area after dark. Early in the afternoon he took a walk, touring the streets of Glenville for the first time since the trouble began July 23, urging residents to keep their children at home Thursday night. At 4 p.m. he met with Baxter Hill and other Negro leaders at the office of Pride, Inc. He sought their counsel on a strategy for Thursday night. Most agreed that additional enforcement was necessary. With some reluctance, stemming more from concern for the unpredictable behavior of white policemen than of black nationalists, they agreed that National Guardsmen and white policemen should be allowed to remain in the area after nightfall.

Mayor Stokes announced his decision at a press conference about 6:30 p.m. A curfew would be imposed on the cordoned area, beginning at 9 p.m. and extending to 6:30 a.m., Friday morning. The National Guard would stay in the area, and no policemen would be constrained from entering the area.

Though the announcement was carried on television and radio stations, it was a late-hour decision that caught many unprepared. Some police first learned of the curfew from a police radio broadcast 20 minutes before the curfew was to begin. Sound trucks were sent into the area to announce the curfew, but did not reach some neighborhoods until 10:30 p.m. People were still walking the streets after 10 p.m. and some businesses were still open. A reporter saw a National Guard unit still encamped in Rockefeller Park at 10:30 p.m.

Stokes had disbanded the Mayor's Committee, but a number of Negro leaders worked Thursday night to keep the peace, patrolling the area in nine cars.

Though the peacekeeping operation on Thursday night was massive, according with the wishes of those who had urged strong enforcement, it was not 100 percent successful. At a predawn press conference, John Little, the mayor's executive secretary, gave a summary report of the night's violence. A major fire had occurred on East 55th Street; there had been four minor fires, of which two were described as "flareups" toward the eastern end of Superior Avenue. Thirty people had been arrested: one for attempted arson, two for looting, the rest for curfew violations. Guardsmen had been sent to disperse more than 200 youths roaming the streets in the southeast corner of Cleveland, far from the cordoned area. There were no reports of sniping.

Friday was a time of relative calm. There were indications the community was returning to normal. The liquor ban was lifted in the suburbs of Cuyahoga County, and Mayor Stokes was expected to approve a lifting of the ban in Cleveland the next morning. (He did.) The Friday-night curfew was delayed until midnight, permitting residents of the cordoned area to attend a Cleveland Indians baseball game.

For the forces of law and order, Friday was not completely a dull day. That afternoon, an army of about 35 policemen and 100 National Guardsmen, equipped with rifles, shotguns, and tear gas, surrounded the Esquire Hotel at 10602 Superior Avenue. They were there in response to a tip that a number of snipers involved in Tuesday night's shootout were hiding in the hotel. A police bullhorn urged the men to give themselves up. The episode turned seriocomic when three unarmed teenagers emerged from the hotel. Nothing incriminating was found in their rooms but they were arrested anyway, on suspicion of possessing stolen property (a radio, a camera, and two adding machines).

On Friday night, at the Afro Set, Harllel Jones and six youths were charged by police with violating the midnight curfew. The police searched Jones and said they found brass knuckles in his pockets; without a warrant they searched his car and claimed to find a .38-caliber revolver. (Police later changed their report to read that they found brass knuckles. The court dismissed the case against Jones on September 16 on grounds that the search was illegal.) Mayor Stokes, having gotten word of the arrest, arrived while Jones was being held, assured the watching crowd that no harm would befall Jones, and assigned a Negro policeman to accompany Jones through the arresting process. After the mayor left, according to Jones' followers, police kicked down the door of the Afro Set, gassed the shop, broke the front window, and damaged articles in the store.

There were few other incidents of violence Friday night, and on Saturday morning Mayor Stokes pronounced the crisis past. National Guardsmen had begun to leave the area. Police were restored to 8-hour shifts. There would be no curfew Saturday night. The mayor, other City Hall officials, and hundreds of policemen went to a Catholic church to attend a memorial service for the three policemen slain Tuesday night.

Not all the tensions had subsided. Cleveland had not seen the last of violence. . . . . .

*　　*　　*

On Sunday, July 28, Cleveland began to assess the damage from 5 days of violence. A task force of architects and contractors walked through the disturbance area, examining damaged properties, using as their guide a list of 73 properties that had been reported damaged to the police department, the fire department, the mayor's office, or listed as damaged in newspaper accounts. A group of alumni of the Harvard Business School also analyzed the property damage, and in their report to the mayor's office listed damage to 63 separate business establishments. Their list contained 10 fewer names than the task-force report because two of the properties were empty stores with apartments above them damaged by water, four were not privately owned businesses, and four were businesses with two locations, both damaged, but listed only once.

The task force of architects and contractors had surveyed damage and destruction of buildings and estimated the total property loss to be $1,087,505. To this, the Harvard Business School alumni added an estimate of $1,550,225 for losses in equipment and inventory so that, in total, dollar losses exceeded $2.6 million.

Of the 63 business establishments burned or looted, two-thirds were on Superior Avenue. There were 11 damaged businesses on East 105th Street, 10 on St. Clair; the rest were scattered. The damage tended to be clustered. Half of the damaged businesses on Superior Avenue were in a four-block ara, between 101st and 105th. In another cluster, between 121st and 124th, 14 businesses were damaged.

Despite the clustering, the damage was far more widespread than during the Hough riots of 1966. Then the burning and looting had been concentrated in a smaller area with only furtive attempts to spread the violence. The unlawful activity in 1968 seemed born of greater self-confidence, less fear of getting caught, than in 1966, and this was interpreted by some as an indication that Mayor Stokes had made a mistake in withdrawing Guardsmen and white policemen.

In defending his policy of withdrawing troops Wednesday night, the mayor admitted that there was property damage, but said he valued life over property. Nonetheless, it would be valuable to know *when* the incidents of property damage took place. Unfortunately, the task force and the Harvard Business School group did not investigate the question, and the only analysis of the timing of looting and arson is one presented by the mayor's office on August 9. According to that analysis, of a total of 47 looting incidents, 26 occurred during the first 24 hours of violence, 17 during the second 24 hours (essentially when the Mayor's Committee was patrolling the streets), and 4 during the remaining days of trouble. Of the 34 fires blamed on vandals and other incendiaries, 14 occurred during the first 24 hours, 7 during the second 24 hour period and 13 during the rest of the week.

The analysis by the mayor's office would indicate that violent activity had been reduced Wednesday night. The figures, however, do not concur with those presented by others, including a statement published by the *Plain Dealer* on July 26, that "at least forty-seven stores in the cordoned area were either burned or looted yesterday." The precise amount of damage Wednesday night will probably never be confirmed.

Hardest hit among the 63 businesses were groceries (17), furniture stores (10) and clothing stores (8). The Lakeview Tavern, involved in the Tuesday-night shootout, was the only bar reported looted, although the State Liquor Store on East 105th Street was looted twice. (It was not included among the list of 63 damaged establishments, since it is not a privately owned business.) Opinions vary on whether Negro-owned businesses were carefully spared from damage, as they had been during the Hough riots of 1966. A reporter for the *Call & Post* cited evidence that Negro merchants were spared, though some of the 63 businesses listed are Negro owned. Certainly racial strife was a contributing factor in the pattern of looting and violence. A 20-year-old Negro college student who participated in the violence told an interviewer: "I burned the corner Jew who had been getting my folks for years. I didn't have a desire to loot. I just had to put that cat out of business." But the choice of targets for looting may have had more to do with the commodities coveted than anything else.

The alumni group of the Harvard Business School talked to 50 of the merchants whose businesses had been affected. Of these, only 4 (8 percent) of the owners believed that they had full insurance coverage; 22 (44 percent) had partial insurance coverage; and 24 (48 percent), the largest group, had no insurance coverage at all. At the time of these interviews, 14 of the merchants (28 percent) were open for business and required no help; 20 (40 percent) said they would reopen in the same area if they got short-term financing or adequate insurance payments; seven (14 percent) had not decided what to do; and nine (18 percent) had closed their businesses and did not plan to reopen in the neighborhood.

A. L. Robinson, of the Cleveland Business and Economic

Development Corporation, cited an effect of the looting that cannot be measured: "I think the looting put fears in the heart and mind of a great many people who under normal circumstances would like to go into business [in the area]." An older resident of Glenville looked at looted buildings and asked in bitterness: "Why do we destroy ourselves?"

*   *   *

In the wake of the violence of July 1968, Clevelanders held a mirror to their city. Few were happy with what they saw, but the impressions formed—and the remedies proposed—were many and varied.

Members of the Fraternal Order of Police were angry. Six hundred policemen attended an FOP meeting on August 1 at the Plumbers Union Hall, where heavily armed cops guarded the meeting from the rooftop. There were denunciations of the Stokes administration and a motion, favorably voted, calling for the resignation of Safety Director Joseph McManamon. A similar motion to oust Police Chief Michael Blackwell was defeated, largely out of consideration of his age (67) and longstanding FOP membership. Two nights earlier, a hastily organized meeting of several hundred police wives had also brought denunciations of the Stokes administration.[1]

The mayor refused to fire McManamon. Partly in response to police pressure, however, he and his administration began taking steps to correct long-standing deficiencies in the Police Department. After studying riot control measures in Philadelphia and New York City, the Cleveland police established a 60-man tactical unit, trained in the use of high-powered weapons and prepared to cope with situations involving heavy gunfire. Early in September, Mayor Stokes announced a campaign to recruit 500 additional police officers, and the NAACP began a program to encourage and prepare Negro applicants for the openings. At the same time, the mayor announced a $186,615 grant from the Ford Foundation to be used for police training, to pay tuition costs for policemen enrolled in college courses of their choosing, and to give 900 city employees (including policemen) training in modern management techniques. Other funds came from the U.S. Department of Justice or a new program to improve police-community relations.

More changes were announced. Safety Director McManamon promised to improve the police department's telephone system so that calls could be answered and responded to more quickly and efficiently. Late in September the city began replacing run-down equipment with 164 new police vehicles, and McManamon ordered that patrol cars on the East Side be integrated. Patrick Gerity, who succeeded Michael Blackwell as police chief in mid-October, began a shakeup of the police department that resulted in the reassignment of 104 men.

Some of the changes made police unhappy. When Cleveland's Civil Service Commission expanded the recommended reading for a police promotion test to 26 books—including works on sociology, race relations, and national crime problems—police rebelled. "What are you trying to make us—social workers?" a policeman asked the secretary of the Civil Service Commission at a meeting of the FOP. Claiming applicants for promotion would not have time to read the books before the exam scheduled for November 16, the FOP sued to have the test delayed and the reading list shortened. The suit was dropped when the Civil Service Commission agreed to reschedule the test for December 14 and reduce the reading list to 14 books.

*   *   *

In an editorial on September 27, the *Cleveland Plain Dealer* called for an end to the tensions and cleavages opened by the Glenville incident.

> This city must not be turned into a mutual aggravation society. It is time for all groups—for their own safety, for their own good, for their children's future—to work together for a peaceable, lawful, orderly community.

The editorial went on to condemn "anyone who tries to keep up the vendetta."

Three days later the *Plain Dealer* began a series of front-page articles, entitled "The Cleveland Police: What's on Their Mind," that effectively kept the vendetta going.

The first installment of the series contained a barrage of quotations from policemen critical of Mayor Stokes, Safety Director McManamon, and Police Chief Blackwell. The article cited pernicious claims that the mayor was "protecting" black nationalists. "He wants to get them in the police department," one officer was quoted. Though it had been promised that the series of articles would separate fact from rumor and myth, the few facts interspersed among the critical opinions were negative ones —for example, concerning outmoded police vehicles. Nothing was said of reforms and improvements then in progress. (The next day, in a side article, the *Plain Dealer* did point out that Cleveland had recently acquired 164 new police vehicles, and that many of these were already in service.)

The second installment, which purported to be about inadequate equipment, opened with a quotation in 14-point type that perhaps unintentionally, had racist overtones: "We're like a British outpost in Africa." Like the first article, the second published comments of policemen alleging lack of leadership and inadequate equipment.

The third installment, on October 2, frankly discussed racial attitudes in the police department. It began with a quotation in large type: "This business about putting a white and Negro policeman in the same car won't work. You got to have a close relationship between partners. If you're not buddies, forget it." There were several quotations of the most-colored-people-appreciate-us sort. Of the troublesome minority of black militants, a police lieutenant offered this analysis: "I think these black nationalists are financed directly by Communists or front groups."

The next installment of "The Cleveland Police: What's on Their Mind" repeated the charge that the mayor was pushing black militants into the police department and contained the allegation that standards were being lowered to let them in. The fifth and last article in the series expressed police dissatisfaction with the courts and with U.S. Supreme Court rulings affecting police procedures.

At the beginning of the series, the *Plain Dealer* had announced that seven reporters—three police reporters, two city hall reporters, (one oft hem a Negro), and two general assignment reporters—were compiling and writing the series. Nearly all of the work, however, was done by the three police reporters. It has been noted in sociological studies that policemen often develop a conspiratorial outlook on the world and a persecution complex about themselves as a group. ("We're alone, we're a football," a patrolman told one of the reporters.) While police reporters do not necessarily develop the police attitude toward the community, they tend to reflect that attiude as an unconscious or unstated condition of their continuing rapport with the police. "The Cleveland Police: What's on Their Mind" gave free rein to expressions of cynicism, conspiracy, and group paranoia.

The series of articles in the *Plain Dealer* was defensible as "news" because it brought to the attention of Clevelanders serious problems, especially problems of morale, in the police department. It is noteworthy, however, that the police had publicly aired their grievances in the days and weeks following the Glenville incident, that tensions had begun to subside at the time the articles were published (and deserved no rekindling), and that steps had already been taken to improve the situation in the police department. While the series of articles led readers to an impression of a police department suffering stagnation, much of the discontent may actually have stemmed from the uncertainty and insecurity that impending changes and improvements in the department were then creating.

Many Clevelanders who regard the *Plain Dealer* as the city's most responsible newspaper were shocked by the content and tone of "The Cleveland Police: What's on Their Mind." Negro leaders were outraged. The local chapters of the NAACP and CORE announced boycotts against the *Plain Dealer*.

*   *   *

Other articles appearing in the *Cleveland Plain Dealer* fed suspicions that the newspaper was carrying on a vendetta of its own.

On October 3, concurrent with the fourth installment of the police-gripe series, a front-page, five-column headline read: "FBI Is Refused Warrant in Glenville Riot Probe." The article told of the refusal of the U.S. Attorney General in Washington to grant a warrant to the FBI to search a farm in Ashtabula County, 50 miles east of Cleveland, allegedly used by black militants involved in the Glenville incident. A source within the police department was quoted as saying, "Our information was that the FBI felt there were weapons and possibly dead bodies [at the farm]." The implication was made that the Justice Department had thwarted the legitimate work of the FBI, possibly because of racial sensitivities.

According to reporters interviewed for this study, the editors of the *Plain Dealer* had known of the warrant refusal for some time but had saved the story to use as a "tie-in" with the series on police complaints. The *Cleveland Press* investigated the matter and came up with a different story. The *Press* article reported that 50 locations had been reported to Cleveland police as possible gun locations, but there was insufficient information to link the Ashtabula farm with the Glenville shootings. "If we did [have enough information]," a police official said, "we would have sought our own search warrant."

The next day the *Plain Dealer* reported that U.S. Representative William E. Minshall, a Republican running for reelection in a predominantly white suburban area of Cleveland, was calling for a special session of the Federal grand jury to investigate the Glenville incident. Minshall accused U.S. Attorney General Ramsey Clark of "shielding" the guilty parties in the incident. On October 5, the *Plain Dealer,* under an eight-column headline, reported that U.S. Attorney Bernard J. Stuplinski had responded with the promise of a Federal grand jury investigation into the circumstances surrounding the Glenville incident. That afternoon, in the *Cleveland Press,* Stuplinski denied that he had any intention of calling a special Federal grand jury to probe the incident.

Federal agencies, including the FBI and the Alcohol Tax

Unit have been gathering information as to possible violations of Federal law since the first shot was fired in Glenville.

If any violations of Federal law are found, Stuplinski indicated,
they would be presented to a regular session of the grand jury.

On October 16, the *Plain Dealer* unleashed a major exposé,
revealing details of an incident, embarrassing to the mayor and
other high officials, that had taken place 5 months earlier. Under
a five-column headline, "CORE 'Bodyguards' Freed by City Hall
in Gun Case," the *Plain Dealer* told of the dropping of concealed
weapons charges against two Negroes "at the request of unnamed
officials at City Hall" in May 1968.

The two East Side Negroes were temporary bodyguards for
CORE's former national director, Floyd B. McKissick. They were
arrested during the early morning hours of April 5, 8 hours
after the assassination of Martin Luther King, outside the home
of a prominent Negro stockbroker where McKissick was sleeping.
Shortly after they were arrested, Roy Innis, then associate national director of CORE, showed up at Sixth District headquarters to appeal for their release, saying that McKissick had announced on a nationwide newscast that his life had been threatened and that the two arrested men were protecting him. Noting
that McKissick had not requested police protection, the officer-in-
charge at Sixth District headquarters declined to release the two
men. Later in the morning, however, they were released on
orders from Chief Prosecutor James S. Carnes.

A jury trial on the concealed weapons charge was scheduled
for May 21. On checking the court records on May 16, one of
the arresting officers found that the case had been advanced to
May 6 and the records marked "Nolle Pros," indicating that the
charges had been dropped by Prosecutor Carnes.

After the *Plain Dealer* revelations on October 16, John T.
Corrigan, prosecutor of Cuyahoga County, proceeded to take over
the case dropped by the city of Cleveland, an unusual move
considering the charges were only for a misdemeanor. Corrigan
succeeded in getting indictments against the two men from the

county grand jury. Carnes, who had resigned as city prosecutor in September, was unresponsive to reporters' questions about the case. Mayor Stokes at first refused to comment on the case, then admitted he had been instrumental in having the charges dropped. But he defended the move as necessary during the volatile hours following the King assassination, when "we were . . . trying to hold the city together and trying to keep down any issues that might erupt."

That seemed a reasonable explanation to many Clevelanders, and reason enough for allowing the issue to die quietly. Reporters interviewed for this study indicated that the editors of the *Plain Dealer* had knowledge of the dropped charges months before they decided to publish their exposé.

*   *   *

The *Plain Dealer* articles, opening old wounds, suggesting conspiracies, casting doubt on the integrity of the Stokes administration, may have increased the credibility of a racist pamphlet widely distributed in the white neighborhoods of Cleveland's West Side. Entitled "Warning!," the bulletin detailed an alleged plot by black nationalists to attack the West Side to "get the white man where he lives." Weapons and ammunition for the attack, it said, had recently been moved from a farm in Ashtabula County. The plot would include planned auto accidents to block streets, fire bombings in a concentrated area to draw police into an ambush, and a main attack by 50 to 75 carloads of black nationalists, shooting at every white person in sight as they rampaged through the West Side and escaped through the western suburbs.

The warning was built upon distrust of the Stokes administration. The anonymous authors said they had warned the Cleveland police of the plot, but the police has replied that "with this administration they probably won't be allowed to take any action." Because the black militants have a friend in City Hall, the pamphlet said, they are better equipped and organized than they were in July. "Because we can expect no preventive action or help from Cleveland City Hall, it has become necessary for you, the potential victim, to protect yourself and your property."

Others were busy during the fall of 1968 polarizing the Cleveland community in other ways. Robert Annable, a telephone company employee and the president of the United Citizens Council in Cleveland, organized a rightwing group called the Citizens Committee for Law Enforcement. The purpose of the new organization was to back police in their demands for heavy weaponry, to provide financial support to policemen in civil suits and disciplinary actions, to "investigate" the liberal organizations that were pressing for investigation of the police department, and to set into motion a campaign to have Mayor Stokes removed from office. At the end of September, Roy Richards, head of the new group and chairman of the Cleveland branch of the Wallace for President Committee, filed a recall petition in probate court, stating that Stokes had acted illegally "in allegedly channeling 'Cleveland: Now!' funds to Negro militant groups, allegedly appearing at a public function with armed black nationalists, and allegedly mishandling the restoration of order during the Glenville disorders last July."

The Citizens Committee for Law Enforcement also printed up posters portraying Mayor Stokes and Safety Director Mc-Manamon, with the caption, "WANTED to answer questions for the murder of three policemen." The poster began showing up on bulletin boards in police stations, alongside another which showed Mayor Stokes marching in a parade on the anniversary of the Hough riots behind armed black nationalists and captioned, "These pictures show how to start a riot which KILLS, wounds and maims policemen who are replaced by BLACK POWER social workers by the Mayor."

Through the fall of 1968, white residents of Cleveland's West Side who put credence in rumors and anonymous pamphlets waited fruitlessly for an invasion by black nationalists. What came instead were further instances of polarization, instigated by the anonymous pamphlets and several racially oriented beatings on Cleveland's West Side. A rumor spread among parents of white students at Shuler Junior High School and John Marshall High School that their children were threatened with mass attacks by black nationalists called in by Negro students to protect them. Negro parents were told that white gangs were assembling to attack Negro students. On Monday, October 21, 70 Negro students walked out of John Marshall High School and a smaller number walked out of Shuler High School. Amidst this walkout, rumors spread over the West Side that students and principals had been beaten up.

Negro groups contributed to Cleveland's polarization. In September, noisy interference of a City Council meeting by black militants did little to win sympathy for their grievances, however meritorious. And in October it was revealed that a group of black nationalists calling themselves the Black Information Service were attempting to coerce some East Side merchants into turning over 10 percent of their profits, allegedly for neighborhood-improvement projects. The extortion shamed the Negro community and brought condemnation from its leaders.

*   *   *

Many months after the violence of July 1968, the neighborhood of Glenville bore the scars. On Lakeview Road there was a large vacant area where two houses burned to the ground during the gun battle, giving the block the appearance of a row of teeth with two incisors missing. On Superior Avenue there were stores that were black, gaping shells, others that hid protectively behind plywood panels at their windows. Graffiti scrawled on the plywood told of hatred and smoldering violence. "Black people buy Protection: 20-20 shotguns Passport to freedom" was scribbled on a boarded-up drycleaning store. Said another: "Kill Wild Beast. Stand and be counted in the war against the Beast." Here and there were more positive evidences of the new black pride. The marquee of an old move theater that had become Muhammad's Mosque proclaimed: "Allah is the Greatest." Among the stores doing business on the avenue a number bore Muslim names, some incongruously: The Shabbazz Market advertised kosher meat. Some stores sold African handicrafts, as Ahmed once had done.

Though they had cause for bitterness and fear, many merchants elected to stay on in Glenville. One who had particular cause for bitterness was Jack Friedman, owner of a department store at East 105th and Superior. Friedman had been active in the community affairs of Glenville, a white man seeking racial harmony and better conditions for Negroes of the neighborhood. Most of his employees, including several top managers, were black. Friedman made many of them stockholders in the enterprise. A Negro businessman said to him once, "Friedman, why don't you put on burnt coffee? You're one of us." During the Hough riots of 1966, Friedman's store had been spared while others nearby had windows smashed.

In 1968, his department store was hit on the first night of violence, some time after Friedman had returned home from a meeting at the Office of Economic Opportunity. It was "like the feeling of cold ice," he recalls, when he learned of the damage. The store was a shambles. Display cases were smashed, their contents gone. Vandals broke into a case displaying shoes only to discover that all the shoes were for right feet. Looters grabbed clothes even from the mannequins, sometimes taking pajama bottoms and leaving the tops. Friedman estimates that, of $60,000 worth of merchandise in stock, he was left with less than $500 worth.

But Friedman decided to stay. "I have faith in Glenville and a small bunch of hoodlums isn't going to destroy my faith in it." He wanted to help heal the wounds and continue to work for the betterment of the Negro community. "I happen to be of a minority group myself," he said. "I know what they've gone through."

Notes

1. A police sergeant, Louis Bors, took matters into his own hands 2 weeks later. He went to the Governor's office in Columbus (wearing his uniform), carrying a 10-page petition calling for the ouster of Stokes, McManamon, and Law Director James for "willfully neglecting to enforce the law, gross neglect of duty, malfeasance, misfeasance, and nonfeasance in office." Governor Rhodes refused to act on the petition.

2. 'NO!' SAYS THE P.B.A.—NEW YORK CITY

Thomas R. Brooks

On Election Day the voters of New York City will decide whether they want civilians to sit on a board to hear citizens' complaints against the police. Civilian review is one of this year's hottest election issues, crowding even such controversial subjects as the Vietnam war, the rising cost of living and the resurgence of the new conservatism. Voters owe much of the excitement of this campaign, as well as the opportunity to have their say on Election Day, to the Patrolmen's Benevolent Association, the oldest and largest line organization, representing 25,000 uniformed men in the Police Department, which secured a place on the ballot for a proposition that would bar civilian review of police actions.

The referendum is considered by many a focus for the white backlash in the city. Mayor John V. Lindsay is worried lest agitation on the referendum create an "inflammatory situation." Civil-liberties and civil-rights spokesmen have accused the P.B.A. of injecting "racism" into the fall's campaign in much the same way an anti-open housing referendum did in California two years ago. (The California bill passed.) The California referendum and the P.B.A.-sponsored referendum, it is charged, exacerbate and exploit the fears of Negroes and Puerto Ricans that exist among lower-middle-class whites.

Indeed, such fears appear to be at the root of the P.B.A.'s opposition to civilian review. There is considerable resentment among policemen over civil rights, as well as over pressures on the police to handle criminals—especially members of minority groups—with what they consider kid gloves.

When the new civilian review board began operations in August, most policemen felt "the minorities" had won another victory, an unjustified one based on unsubstantiated claims of police brutality. P.B.A. President John J. Cassese spoke for them when he snapped at reporters: "I am sick and tired of giving in to minority groups with their whims and their gripes and shouting." He has also asserted: "Any review board with civilians on it is detrimental to the operations of the Police Department."

The P.B.A. has been vigorously fighting public review for several years now. Last year, on June 29, when several civilian review bills came up before the City Council, the P.B.A. mustered 5,000 off-duty policemen to picket City Hall. That morning, an unauthorized voice on the police radio exhorted listeners: "Everybody to City Hall!"

The P.B.A. followed up the demonstration—"the largest police turnout ever," according to a spokesman—with a drive that collected 500,000 signatures protesting the civilian review plan up for Council consideration. Then the P.B.A. introduced a bill in the State Legislature aimed at blocking civilian review; it did not pass. So, last spring, the P.B.A. went to court seeking to forestall the setting-up of the present review board. When that maneuver failed, the P.B.A. launched its drive for a referendum.

P.B.A. "friends and relatives" gathered 51,852 signatures in order to provide the 30,000 "validated" signatures needed to secure the City Council's attention. The Council then could have adopted the proposed law outlawing a review board, but it chose not to. Thereupon, P.B.A. friends and relations collected 45,036 additional signatures (15,000 of them validated) to force a referendum. The city challenged its legality, but the courts held that Question No. 1, as it is called, had a place on the ballot. Another proposition put forward by the Conservative party was withdrawn to prevent "confusion" among voters.

The referendum, though aimed at the present review board, is actually much broader in scope. The proposed law would amend the City Charter so as not only to bar civilians from boards reviewing police actions but also to limit severely, if not eliminate, the right of any city agency to investigate the police for any reason. If the proposal is passed, for example, investigations of citizens' allegations of graft and corruption—and there are many more of these than charges of brutality—could be carried out only by the police themselves, not by, say, the Mayor's office or the City Department of Investigation.

Meanwhile, on July 11, Mayor Lindsay and Police Commissioner Howard R. Leary appointed a seven-man board to hear citizens' complaints about police behavior. The board was set up under an executive order issued by the Police Commissioner amending the department's rules and regulations.

Although civil-liberties and civil-rights groups were disappointed by what they termed a "compromise" that fell short of fully independent civilian review, they hailed the appointment of Algernon D. Black, senior leader of the New York Society for Ethical Culture, as chairman, and of Dr. Walter I. Murray, a Negro who is professor of education at Brooklyn College; Manuel Diaz, chief consultant and acting executive director of the Puerto Rican Community Development Project, and Thomas R. Farrell, a lawyer who is a former president of the Bronx chapter of the Catholic Interracial Council, as the other civilian members. Police Commissioner Leary appointed the three police members— Edward J. McCabe, a former F.B.I. man and deputy commissioner in charge of licenses; Franklin A. Thomas, a Negro who is deputy commissioner in charge of legal matters, and Deputy Inspector Pearse P. Meagher, a 25-year veteran of the police force.

The board is authorized to investigate citizens' charges of police misconduct in four categories: unnecessary or excessive use of force; abuse of authority (including depriving a suspect of his civil rights); discourtesy, abusive or insulting language; language, conduct or behavior which is derogatory to a person's race, religion or creed or national origin. An investigative staff of 20 police officers—captains and lieutenants—works under the supervision of Inspector Arthur Savitt. A complaint may also be heard before either of two civilian hearing officers, who take testimony from both sides, with parties entitled to counsel. The board meets each Friday to review all cases and staff recommendations. Its findings are submitted to the Police Commissioner, who has the final word on any action to be taken. The board itself cannot try or punish a policeman.

In view of the mildness of civilian review—cases are coming in at the rate of roughly 100 a month, but the vast majority are unsubstantiated—the police reaction seems excessive, even irrational. It is rooted, I think, in the policeman's sense of authority, which he sees challenged by civilian review. The policeman's inner world is bound by "us" and "them," the latter being all punks or potential criminals at best. And nothing irritates a policeman more than having a punk say, "I got rights, see."

Beyond this, we must recognize that a policeman is a man authorized to carry a gun and to use it when necessary. Should he make a mistake that mistake is sometimes irrevocable. With this in mind—or, rather, buried in his subconscious—the policeman would rather his actions be judged by someone he considers one of his own. Departmental trials of policemen who have shot suspects, or even innocent bystanders, rarely find against the officer. The policemen, however, fear that under civilian law, especially in cases involving members of the city's minority groups, they would not fare so well. All this is bound up with police resentment, a feeling that they are "picked on" and "have no civil rights" in contrast to "the minorities."

When the Mayor's moderate version of civilian review came under attack, civil-rights, civil-liberties, labor and liberal organizations came together to form the Federated Associations for Impartial Review (FAIR) to combat the referendum. Senators Jacob Javits and Robert F. Kennedy, gubernatorial candidates Frank O'Connor and Franklin D. Roosevelt Jr., former U.S. Attorney General Herbert Brownell, Bronx Borough President Herman Badillo and a host of other prominent citizens are also committed to the campaign against the P.B.A. sponsored referendum.

"They've got the luminaries, we've got the people," said

Norman Frank, P.B.A. public-relations counsel. But his side has not neglected its own luminaries, either. One of the first moves the P.B.A. made in its referendum campaign was to call together a group of businessmen, State Senators and Barry Gray, the radio commentator, to form an Independent Citizens Committee Against Civilian Review Boards. ("We haven't the initials, either," Frank said.)

Gray, who fears that the city "will become an asphalt jungle" with civilian review, former Police Commissioner Michael J. Murphy and State Senator Martin J. Knorr are honorary chairmen of the committee. Rodney Ettman, the 50-year-old president of the Verde Wallpaper Company and head of the Police Reserve, an organization of police buffs who provide scholarships for policemen and send needy children to camp, is chairman.

"A lot of us feel that this (civilian review) is the straw that breaks the camel's back," Ettman said in explaining his support of the referendum. "We feel we have to do something to free the policeman from all these encumbrances."

While individual policemen may be talking up the referendum to neighbors, storekeeper and acquaintances on the beat, the hard campaign is being carried out by the Independent Citizens Committee. The alliance of forces against civilian review is perhaps somewhat broader, including as it does members of the John Birch Society, the Conservative party, the parents' and taxpayers' groups of anti-school-busing fame, American Legion posts, homeowners' groups and the Brooklyn Bar Association. But the burden of campaigning falls on the committee.

Both the law and Police Department regulations bar policemen from participation in political campaigns although the P.B.A.—like all other police line organizations—is free to lobby for legislation affecting working conditions, pensions, and the like. The referendum is something of a borderline case, or so the P.B.A.'s officers apparently feel. Even in collecting signatures for the referendum petition the P.B.A. was cautious, relying on "friends and relatives" and retired policemen to do the job.

The P.B.A. is on record as being "prepared to spend its whole treasury" of $1.5-million to combat civilian review. But it has no plans for hitting the rank-and-file for contributions, as a union might to beef up a strike fund. When I spoke to Cassese about his commitment of the P.B.A. treasury, he stressed the words "If necessary."

The P.B.A., he said, has total assets of almost $4-million. It has an annual dues income—$2 a month from roughly 25,000 uniformed members and $1.50 a month from 9,000 retired cops —of about $760,000. There is a "contingency fund," which is "for anything the delegate body decides to spend it on," but Cassese refused to divulge how much it contains. He was equally closemouthed about other aspects of the P.B.A. finances. Its annual financial report is "not available" to the public. "We're a membership corporation and we're not required to report to the state (with the exception of health and welfare funds), only to our membership," I was told.

Whatever the state of P.B.A.'s finances, which seem healthy, its officers have high hopes of not having to tap its resources too deeply. "We expect to raise enough public funds (through the Independent Citizens Committee) to obviate the need of the P.B.A. to spend its own money," Frank told me, adding somewhat cryptically that the "P.B.A. has responsibilities of its own in the campaign." Questioned about this, he explained, "Somebody must coordinate the various aspects of the campaign. That's my job."

Under Frank's aegis, the committee has drawn up a $500,000 budget ("an opening allotment," according to Frank) and has announced a planned expenditure of $200,000 for TV and plans for 370 prominently placed bill-boards. There is an active speakers' bureau and the committee hopes to open at least 20 storefront—"à la Lindsay"—headquarters around the city. Buttons, placards, bumper stickers, leaflets—all the paraphernalia of a political campaign will pour out of the Independent Citizens Committee headquarters in the Sheraton-Atlantic Hotel at 34th Street and Broadway.

The theme of the campaign was spelled out in the committee's first advertisement, an appeal for funds. The advertisement shows a young, attractive, somewhat apprehensive white girl in a white coat coming out of a subway entrance onto a dark street on a dark night. Across the black bottom of the picture, white type states: "The Civilian Review Board must be stopped! Her life . . . your life . . . may depend on it. Send your contribution today!"

Surely, the picture and text suggest, the girl is going to be in a bad way whether the Civilian Review Board or the police get there first. A police officer, the text of the advertisement reminds us, "must not hesitate. If he does, because he fears the possibility of unjust censure; if he feels his job, pension or reputation is threatened, the security and safety of your family may be jeopardized." In sum, the referendum campaign is pitched to the notion that a civilian review board will make a policeman think twice before he acts—and that this moment of hesitation will cost lives.

The photograph, obviously, was staged. The scare is synthetic, as Police Commissioner Leary made clear after the advertisement appeared: "The suggestion has been made . . . that the existence of a civilian complaint review board reduces the effectiveness of the police and thereby threatens the safety of the people of New York. This suggestion is totally without foundation.

"The review board," the Commissioner continued, "has been in operation now for some three months. During that time there has been absolutely no discernible rise in crime, nor has there been any discernible reduction in arrests."

The referendum campaign will not rest on suggestiveness alone, however. The Independent Citizens Committee plans a doorbell push by some 25,000 volunteers. It hopes they will, in turn, reach a half-million voters.

Every day between Sept. 19 and a week before the election, two shifts of 25 hired telephone solicitors, mostly young women, are working their way through the 96,888 signatures collected on the referendum petition. (Incidentally, the crew I saw in action was integrated. The three young Negro women were just as ardent as their white counterparts in support of the referendum.)

Each signer of the referendum petition is asked to become a volunteer, take a kit and visit anywhere from 12 to 25 homes in order to get out the vote. Naturally enough, I was told by both Frank and the young women that the response was "terrific," a statement that calls for skeptical salt. But a glance at two report sheets filed with the supervisor did show 20 yesses to four noes on one and one no and 16 yesses on the other.

The hucksterism of the campaign owes much to Madison Avenue; the ideological content, however, is pure cop. The differences between style and content show up in the personalities of Cassese and Frank, who between them run the show. These differences are even exploited in the campaign itself. Cassese is the speaker for American Legion meetings, Rotary Clubs and the like.

When it comes to a debate with labor arbitrator Theodore Kheel or the New York Civil Liberties Union director, Aryeh Neier, Frank gets the assignment. He is articulate, sharp and suave. Slim, handsome in a dark suit, button-down shirt, striped tie and Continental black loafers, Frank is Madison Avenue circa Frederick Wakeman.

His firm, Norman Frank Associates is indeed on Madison Avenue, and represents the Congressional Life Insurance Company (Frank is on the board of directors), a large, diversified West Coast financial concerned construction company and an electronics company, among others. Frank formerly "was in television and radio," working with the CBS "21st Precinct" show and other programs dealing with the police.

Frank advances the sophisticated arguments—for example, "if it is better jobs or housing one wants civilian review is a very poor substitute. It is not an answer to social injustice or inequality." The cruder arguments come from Cassese: "if we wind up with a review board, we'll have done Russia a great service whether by design or accident."

Cassese, a brawny, 6-foot-1-inch 53-year-old who keeps an eye on his waistline successfully and wears his customary gray suit, white shirt and slim black tie uneasily, fits the police prototype—a patrolman out of uniform and feeling awkward, dressed in his Sunday best. Taciturn, grave faced, with strands of gray hair brushed across a high-domed forehead, he is likable, a person of considerable warmth. On the platform, he is a dullish speaker who comes across with undoubted sincerity.

Although some policemen have been known to wince when watching Cassese on television, there is not much doubt that he represents the uniformed men on the force. His stand on civilian review is, by and large, their stand. The all-Negro 1,500-member Guardians is the only police organization to have come out for the review board. Individual white policemen may also be in favor but I have yet to meet one.

Cassese's career is typical for the men of his generation who joined the force during the Depression; policemen do feel that Cassese is one of their own. He has, on occasion, at police functions, received more applause than the Police Commissioner.

He was born Jan. 20, 1913, in the Greenpoint section of Brooklyn, the son of two immigrants from Naples. His father was a moderately successful baker and the young Cassese went to school, first at P.S. 17, then to Boys High, and on to a pre-medical course at New York University. "Dad got sick," he recalls, "and we had to give the bakery up. That's how we quit school, and everything."

Cassese was appointed to the force on March 1, 1937, and considered himself lucky. "It was a happy day for me. My mother, though, she was against it. She wanted me to be anything but a policeman."

Cassese spent the next 18 years in Brooklyn's 83d Precinct based at the station house at DeKalb and Wilson Avenues. "Mostly I was on foot patrol," he recalls, "but I got my share of radio-car work." He remembers "many a time chasing fellows over roofs, going into basements to get prowlers."

But the incident that sticks in memory is the day when Patrolman Cassese, as the story goes, "shot a cow." The shooting took place early one March morning back in 1945 when, as newspapers pointed out, a 1200-pound steer was "worth 2200 red ration points on the hoof." The steer busted out of a Brooklyn slaughter house and thundered away with six employes in pursuit. Cassese took up the chase, riding the running board of a car for three-quarters of an hour, emptying his gun twice before the steer fell dead. "We went a full mile and a full circle," Cassese recalled. "We ended up two blocks from where we started." He laughed. "You know, I almost got a complaint for that."

The young patrolman met, courted and married the former Sally Rudman. They had two children, Roberta, 23, a physical-education teacher at City College, and Rhonda (Ronnie), 15, a student at Ditmas Junior High School. Mrs. Cassese died last March. Cassese still lives in a modest four-room apartment at 10 Ocean Parkway, "across the street from the 74th Precinct." Evenings, he relaxes in a rocker, watching such television favorites as "Bonanza" and "The Man from U.N.C.L.E."

Like most policemen, Cassese joined the P.B.A. when he joined the force. In 1944, "there was an opening (for P.B.A. delegate) and I ran for it." He became the Brooklyn trustee in 1951, the second vice president and then the first vice president in the administration of his predecessor, John E. Carton.

In 1956, the department suffered a thorough shake-up at the hands of a former policeman, Commissioner Stephen P. Kennedy, who wanted to clean up both corruption and inefficiency. "Mass transfers were going on," Cassese recalls, "hundreds at a time." Commissioner Kennedy also had the temerity to try enforcing a departmental ban against moonlighting. (Cassese estimated some years later that 60 to 70 per cent of the force held second jobs in defiance of the department's regulations.)

The resulting turmoil within the department was reflected within the P.B.A. Considerable opposition developed to the Carton administration. The P.B.A., many younger men felt, was not militant enough. Cassese and a group of fellow officers decided to break with Carton and run an opposition slate. Cassese won, becoming president of the P.B.A. in 1958.

The job is a nonpaying position—as a first-grade patrolman, Cassese earns $8,348 a year—though the P.B.A. president may draw up to $10,000 a year for expenses. All P.B.A. officers and delegates must be active members of the force. However, although Cassese is officially "on duty," he does spend a good deal of his time on P.B.A. affairs. "This is something the P.B.A. president has been doing for years," he explained. "The reason they give him this kind of job (Cassese's is at the Safety Records Bureau) is so he can coincide his police work along with this P.B.A. work."

But things were not so cozy under Commissioner Kennedy. The clash between the P.B.A. and the Commissioner resulted in a series of donnybrooks, many of them totally confused. This much is clear, however, Commissioner Kennedy's strictness evoked a greater militancy from the P.B.A. than it had ever shown.

The high point of the hassle came when patrolmen—they had "charitably conceded the right to strike," a high department official told me—slowed down the issuance of summonses on Oct. 24, 1960. There was a 23 per cent drop from the corresponding day of a year before. Five days later, in a continuing effort to embarrass the Commissioner, the police "blanketed the town in green," writing 132 per cent more parking tickets than on the corresponding day the year before.

Commissioner Kennedy tore up his P.B.A. membership card, put it together with Scotch tape and did it all over again for television. The P.B.A. countered by ousting the Commissioner officially. Cassese, somewhere along the line, broke his toe. Legend has it that he did so kicking his television set. (Cassese told me he couldn't recall the exact circumstances of the accident. "I guess they wanted to make a story," he said.) He went on sick call and was confined to his home by order of the Commissioner. He could not go to his sister's house for Thanksgiving dinner, nor attend the monthly P.B.A. delegates' meeting. So the delegates went to Cassese, meeting in the basement of his apartment house. When Cassese returned to duty, Commissioner Kennedy transferred him to a windy traffic spot at 11th Avenue and 18th street, where he remained for eight months. When I asked how the dispute with Kennedy was resolved, Cassese said: "He quit."

After Kennedy resigned, the P.B.A. did make some real gains. It secured a dues checkoff and, ultimately, recognition as the certified bargaining agent for patrolmen. Up until then, the P.B.A. had bargained, more or less, with the Mayor and in conjunction with the budget hearings. Today, it negotiates with the Budget Director and head of personnel under the city's recently adopted labor-relations procedures.

This year, the P.B.A. and the Uniformed Firemen's Association, negotiating jointly for the first time, have asked for a pay increase of 10 per cent for beginning policemen (who start at $6,347 a year) and a 20 per cent hike for men with three years or more on the force. The present base pay of $8,483 would go to $10,500 under the proposal. The P.B.A. also has asked for an increase to 5 per cent from the 2.5 per cent that the city now pays into the police pension fund. Additional length-of-service increments, higher uniform allowances and increases in health and welfare benefits are among the other demands sought in an estimated $200-million package for the policemen and firemen.

Ironically, in the light of the P.B.A.'s opposition to civilian review of citizens' complaints, the P.B.A. has also demanded that an impartial arbiter from outside the Police Department be appointed to hear patrolmen's grievances. Actually, such grievances, post-Kennedy, are few. According to Deputy Commissioner McCabe, whose duties include heading the department's Joint Personnel Board, on which Cassese also sits: "Unusual as it may seem, we've had only about four grievances reach the third stage since we've been in operation (1961)." And most of those occurred in the first year. The Joint Personnel Board does, however, make recommendations for changes in personnel practices. Most grievances are, apparently, resolved in the station house, with the men going directly to their captain with their problems.

Current P.B.A. negotiations are in abeyance while Peter Seitz, an outside arbiter, decides whether or not three P.B.A. demands are negotiable—no radio car with fewer than two men; increased pensions for retired men; wiping the "jacket" clean of complaints lodged against policemen if they prove unfounded, and the expunging of minor infractions after a year. These are propositions of a kind that unions long since have had some say about.

The P.B.A. founded in 1894 when Theodore Roosevelt sat on the Board of Commissioners, has some of the attributes of a union. But there are significant differences. For one thing, rank-

and-file members do not meet regularly, if at all. Each command is entitled to one delegate for every 50 men, up to a maximum of three. There are 306 delegates, all told, who meet monthly. Delegates get 15 per cent of the $2 a month in dues collected from the men they represent—"for expenses." A delegate may call a meeting of the men in his command if he wishes. Such meetings, as far as I can discover, are rare.

To inform the rank-and-file, the P.B.A. publishes, erratically, New York's Finest, and a mimeographed digest of meetings of the delegates is posted on precinct bulletin boards. Some of the information so posted is cryptic, like the account of the treasurer's report, which reads: "Accepted as submitted." The men in the command, of course, may ask for elucidation. Whether they know of their rights as P.B.A. members is not clear. When I asked for a copy of the P.B.A. constitution, I was told: "It's at the printer's." One patrolman assures me that he has been getting the same answer for several years.

P.B.A. delegates are elected "whenever the men want an election." In practice, this means that once a man is elected he is in until transferred, promoted or retired. "I can recall only two elections (for delegate) in 11 years," one patrolman told me. There is, however, a turnover of about 60 delegates a year. Yet, the turnover has not been sufficient to keep up with the changing ethnic composition of the Police Department. There is one Negro delegate and one Puerto Rican delegate; neither minority is represented among the officers. Most Negro and Puerto Rican patrolmen, nonetheless, belong to the P.B.A.

One delegate I met has been on the force 30 years and a P.B.A. delegate for 25 years. Like many, but not all, of the delegates, he is an "inside man." He holds down a clerical job as a "124 man" assisting a desk sergeant. The captain in his precinct has been there all of a year and a half. Several policemen told me that a new captain often relies on the P.B.A. delegate to clue him in. "Policy is made in the station house," a patrolman explained, "and the delegate is consulted, so to speak. He has an in when it comes to saying who gets a radio car or a good beat."

The 18 officers of the P.B.A. serve two-year terms. To run for office, a man must first be a delegate. Nominations are made at a delegates' meeting. If there is no opposition, the slate of candidates is declared elected unanimously. If there is a contest, the rank-and-file votes. Cassese has survived two contested elections, one his first, and has been unopposed in the last two.

There is, however, an opposition—a committee chaired by Patrolman Frank Clark. It puts out an irregularly published newsletter, called Change. This opposition group is adamantly against civilian review, but it also opposes what it considers Cassese's domination of the P.B.A. "The delegate has in essence today very little to say," a recent issue of Change complained. "Everything done by the P.B.A. must have John Cassese's stamp on it." Change has called for "mandatory two-year elections of delegates to assure us of the best possible men to represent us at all times." Change's strength is uncertain, while Cassese's certainly is high.

Cassese's popularity is based on both his standing up to Commissioner Kennedy and on his successes as a lobbyist. According to one fellow lobbyist, Alice Marsh of the United Federation of Teachers, "Cassese is very effective. He's not loud, carries himself very well and has the respect of legislators."

Normally, lobbyists for the city's civil-service organizations try for "home-rule" messages of support from the Mayor, largely because in most instances the Legislature will dispose in the city's favor. But the P.B.A. circumvents home rule by having changes it seeks—in the pension law, say—adopted under the general municipal code that applies to all cities. As one lobbyist explained: "Since there are not many policemen in cities outside of New York, upstate legislators don't mind passing bills that will cost New York City money."

Legislators too, tend to sympathize with the policeman's lot. "They have a rough ob." Al Blumenthal, a Manhattan Reform Democrat, told me. "Those of us who are very tough on civil-liberties questions often feel we have to make it up to the police by voting for those measures that improve police working conditions and benefits."

Cassese, says Blumenthal, "is there every week." The P.B.A. lobbyists, usually Cassese and a vice president or two, take the legislators out, county by county. "They'll feed you and tell you what they want," Blumenthal said. "The P.B.A. touch is lighter than most; it's a soft sell." The P.B.A. also holds, as do most other lobbying groups, an "annual feast" for the legislators; it is "not elaborate as these things go," according to a faithful guest. The P.B.A. also gives them each a small gift—a wallet one year; this year, a silver penknife. "If they spend $10 to $12 a legislator a year," a legislator told me, "that's a lot."

The P.B.A. usually confines itself to lobbying for measures specifically aimed at police welfare—retirement, pensions and so on. On policing issues—the rules governing confessions, search and seizure problems and the like—the P.B.A. works through the State Police Chiefs, the Combined Council of Law Enforcement Officers and the State District Attorneys Association. "The P.B.A. never directly lobbies on these things, as far as I can recall," Blumenthal said.

The P.B.A., nearly everyone agrees, has been remarkably successful in Albany. It succeeded, for example, shortly after Cassese came to office, in knocking out residency requirements, so that policemen might flee to the suburbs along with the rest of the white middle class. Today, some 8,000 New York City policemen live as far afield as Orange County or the tip of Long Island. (They cannot, however, live in New Jersey.) Policemen may also retire at half pay, based on their final year's annual earnings, including overtime. Since last year was a very good year for overtime, a fair number of policemen have chosen to retire this year. This run on retirement has been blamed on bad morale stemming from changes made under Mayor Lindsay and from the pending threat of civilian review. The P.B.A. has not stepped forward and claimed the credit due.

The police had no paid holidays in 1958; now they enjoy 11. There has been a 2.5 per cent reduction in pension contributions from the patrolmen . . . and so the record goes. The P.B.A., however, does not win them all. A bill legalizing moonlighting failed to pass the last session of the Legislature.

Cassese clearly is proud of the achievements on behalf of the patrolmen. "I know what it is like out there," he told me. His stand against civilian review has not hurt his standing with the P.B.A. rank-and-file. He's pretty sure of winning on Nov. 8. I asked him what the P.B.A. would do if the referendum lost. "We'll accept it," he said. [The referendum passed by a vote of 1,313,161 to 765,468—Ed.]

3. BLUE POWER—DETROIT

Art Glickman

"Everybody else can indulge in politics—every black group, every political party group, every church group," says Carl Parsell, president of the 3,500-member Detroit Police Officers Association (DPOA). "Why are police officers so different?"

Maybe they aren't. Political activism by the heavily white DPOA has become a lively issue in the race for mayor between Wayne County Sheriff Roman S. Gribbs, who is white, and Wayne County Auditor Richard H. Austin, a Negro. The policemen's group has endorsed Mr. Gribbs, as well as eight other whites running for seats on the city Common Council.

Off-duty patrolmen are performing chores such as helping to register voters. On Nov. 4, they will help get voters to the polls. The 525-member Detroit Police Lieutenants and Sergeants Association and the 500-member Detroit Police Detectives Association also are contributing manpower—plus several thousand dollars—to the Gribbs campaign.

Irritated Candidate

Never before have the three organizations openly campaigned for a mayoral candidate. Mr. Austin, the black con-

From "Blue Power," by Art Glickman, *The Wall Street Journal*, October 30, 1969, pp. 1, 29. Copyright © 1969 by *The Wall Street Journal* and reprinted with permission.

tender, is angry. So are black police officers, who complain that
they have no policy-making influence in the DPOA.

Mr. Austin has charged that political activism by "men who
have the power of life and death over individuals" does "violence" to the concept of civilian control over police. And he has
suggested that Mr. Gribbs might have promised the policemen
special treatment. Mr. Gribbs denies any promises of favors,
asserts that policemen have a constitutional right to engage in
political activity in their off hours, out of uniform and scoffs
at the notion of a developing police state. "I have too much
faith in the policemen and their goodwill and their common
sense," he says.

The debate over police and politics reaches into many cities.
For decades, state or local laws in many areas have banned policemen from activism. A tradition of nonpartisanship has inhibited
others. But now policemen in ever-increasing numbers are shed-
ding their nonpartisan stance—often flouting the law—to take
part in municipal elections.

The trend became evident last spring when white police
officers campaigned for the re-election of Mayor Sam Yorty in
Los Angeles, and for the election of Charles Stenvig, a detective,
as mayor of Minneapolis.

The Crime Rate

Rising crime tolls and the heated issue of "law and order"
seem to have provoked many officers to political activism. "People are fed up with this growing crime rate, and there's nobody
more frustrated about it than the policeman," says Norm Moore,
a former Los Angeles detective who helped organize policemen
and firemen to work for Mr. Yorty. Policemen particularly seethe
over Supreme Court decisions that they believe favor the rights
of suspects to the detriment of effective police work.

Many white policemen also believe that the prominence of
the civil rights cause has disrupted the political balance in
their cities. All too often, they complain, the arguments of the
black militants prevail at city hall.

This fall there is political activism by policemen in many localities. The Seattle Police Officers Guild is working for the election of its president to the city council. Police in Hartford, Conn., are prohibited from political activity, but the wives of policemen are working for the election of George (Pete) Kinsella as mayor, and, one officer says, "They're probably getting a lot of help from their husbands."

Texas law forbids police activity in politics, but many Houston officers are edging toward overt support of Mayor Louie Welch for reelection. "Lots of us would like to go out and openly campaign for him," says Sgt. J. A. Knigge, secretary of the Houston Police Officers Association. "I'm pretty sure some of us will."

The usually nonpolitical Fraternal Order of Police in Cleveland recently took out a full-page newspaper advertisement listing shortcomings in police administration and calling on Mayor Carl Stokes, a Negro, to make improvements. The FOP says the ad wasn't politically motivated, but some observers suspect that it helped Mr. Stokes' challenger, Ralph J. Perk. In Pittsburgh, some officers were directed to remove from their patrol cars bumper stickers that supported Eugene Coon, a former assistant superintendent of police who is running for county sheriff.

"Bargaining and Campaigning"

Royce Givens, executive secretary of the International Conference of Police Associations, believes that policemen are becoming more political as they win the right to organize and bargain collectively. Carl Parsell, whose association is exclusive bargaining agent for Detroit's patrolmen, says, "We have found our negotiating power is tied together with political power." Mr. Givens sees a big increase in the number of policemen running for office and says he expects the trend to grow.

For policemen to engage in politics isn't new. Arthur F.

Brandstatter, head of the department of police administration at Michigan State University, says that three or four decades ago policemen in most big cities were chosen for their jobs largely on the basis of political party and religion. They were expected to do political chores for the party in power.

That led to abuses and dissatisfaction. Sgt. Knigge of the Houston police recalls that in the 1940s one man who was active in local politics "went to 7 a.m. roll call as a patrolman, and at 11 a.m. he was chief of police." Civil service procedures eventually were instituted in most departments, calling for hiring and advancement on the basis of ability. Such regulations often prohibited policemen from political activity, singly or in groups. In many states the prohibition was written into statutes.

Now there is a growing feeling among policemen that such regulations deny them their constitutional rights. The Patrolmen's Benevolent Association of Nassau County, N. Y., has embarked on a test case, challenging in state supreme court a local restriction against off-duty politicking. The PBA expects to file in Federal court against a state law that forbids political activity by policemen.

The association lost the first round in its challenge when Justice Sol Wachtler of the state supreme court upheld the local restriction, ruling that police shouldn't engage in partisan politics "for fear that the authority and influence with which they are invested by the public could be used unfairly." The PBA has appealed the decision.

How effective police politicking is seems to depend on the city and the circumstances. Thomas Bradley, the black Los Angeles city councilman who lost to Mayor Yorty last May, says police had a "significant impact" in the race. Mr. Bradley, a former police lieutenant himself, charges that his old colleagues used "purely racist" tactics, exploiting the fears and prejudices of white voters.

Mr. Bradley believes that policemen can swing a lot of weight at the polls. "Many people respect them," he says. "They look at them as the champion and protector against the threat from minority communities, from militants, from students, from whoever is engaged in activities associated with unrest in our society."

Mr. Moore, the former Los Angeles detective who helped organize police and firemen to campaign, disputes the racist label. He says policemen opposed Mr. Bradley because they were fearful of the men surrounding him and because they believed he favored a civilian review board that would monitor police actions. "I don't think it hurts a thing to have policemen and firemen knocking on doors in precincts that went to Bradley in the primary," Mr. Moore says.

No Difference

In Minneapolis, Mr. Stenvig, the former detective, won the mayoralty by a big margin. Former Alderman Dan Cohen, the losing candidate, got less than 40% of the vote. Mr. Cohen traces his defeat to running against a policeman, rather than to politicking by off-duty officers. "The margin was too great for me to feel the police department tipped the scale," Mr. Cohen says.

Mayor Stenvig (who turned out on Moratorium Day in Minneapolis to personally direct a riot squad dispersing demonstrators) has become something of a hero to politically inclined policemen elsewhere in the nation. Mr. Stenvig has expressed his philosophy thus: "People are sick and tired of politicians and intellectuals. They want an average workingman from the community to represent them, and that's me."

In Detroit, nobody is certain how much effect the open police support for Sheriff Gribbs will have on the outcome of the race. However, supporters of Mr. Austin says that police and firemen mounted a well-financed campaign last year against a ballot proposition that cut their pension benefits. Although the change saved the taxpayers money, it passed only by about 20,000 votes.

Both Mr. Austin and Mr. Gribbs agree that law and order

is a prime issue in the present campaign. Mr. Gribbs has avoided comment on the race issue, but many black politicians and black policemen see race as the underlying reason white policemen support Mr. Gribbs. Coleman A. Young, Negro minority whip in the Michigan senate, sees the white police involvement as "a call to arms against a black takeover," of the city.

Black and White

About 40% of Detroit's 1.5 million residents are black, but about 75% of the registered voters are white. More than 90% of the policemen are white. Mr. Young sees dire implications in the recently formed coalition called "Real Detroit." Its members: The Detroit Police Officers Association, the Police Detectives Association and the Greater Detroit Council of Homeowners, an all-white cittizens' group.

In 1965, the homeowners group attempted unsuccessfully to get a proposal on the ballot that would have given property owners the right to refuse to rent or sell to any person for any reason. Mrs. William Otenbaker, executive secretary of the council, explains the motive for joining with the policemen: "They should be able to get out and do a job without having all the minority groups on their backs."

Patrolman Ronald Turner, leader of a dissident group of black policemen who may bolt the DPOA, says the coalition only reinforces the widespread belief among blacks that white policemen are the enemy, standing for "suppression by the white, middle-class community."

The police deny that racism is involved. "The number one issue is law enforcement," says Eljay Bowron, president of the detectives' association, "and there's never been a candidate who knew more about the problem of law enforcement than Roman Gribbs." Mr. Bowron says he opposes Mr. Austin for advocating a civilian review board.

Mr. Parsell, the DPOA leader, is pushing for more police

activism in Michigan. He has organized several groups into the Michigan Police Officers Association, which intends to lobby for legislation that will help police and support political candidates sympathetic to police. [Roman Gribbs won the election by a very small margin of 3,500 votes—Ed.]

4. MODELS OF POLICE POLITICS—
NEW YORK CITY, CHICAGO, PHILADELPHIA
Leonard Ruchelman

Though police militancy is in many ways similar to the militancy of other public employees, there are some important differences which pose considerably greater potential for the police as a political force. First, virtually all police organizations are essentially closed systems. Policemen must enter the force from the lowest rank, irrespective of previous experience, and work their way up through the organization. Contrary to most other forms of public and private employment, policemen usually cannot transfer to another police organization as a way of furthering their careers. Under such circumstances, pressures of conformity —the need to "get-along" and "go-along"—are substantial.[1]

Second, the semi-military form of organization and the consequent stress on hierarchy and chain-of-command is pervasive in police work. Compared to other bureaucracies, there tends to be greater control from the upper levels of the command structure. In this light, "Control over promotions and disciplinary action could make coercion possible, and pressure might be exerted on lower ranking members to adopt, contribute to, or work for a particular cause."[2]

A third factor which bears on police power, actual or potential, is the fact that ". . . the police have a practical monopoly on the legal use of force in our society."[3] Consequently, the

This is a revised version of a paper delivered at the 1971 Annual Meeting of the American Political Science Association, Chicago, Illinois, September 7-11.

growing politicization of the police poses a fundamental threat of coercion in community affairs. Persons who oppose the police could be intimidated with arrest or warnings of arrest.

Research Approach

The special dimensions of police politics, vary from city to city. As communities differ in political style (loosely defined here as the way in which issues are resolved), so too will police politics differ. The police, after all, are not immune to forces in the political environment and are subject to pressures and demands that emanate from elected officials, political executives, parties and interest groups.

However, the converse of this must also be considered: namely, the idea that police politics affects community politics. As a power bloc in its own right, the police have a stake in the political process. For example, they have an interest in the kinds of laws that are passed and whether these laws will be likely to restrict them in their jobs or give them wider lattitude of discretion. The research problem that we have defined, then, is to assess the impact of police on the political environment. In this light, we try to discern patterns of political behavior among the police and to weigh the implications of this for the larger community. Matters which are essentially internal to the workings of the police bureaucracy are not considered, e.g., promotions, salaries, time schedules.

The basic approach is to investigate and compare important issues of police policy in three cities: New York City, Philadelphia, and Chicago. Covering the years 1966 to 1969, we focus on three over-lapping issue-areas which have received a great deal of attention in the news media of all three cities. They have been selected for study because they vividly demonstrate the changing political role of the police in society. However, this does not preclude the possibility that other issues may be equally revealing. The issue-areas are as follows:

1. *Civil review and accountability of the police:* This subject goes to the heart of any democratic system since it focuses on the issue of civil watchfulness and control of the military arm of the community. A fundamental question here is who watches and commands the police and how do the police respond.

2. *The law and order issue:* This subject is also crucial to a democracy but more complex since it has come to mean different things to different people. For purposes of this study we define it as the rights of the individual versus the obligation of the community to protect life and property. Decisions are observed in three types of situations: conditions of civil protest; conditions of civil disorder; conditions of due process, e.g., matters of bail, self-incrimination, legal counsel, search and seizure, cruel and unusual punishment.

3. *Police-community relations:* Here we are interested in the way the police are structured into the community. We consider decisions which determine how the police relate with other groups and participate in other jurisdictions, e.g., minority groups, education.

Methodology

This study concentrates on the process by which issues are resolved rather than on a detailed treatment of the issues themselves. Such an approach requires careful scrutiny of the mayor, the police commissioner and police personnel as they interact with each other and with other decision-making participants. In each issue-area we attempt to discern the nature of participation which includes the point of view of key participants and the degree of success as measured by the outcome of an issue. We also try to generalize about the power resources which are brought to bear. Careful attention is directed to determining which individuals or agencies "most often initiated the proposals that were finally adopted or most often successfully vetoed the proposals of others." [4] (In a few cases a particular decision is judged applicable to more than one issue-area and is therefore considered more than once.) We ask, for example, was the mayor successful, on what kinds and how many proposals, why, and if not, why not? Furthermore, the pursuit of such questions in three cities rather than one affords opportunity for more enriched insights; for a comparative focus permits inquiry into why certain patterns are revealed in some places or situations but not in others—e.g., why is the mayor successful in city A but not in city B?

While there were many decision-making cases, we consider only those that were of community-wide significance. Cases that were essentially parochial (e.g., limited to a few individuals) or temporary in nature (e.g., experimental programs) are excluded. Furthermore, we focus on decision-making as an aspect of open conflict. Important as it may be, we do not purport to generalize about the more covert qualities of power.[5] Data was derived from the newspapers of the three cities, relevant documents and studies, as well as interviews.[6]

Before proceeding to the data, we should take cognizance of some other difficulties which are inherent in our methodology. For one, political confrontations can result in mixed outcomes thereby making it difficult to assess success or failure. In the few cases where this did appear as a problem, we relied on the assessments of observers who could judge outcomes in light of the surrounding circumstances. Secondly, where more than one participant seemed to share in an outcome and where fine distinctions could not be made, we attributed multiple scores. Because of the controversial nature of our subject matter, however, and the publicity and discussions which naturally follow controversy, coding was not as difficult as might ordinarily be supposed.

Locales.

The selection of New York City, Chicago and Philadelphia for study is basically a choice of convenience. Nevertheless, ranking first, second and fourth among the largest metropolitan centers in the nation, they evidence a history of what we have defined as police politics and especially a preoccupation with civilian review board and "law and order" issues. Such concerns, we should note, grow out of environmental conditions and particularly what has come to be recognized as urban crisis conditions; namely, high crime rates and civil disorder. The statistics in Table 1 give a general picture of this and are presented as useful background for the analysis which follows.

Civil Review and Accountability of the Police

Civil review and accountability in the police policy area is analogous to the American principle of civilian control of the military. But while tradition and the United States Constitution clearly support the President as "Commander-in-Chief of the Army and Navy," the idea of external control of the police on the community level is surrounded with ambiguity. The purpose of this section is to treat the question: how much review and how much accountability in our three sample cities? More specifically, we try to assess the extent to which the civil authorities assert themselves in procedures of review and command and the ways in which the police respond.

Civil Review

As a measure of public watchfulness, we first inquire into the number of reviews which have taken place and whether they were initiated by forces external or internal to the city during the period 1966 to 1969. The kinds of procedures referred to here are hearings, studies, and investigations undertaken by both public and private agencies which are intended to have some important impact on public control of police activities. Indeed, grand juries, "blue-ribbon" committees, and special task force study groups have come to intervene often and sometimes dramatically in the law-enforcement affairs of communities. Where effectively done, such endeavor can lead to reform of

Table 1

Law enforcement profile of three cities by selected characteristics

Civil disorders— intensity index of more than 5 (January, 1967-August, 1968)*	Date civil disturbance began	Length of disturbance in days	Number arrested, injured, killed	National guard called	Intensity index*
Chicago**	5/12/67	1	37-12-0	no	8
	7/26/67	2	80-0-0	no	11
	2/27/68	1	49-0-0	no	6
	4/4/68	8	2931-500-9	yes	457
	7/25/68	1	3-12-0	no	5
Philadelphia	1/20/68	1	7-11-0	no	5
	4/4/68	7	100-37-0	no	28
New York City	7/23/67	3	47-150-2	no	54
	7/29/67	3	76-58-0	no	28
	9/4/67	5	76-58-1	no	31
	4/5/68	2	400-0-0	no	42
	4/9/68	2	515-97-1	no	83
	4/23/68	4	1000-231-0	no	173

Crime rate per 100,000 inhabitants	1966	1967	1968	1969
Chicago	3012.0	3244.6	3334.4	3627.9
Philadelphia	1490.8	1472.8	1638.4	1823.5
New York City	4059.1	4850.2	5983.0	5867.9

Number of police officers	1966	1967	1968	1969
Chicago	11,113	11,428	12,006	12,205
Philadelphia	7,234	7,393	7,319	7,439
New York City	27,418	27,462	29,939	31,578

SOURCE: J. Robert Havlick and Mary K. Wade, "The American City and Civil Disorders," *Urban Data Service* (Washington, D.C.: International City Managers' Association, 1969); Federal Bureau of Investigation, *Uniform Crime Reports*, 1966-1969 (Washington, D.C.: U.S. Department of Justice).

* According to the scheme of Havlick and Wade, *ibid.*, the intensity index is determined in the following way: 10 points for each day of disturbance; 1 point for each arrest; 3 points for each injury; 5 points for each death; 10 points if the national guard was called.

** Figures for Chicago do not include the results of the disorders during the Democratic National Convention.

established police practices. (Reviews which do not affect the police force as a whole or which do not have some broad community significance are not included in our data.)

The findings in Table 2 become more meaningful with explanation. While there appear to be no great differences between the cities in the number of reviews, it is revealing that

Table 2

Civil review of police activity: investigations, studies, inquiries

	New York City	Philadelphia	Chicago
Number of reviews	12	8	13
Number of reviews initiated by forces external to the city	2	3	9
Number of reviews initiated by forces internal to the city	10	5	4
Number of reviews essentially critical of police and/or recommend limitations	8 (1 external*) (7 internal**)	5 (3 external*) (2 internal**)	8 (7 external*) (1 internal**)

* This referse to number of reviews initiated by forces external to the city.

** This refers to number of reviews initiated by forces internal to the city.

in Chicago most of them were initiated by forces external to the city. Seven of the nine external reviews were critical of the police and comprised almost all critical assessments made during the entire four year period. Studies and investigations initiated internally were essentially favorable, justifying police behavior under controversial conditions, e.g., demonstrations, riots. Interestingly, all of the latter were called for either during or immediately after major civil disorders in Chicago: two were initiated in 1966 by Mayor Richard Daley during summer demonstrations and riots; and in 1968, one was authorized by Mayor Daley and another by Police Superintendent O. W. Wilson and the Chicago Bar Association after the violence of the Democratic

National Convention. (Listings of these reviews can be found in Appendix C.)

This is in contrast to New York City where most of the reviews were authorized by forces internal to the city. What's more, most of these—seven out of ten—were essentially critical and recommended change in police affairs, e.g., reorganization, new procedures to safeguard the rights of the accused, findings of police corruption. (See Appendix A for listing of reviews.) Mayor John Lindsay played a prime role in instituting three of these. But critical assessments also came from a variety of other city participants: the Manhattan and Bronx district attorneys (in conjunction with the county grand juries), the New York Civil Liberties Union, and the City Controller and Corporation Counsel. For the most part, defense of police behavior and practices in the face of criticism was forthcoming from the Patrolmen's Benevolent Association.

In Philadelphia, all three external reviews occurred early in 1966 and were essentially critical of police activities. In each instance the report, or follow-up attempts to effect change in light of the report, was criticized or refuted by the Police Commissioner, the Mayor, and others who ranked high in the police establishment, i.e., the president of the local policemen's association (the Fraternal Order of Police) and top police officers. (See Appendix B for a listing of these reviews.) The pattern of refutation was generally the same: The police department would assume the responsibility of investigating allegations made by the outside agencies and would subsequently report no validating revelations. Strong supporting pronouncements from Mayor James Tate effectively served to conclude further debate.

Subsequent to 1966, five reviews originated from within the city with some revealing results. One inquiry was authorized by the Mayor into charges of police brutality in the city's public schools and, in addition, the police department authorized two studies of police management and needs by a private research corporation. In the former case the police were absolved of any wrongdoing, and in the latter two studies the police department passed muster with high ratings and recommendations for increased manpower. Thus the Philadelphia pattern compares quite closely with Chicago: while external reviews tended to find fault, internal reviews were supportive of the police. In only two cases after 1966, critiques from the city's Human Relations Commission and the Americans for Democratic Action, do we see any criticism coming from within the city. It is indicative that the Human Relations Commission report on police-community relations was never officially released but was "leaked" by the staff. The commission's executive director explained that "there were some things in it that would really upset some people like the Police Commissioner." [7]

Civil Review and Accountability

Table 3 gives us some broader perspective into the subject of civil review and accountability. Here we are primarily concerned with two questions: Who successfully initiates or vetoes police reviews? Who successfully initiates or vetoes procedures and methods which would affect police accountability? This in-

Table 3

Civil review and accountability of police: leaders

	New York City successes	defeats	Philadelphia successes	defeats	Chicago successes	defeats
Mayor	7	4	4	—	5	—
Cmnr./Supt.	7	6	2	—	—	2
Police officers/Dept.	0	3**	2	1**	—	3**
Policemen's assns.	4	6	3	1	—	—
Others	10	***	6	***	12	***
Total successes*	28	***	17	***	19	***

* Number of successes do not equal the total number of decisions as more than one person can be attributed with having been successful in a particular decision.
** This includes damaging revelations *via* civil review of police malpractices, e.g., corruption.
*** Not estimated.

cludes actions already discussed in Table 2 as well as other
important issues that have generated conflict. For example, a
continuing source of contention in New York City and Philadelphia has been the argument over the uses and abuses of civilian
review boards. Blacks and civil rights groups, complaining of
police brutality, have been dissatisfied with police internal review procedures and have been insisting on the use of civilian
dominated boards to investigate and judge citizen complaints.
The police, on the other hand, have resisted such efforts to institute outside watchdog agencies. Mayor Lindsay of New York
has had the additional problem of open challenges to his authority to direct police affairs. (Consult Appendices A, B & C
for listings of decision-making cases.)

In New York City, the leading participants have been the
Mayor, the Police Commissioner and officers of the Patrolmen's
Benevolent Association (PBA), an organization whose membership includes 99 percent of the uniformed force of the city's
Police Department. But while they all evidence substantial power,
as measured by the number of decision-successes, the same set of
actors have also been subject to setbacks—much more so than
is the case for the other two cities. In addition, and this is not
shown in Table 3, most of the defeats were inflicted by the same
three participants. (Table 7 gives some idea of this for all issues.)
With few exceptions, the alignment of forces has been one where
the Mayor and the Commissioner have stood opposed to the
PBA and its allies. Exemplifying this was New York's civilian
review board controversy where the PBA scored all of its wins
and which culminated in a referendum defeat of the board. Because Commissioner Vincent Broderick was opposed to the idea
of civilian review, Lindsay replaced him in 1966 with Howard
Leary who was Commissioner in Philadelphia.

Another issue of significance to our discussion of police
accountability in New York City is the continuing allegation
of political interference with the police. This charge has haunted
the Lindsay administration from the time the Mayor decided to
bring in a new commissioner who would condone a civilian review board. While there have been a number of incidents over

this question, two led directly to confrontation decisions of considerable importance. In December, 1967, accusations were made by leaders of the PBA that two aides of the Mayor had issued orders to the police during anti-draft demonstrations which restrained them from taking effective action. The PBA demanded they resign from office. As part of his rebuff, Lindsay advanced the theory that he is the chief executive of the city and therefore his relationship with the Police Commissioner should be the same as the President's relationship with ranking military advisers. "I believe the Mayor has a role to play in the fixing of policy in all matters in the city. We have a policy role to fill, just as the President does with the Joint Chiefs of Staff." [8]

The other challenge took place in August, 1968, and was directed toward Police Commissioner Leary though the Mayor was also involved by implication. In response to complaints from his PBA followers that the police were being restrained in the face of criminal acts, President John Cassese issued instructions to members to disregard any orders from superior officers to ignore violations of the law. Instead, Cassese planned to offer his own orders on the handling of demonstrations and disorders. But after Commissioner Leary warned of disciplinary action against those who would interpose themselves this way, the PBA sent its members excerpts from the Police Department's rules and state laws. While it was clear that Cassese had retreated, it was also clear that he retreated from a position unprecedented in the history of the New York police force.

Similar things do not happen in Chicago where Mayor Daley rules with little threat from others in the city. Certainly there is no evidence of opposition from the city's police organizations. The only real challenges to be observed are from the outside such as a federally sponsored inquiry or a federal grand jury investigation. Even more indicative than the number of successes by Daley is the complete absence of visible defeats. Only the Police Department has suffered damage as experienced through revelations of malpractice and corruption. A controversy still raging (at the time of writing) is the raid of December, 1969 by Chicago policemen who were attached to the Cook County State

Attorney's office. Two members of the Black Panther Party were killed, one of them the chairman of the party. While a coroner's jury declared the killings justifiable, a federal grand jury investigated shortly after and issued a report suggesting that the police had assassinated the two and that the Chicago Police Department had tried to destroy the evidence. (Subsequently in September 1971, the Illinois Supreme Court ordered a Chicago judge to release a long-suppressed Cook County grand jury indictment that charged fourteen lawmen, eight of them Chicago policemen, with conspiring to obstruct justice in this case.)

The closest that the Mayor has ever come to being implicated was as the result of the Walker Report.[9] This study was authorized by the National Commission on the Causes and Prevention of Violence to investigate the Chicago confrontation of demonstrators and police during the Democratic National Convention in the summer of 1968. Mayor Daley was criticized for indirectly instigating violence by his "shoot-to-kill" orders to the police during riots which had occurred earlier in the year. But Daley was ready with his own vindicating report, "The Strategy of Confrontation," which was prepared by his Corporation Counsel.

Philadelphia differs from Chicago in that its policemen's oragnization, the Fraternal Order of Police (FOP) Lodge 5, has scored almost as many successes in matters of civil review and accountability as has the Mayor. Moreover, its record of three victories over one defeat is substantially superior to New York's Patrolmen's Benevolent Association. All of the FOP's victories here were the result of a series of battles over Philadelphia's Police Advisory Board (PAB), the name of the city's civilian review board. Until it was dissolved by order of Mayor James Tate in December of 1969, the FOP vehemently opposed its very existence on the grounds that the board harassed the police, lowered their morale and reduced their effectiveness. One particular charge which President John Harrington had repeated again and again was that the Police Advisory Board was a hindrance to law enforcement during the Philadelphia riots in the summer of 1964.

In assessing the roles of the Mayor and the Police Commissioner in Philadelphia, that which is most striking is the shift from an attitude of tolerance towards the idea of civilian review to one of opposition. During his first term in office (1963 to 1967), Tate expressed the view that the board protected the police from abuse as well as the public. Tate's commissioners—Howard Leary and Edward Bell—also evidenced willingness to cooperate. But a new perspective became noticeable after Tate's reelection in November, 1967. At that time he was reluctant to press for an appeal of the city's Common Pleas Court decision which upheld an FOP suit charging that the Police Advisory Board violated the city charter and was therefore illegal.

In speculating on the circumstances which induced this change of mind, the Mayor's uphill battle and his narrow margin of victory in the election of 1967 appear to be of great significance. For it is unlikely that he could have won without devising a new "get-tough" strategy during a time of racial unrest. Having been denied his party's endorsement, Tate appointed Frank L. Rizzo, widely known as a "no-nonsense" policeman and someone notorious to civil rights groups, to the position of Commissioner. Using Rizzo's reputation in his campaign, Tate unexpectedly won both the primary and the regular election. The FOP leadership claimed part of the credit: "Tate won by only 12,000 votes and we think it's because we went out on a limb. Police and firemen, wives and families—that's 50,000 votes." [10]

Thereafter, the Tate-Rizzo-FOP coalition has functioned with surprising cohesiveness. When the Pennsylvania Supreme Court overruled Philadelphia's Common Pleas Court and said that the board had been legally constituted, Mayor Tate refused to reactivate it. And when the chairman of the PAB attempted to revive the board with the assistance of a volunteer staff, the Mayor announced formal dissolution by executive order. Having achieved success in this important area, the coalition, as we shall see, has continued to operate on other fronts. Contrary to the New York City experience, moreover, the Mayor of Philadelphia has felt no need to promulgate a chief-executive theory of police supervision.

The Law and Order Issue

The sense of frustration which comes from the contradictions of their daily work has, in many instances, encouraged the
police to enter the political arena. There they seek to influence
affairs which have traditionally been considered outside of their
jurisdiction. One special target has been the criminal laws and
judicial procedures which appear to them to "coddle criminals"
and to sanction "permissiveness." How successful they are in
effecting themselves in places like New York, Philadelphia and
Chicago is something that we shall now consider. (Refer to
Appendices A, B, and C for listings of decision-making cases.
Law suits in behalf of individual rights are considered only where
they are of broad community significance.)

If the traditional expectation is that it is the Mayor, like the
President, who is protector of the public peace, then Philadelphia appears to be something of an exception. Table 4 shows
the strong leadership which has been exercised in that city by
the Police Commissioner; more leadership, as measured by the
number of successes, than the Mayor or anyone else. All this was
achieved by Frank Rizzo who, as we previously noted, served
as Commissioner from 1967 to 1971.

Much of Rizzo's record here is attributable to a series of
winning confrontations with other groups and organizations
ranging from the city's Board of Education to the local legal aid
group to civil rights groups. For the most part, however, Philadelphia's black population, organized and unorganized, has been
at the center of most of the battles with the Commissioner. Law
suits against Rizzo and the police, charging denial of free speech
and assembly were, up to 1969, to no avail. To preserve order
in the schools, the Commissioner succeeded in assigning police
to the public schools over the opposition of the school board.
The Commissioner also established the practice of personally
requesting legislation from the City Council: one ordinance which
was passed banned the open display in streets or meeting places
of any weapon with a cutting edge; another empowered the

police to enter colleges and universities on evidence of persons bearing arms.

In virtually every public confrontation we find unanimous support of Rizzo from the Mayor and the local chapter of the Fraternal Order of Police. If, from the data on Table 4, the Fraternal Order of Police appears to be dormant, this is primarily because of the organization's endorsement of policies

Table 4

Law and order leaders

	New York City		Philadelphia		Chicago	
	successes	defeats	successes	defeats	successes	defeats
Mayor	4	—	5	1	16	—
Cmnr./Supt.	4	—	7	2	1	2
Police officers/Dept.	—	—	1	—	2	4
Policemen's assns.	1	3	—	—	—	—
Others	10	**	6	**	6	**
Total successes*	19	**	19	**	25	**

* Number of successes do not equal the total number of decisions as more than one person can be attributed with having been successful in a particular decision.
** Not estimated.

which were being clearly articulated by the Commissioner and the Mayor. The only evidence of disagreement was when Rizzo ordered two tank-like riot control vehicles. Following a public outcry over "tanks in our streets" from the leaders of black organizations, Tate was forced to cancel the order. Another defeat that Rizzo experienced together with the Mayor and the local district attorney, was over a program urged upon the city's judiciary to meet the problems of gang war and criminal repeaters. The Judges considered proposals of maximum sentences, preventive detention and the elimination of bail under certain circumstances as being unduly harsh and in violation of legal standards.

In Chicago, as Table 4 shows, it is the Mayor who is clearly ascendant in the role of protector of the public peace. Only the Police Department and the Superintendent of Police have been subject to defeat—primarily the result of law suits charging violation of constitutional rights. Contributing to this were the demonstrations led by the Rev. Martin Luther King in 1966 and the riots and violent confrontations of 1968. During this period, Daley acted in the following ways: He demanded and got a variety of new laws permitting more inclusive city government control of demonstrations and riots; he induced the City Council to pass a "stop and frisk" ordinance; he called in the national guard on five occasions and federal troops on two occasions to assist the police; he vetoed the demands of black groups for black policemen and a curfew on whites in black neighborhoods; and he overruled his Police Superintendent, James Conlisk, by giving orders to the police to "shoot to kill" arsonists and to "shoot to maim and cripple" looters.

The latter event provoked wide national controversy. Lindsay was one of many persons to criticize Daley and his statement serves to illustrate the contrast in styles of leadership in New York and Chicago: "We happen to think that protection of life, particularly innocent life, is more important than protecting property or anything else. . . . We are not going to turn disorder into chaos through the unprincipled use of armed force." [11] This attitude was reflected in the actions of both the Mayor and Commissioner Leary. During the period 1966 to 1969, both persons were occupied with proposals which would assure equitable law enforcement procedures under conditions of stress. We can refer to the creation of a new agency to study ways of assuring individual rights under emergency conditions (the Commission on Administration of Criminal Justice Under Emergency Conditions), new arrangements with the Legal Aid Society to provide counsel for the poor, a new arraignment plan to eliminate the possibility of coerced confessions, and a directive warning police against unlawful actions with regard to any person or group, e.g., the Black Panthers. To be noted also is that Lindsay, like Daley, requested and received from the City Council sweeping powers to control civil disorder, e.g., authorization to impose curfews and to ban the carrying of firearms.

But in spite of such efforts, the Lindsay administration has had its own special set of critics. For example, a faction within the Patrolmen's Benevolent Association had been pushing the parent organization toward a more restrictive stance on questions of civil liberties. Known as the Law Enforcement Group (LEG), this dissident wing came into existence in the summer of 1968 when a group of policemen demanded the removal of a criminal court judge because he was alleged to have permitted disorderly conduct in his court during the arraignment of two members of the Black Panther organization. This move failed. Nevertheless LEG's other goals have been the creation of a grand jury investigation of alleged coddling of criminals in the courts, the abolition of the all-police Civilian Complaint Review Board (the successor to the Civilian Review Board which was defeated in a referendum) and support for Senators who were seeking to prevent creation of "another Warren Court" by blocking the appointment of Justice Abe Fortas as Chief Justice of the United States Supreme Court. As a sop to this group and in order to maintain control of its members, the PBA leadership took steps of its own including direct challenge to the authority of the Police Commissioner and the Mayor who, they claimed, has encouraged "permissiveness." In all, PBA and LEG have lost a total of three battles with the Mayor and the Commissioner and have attained success in one instance—they helped to defeat a Civil Service Commission proposal to ease criminal record restrictions which would have made jobs available to a greater number of minority group persons.

It is this ongoing conflict, then, between the Mayor and the Commissioner on the one hand and the policemen's organizations on the other which continues to distinguish New York City from the other two cities. But while the policemen's organizations of Chicago are barely heard from, the FOP of Philadelphia has been able to count on the Mayor and the Commissioner to represent its special interests.

Police and Community

Since the ghetto riots of the mid-1960's, there has been a great deal of discussion about the need to strengthen police relations with the community.[12] For the most part, such discussion has centered on minority group hostility towards the policeman and the ways and means of alleviating this hostility. As such, the subject tends to be rather narrowly defined as a sociological problem in intergroup relations. The present study attempts to broaden the focus by viewing police-community relations as a power phenomenon. This is to say that the police may in some instances be quite willing to establish themselves in the community for purposes of influence and control. At the same time there may be those who resist such efforts because they fear police power.

In Table 5 we observe decisions by key participants which structure police involvement and accessibility to other groups and jurisdictions. (Temporary and experimental programs of limited scope are not considered. Consult Appendices A, B, and C for specific references.) The data for Philadelphia shows the strong role played here by the Police Commissioner and the Fraternal Order of Police. What the data in the table do not show, however, is the combined efforts of the Commissioner and the FOP leadership in working together to establish police influence in places not ordinarily within the police orbit. In the face of opposition, they succeeded in the following ways. For purposes of security, they placed police in the public schools as a substitute for school guards who would otherwise have been entirely beholden to school authorities. They persuaded the United Fund of Philadelphia to agree to forward all complaints of police brutality to the Police Commissioner rather than agencies like the American Civil Liberties Union or the Legal Aid Society. Primarily through the efforts of the FOP, the Philadelphia General Hospital was reorganized to provide improved facilities for policemen and firemen and President John Harrington was appointed to the Board of Trustees. Largely through the efforts of Rizzo, the police were empowered by law to enter into colleges and universities on evidence of persons bearing arms. We should note that in most of these cases Mayor Tate provided open support.

In Chicago, on the other hand, the police establishment as well as the Mayor appear to be uninterested in police-community relations—there is little evidence of action whether it be successes or defeats. A careful viewing of successes, furthermore, reveals as much effort directed toward the vetoing of proposals as toward the initiating of proposals, e.g., the success of the police in helping to kill a federally supported gang control program.

In New York City, the major issue on the subject of police-community relations pertains to programs intended to encourage the recruitment of blacks and Puerto Ricans into the police force. While the Commissioner has been the chief proponent of such proposals, the Patrolmen's Benevolent Association has been

Table 5

Police and Community: leaders

	New York City successes	defeats	Philadelphia successes	defeats	Chicago successes	defeats
Mayor	2	1	3	—	—	—
Cmnr./Supt.	4	—	5	—	2	—
Police officers/Dept.	1	—	2	—	1	—
Policemen's assns.	2	2	3	—	—	—
Others	2	**	6	**	5	**
Total successes*	11	**	19	**	8	**

* Number of successes do not equal the total number of decisions as more than one person can be attributed with having been successful in a particular decision.
** Not estimated.

the chief opponent. (The PBA usually argues the case for maintaining "high standards.") As Table 5 indicates, the Commissioner has been successful in overcoming this resistance, at least as measured in overt decision-making. Another controversial decision which he made was to permit policemen to belong to the John Birch Society. Surprisingly, Lindsay shows rather limited involvement in what might be expected to be his strongest field of interest. His one defeat here can be attributed to the PBA's lobbying success in the State Legislature: a law was passed over Lindsay's objections permitting policemen to hold outside jobs as part-time taxi-drivers. Overall, New York City appears as listless in the area of police-community relations as does Chicago.

Summation and Conclusions

Table 6 gives us an overview of all successes and defeats of key participants in the making of police policy. As a first observation, we note the many defeats experienced by all the New York City participants—an important contrast with the other two cities. While the Patrolmen's Benevolent Association appears to lead in defeats (the Law Enforcement Group is repsonsible for one of the nine defeats listed for policemen's associations), it would be a mistake to overlook the fact that it has also scored as many victories as Philadelphia's Fraternal Order of Police. In Chicago, the policemen's organizations—a total of four claim to represent patrolmen's interests—appear to have no visible

Table 6

Total successes and defeats of key participants

	New York City		Philadelphia		Chicago	
	successes	defeats	successes	defeats	successes	defeats
Mayor	11	5	12	1	21	—
Cmnr./Supt.	14	6	11	2	5	2
Police officers/Dept.	1	3	5	1	3	7
Policemen's assns.	6	9	6	1	—	—

NOTE: Totals in this table are a little less than the equivalent of total figures in the previous tables since data were sometimes included twice when found to be applicable to more than one category, e.g., police accountability and law and order.

influence while it is the Mayor who looms forth as a man of unchallenged authority.

In viewing police commissioners, the ones in New York and Philadelphia appear to have asserted strong leadership. But the fact that New York's Commissioner shows six defeats as compared to only two in Philadelphia would seem to indicate a greater degree of countervailing power in the former city. The same can be said in assessing the mayoralty roles in these two cities.

To probe further, it would be useful to consider the special kinds of relationships which exist among the key participants. To what extent have these persons and groups been mutually supportive or mutually antagonistic? The findings in Table 7 provide us with some clues to conflict relations. In looking at New York City we can see that a favorite target of both the Mayor and the Commissioner has been the policemen's association (PBA); and, as to be expected, the policemen's association has managed to inflict the most set backs on the Mayor and the Commissioner. The totals for New York City indicate that here indeed is the source of most of the conflict. Philadelphia, on the other hand, shows only five defeats in all and four of these originated from other sources. Among the key actors—Mayor, Commissioner, FOP, ranking police officers—there is virtually no visible conflict. Chicago presents a similar picture. Almost all contributors of defeats are from outside the mayor-police orbit and, we might add, from outside the city.

Not to be overlooked, however, are some important differences between Philadelphia and Chicago. In the latter place, as we saw in Table 6, it is the Mayor who exercises unchallenged leadership. No one person or group in the police establishment competes or even comes close to competing with him. In Philadelphia, the Mayor shares power with the Police Commissioner; and since 1967 when Rizzo assumed office, the Commissioner has actually shown greater leadership. The FOP and ranking police officers must also be counted among the influential. As a coalition of interests they have all contributed to the making of police policy. But just as important, as noted in Table 5, is the ability

Table 7

Conflict relations in all three issue-areas according to contributors and subjects of defeat

Contributors to defeat	Mayor			Cmnr./Supt.			Police officers/ Dept.			Policemen's assns.			Total*		
	NYC	Phil.	C	NYC	Phil.	C	NYC	Phil.	C	NYC	Phil.	C	NYC	Phil.	C
Mayor	—	—	—	2	1	1	—	—	—	4	—	—	6	1	1
Cmnr./Supt.	—	—	—	—	—	—	—	—	—	6	—	—	6	—	—
Police officers/Dept.	—	—	—	—	—	—	—	—	—	—	—	—	—	—	—
Policemen's assns.	5	—	—	4	—	—	—	—	—	—	—	—	9	—	—
Others	—	1	—	—	1	1	3	1	7	2	1	—	5	4	8
													26	5	9

*Total conflict relations amounts to more than total defeats as more than one person or agency can oppose a particular decision.

of this coalition to establish itself in other community jurisdictions which are only indirectly related to police affairs.

The Police as a Political Machine

In the forward to the second edition of Harold Gosnell's classic study *Machine Politics, Chicago Model,* Theodore Lowi analyzes the impact of the reform movement on the party organizations of America's big cities.[13] Particularly noteworthy is Lowi's contention that the reform movement has been responsible for the "replacement of Old Machines with New Machines. The bureaucracies—that is, the professionally organized, autonomous career agencies—are the New Machines." [14] Lowi continues:

> The modern city is now well run but ungoverned because it now comprises islands of functional power before which the modern mayor stands impoverished. No mayor of a modern city has predictable means of determining whether the bosses of the New Machines—the bureau chiefs and the career commissioners—will be loyal to anything but their agency, its work, and related professional norms.[15]

Indeed, this condition has been evident in New York City since the late 1950's when, with the last throes of the Democratic organization, politics became a free-wheeling, multi-factioned affair. At around this time, the police machine entered the political lists just as other groups and organizations were tempted to do.[16] But it was not until the 1969 mayoralty election that the police reached new heights of political activity. For example, Chief Inspector Sanford Garelik was selected by Mayor Lindsay to run on his ticket for City Council President. (He eventually did get elected along with Lindsay.) Lindsay's strategy was to offset various moves by the Patrolmen's Benevolent Association's leadership and its allies. We refer to Norman Frank, the PBA's public relations director who was running for the Democratic nomination for Mayor. Frank subsequently withdrew to become Finance Chairman for Mario Procaccino who was Lindsay's Democratic opponent and an exponent of the need for "law and order." In addition, John J. Cassese resigned as president of the PBA to devote his full efforts to Procaccino's campaign. Also indicative was the decision by former Police Commissioner Vincent Broderick to compete for the Democratic nomination for City Controller. Broderick was removed as Commissioner when he had earlier opposed Mayor Lindsay on the civilian review board issue and had complained of "political interference" with the police. (He lost in the primary.)

The traditional party machines of Philadelphia have also been subject to deterioration—first the Republican organization which had been dominant until the early 1950's, and most recently the Democrats.[17] The end results of this condition were illustrated in the 1967 elections when the incumbent Democratic Mayor James Tate was denied his party's endorsement in light of pre-election polls which predicted his defeat. Refusing to be counted out, Tate was desperate for any kind of electoral assistance he could get from whatever source. Tate found such assistance in the person of his newly appointed police commissioner Frank Rizzo and he unexpectedly succeeded in winning the primary and the regular elections. Most important, according to our findings, is that what Tate initiated in support of his own cause has since escalated into a new political phenomenon: the coming of age of the police as a power bloc.

As a new symbol of electoral potency, Rizzo was given a free hand and, with strong support from the Faternal Order of Police, he came to exercise strong influence in a variety of issues. Of special significance has been his leadership on the issue of "law and order." With the help of Mayor Tate, who was forbidden by the City Charter from seeking a third term, Rizzo was endorsed almost unanimously by the Democratic Committee to run for Mayor. (Only one dissenting vote was recorded.) Shortly thereafter, in the spring of 1971, Rizzo won a crushing victory in the primary election over the former chairman of the city's Democratic party; and in the fall, he easily won the mayoralty election against his Republican opponent.

In Chicago, the Cook County Democratic Committee as headed by Mayor Richard Daley is alive and well [18]—a very different story from either Philadelphia or New York. Theodore Lowi reminds us that "when New York was losing its last machine and entering into the new era of permanent Reform, Chicago's machine politics was just beginning to consolidate." [19] If the police establishment appears impotent here, it is because the machine is too strong. Even Police Superintendent Orlando Wilson (1962-1967), the academic expert who was called in to clean up police corruption and improve administration, enhanced City Hall control by centralizing procedures and consolidating police districts; thereafter police collusion with ward leaders and neighborhood interests would be more difficult to maintain.

Contributing to the weakness of the Chicago police bloc is the fact that it is poorly organized and lacks unity. Most of the city's policemen belong to four large associations and, so far, all efforts to form a joint council to assert pressure in behalf of police interests have failed.[20] But there is another factor to be noted. Daley, himself, speaks for the police on a variety of issues which, in effect, de-energizes any potential police movement. He is against the idea of a civilian review board and Chicago has never experimented with one; and few policemen, if any (with the exception of black policemen), objected to his "shoot-to-kill" orders during the 1968 riots.

Three Models of Police Politics

During a time in our history which Samuel Lubell calls the "Hidden Crisis in American Politics," i.e., "too rapid and uncontrolled a rate of change . . . (that is) beginning to tear the nation apart," [21] the police of America's largest cities have come to play a more active political role than ever before. In light of this, we have tried to discern the basic patterns of such politics. Having identified the key participants and assessed their behavior in the three cities of New York, Chicago, and Philadelphia, we can now pose three models. The broad outlines as based on our observations from 1966 to 1969 are as follows.

Model 1. *New York City: Mayor-police war.* Through legal suits, referendum battles and lobbying, the policemen's association shows considerable success in opposing the Mayor. Overall, the Mayor and the Police Commissioner remain in control though at any time their authority in police affairs could evaporate. Where the Police Commissioner is unwilling or unable to fulfill the role of the "mayor's cop," he is expected to leave. No one of the contending forces appears to be able to overawe the other. The battle rages on.

Model 2. *Philadelphia: police cooptation of the Mayor.* The Mayor supports the Police Commissioner and the police in virtually every issue, irrespective of the opposition. The Mayor himself has limited power resources: he is a lame duck with a disintegrating party organization. The initiative on police matters has shifted to the Police Commissioner in his role as a "cop's cop." With the close support of the local policemen's association, and with the acquiescence of the Mayor, the Commissioner has been able to assert influence beyond the police policy area.

Model 3. *Chicago: the Mayor ascendant.* Because of the strength of the Democratic party organization as headed by the Mayor, the police are effectively limited in what they can do. The Mayor has the initiative and sets the tone on matters of police policy. The Police Superintendent is only as successful as he has support from the Mayor which structures his role as the "mayor's cop." [22]

APPENDIX A. DECISION-MAKING CASES
IN NEW YORK CITY, 1966-1969

Civil Review and Accountability of Police

Civil review:
1. The Law Enforcement Task Force Report.
2. The Vera Foundation study on police methods.
3. Hearings and report from the New York State Joint Legislative Committee on Election Laws and the New York State Joint Legislative Committee on Corporation Laws.
4. The International Chiefs of Police Report.
5. The New York District Attorney's investigation of police corruption.
6. The Bronx District Attorney's investigation of police corruption.
7. The Rand Corporation study of police operations.
8. Hearings by the New York State Joint Legislative Committee on Crime.
9. The Brooklyn Bar Association survey on political interference with the police.
10. The Brooklyn grand jury investigation into an attack by off-duty police on Black Panthers.
11. The New York American Civil Liberties Union study of police practices.

12. Investigations by the City Controller and the City Corporation Counsel into the Patrolmen's Benevolent Association's health and welfare fund.

Civil accountability:

1. The Civilian Review Board Controversy.
2. The appointment of the Police Commissioner.
3. Controversy over the role of the Mayor's aids during public demonstrations.
4. The PBA's attempt to issue new guidelines for the police on enforcing the law.
5. The Brooklyn Bar Association's request for an investigation of political interference with the police in civil disorders.

The Law and Order Issue

1. The role of the Legal Aid Society in providing legal assistance for indigents.
2. A proposal for a new arraignment plan.
3. Proposed easing criminal standards to enhance police recruitment of minorities.
4. Controversy over the role of the Mayor's aides during public demonstrations.
5. Proposed project to provide free legal assistance in certain kinds of criminal cases.
6. The role of the Committee on Administration of Criminal Justice under Emergency Conditions.
7. Proposed emergency powers for the Mayor during civil disturbances.
8. The attempted ouster of Criminal Judge Furey.
9. Proposed guidelines on preventing unlawful police actions with regard to the Black Panthers.
10. Immunity from prosecution ruling.
11. The PBA's "get tough" guidelines.

Police and Community

1. Controversy over police membership in the John Birch Society.
2. Creation of PACT (Police and Citizens Together) to strengthen police-community ties.
3. Creation of the Criminal Justice Coordinating Council.
4. Creation of the Committee on Administration of Criminal Justice under Emergency Conditions.
5. Proposed easing criminal standards to encourage police recruitment of minorities.
6. Proposal to permit the police to hold outside jobs.
7. The use of grammar questions on civil service examinations for promotion of police.
8. Instituting a Preventive Enforcement Patrol program in Harlem.
9. Proposed Police Cadet program to recruit minorities.
10. Special recruiting drive to attract minorities into the police.

APPENDIX B. DECISION-MAKING CASES IN
PHILADELPHIA, 1966-1969

Civil Review and Accountability of Police

Civil review:
1. Federal grand jury investigation of police collusion with gambling ring.
2. Pennsylvania Joint Legislative Committee Investigating Narcotics views police role.
3. Staff study of police prepared for the President's Commission on Law Enforcement and Administration of Justice.
4. Three-man city committee inquiry into charges of police brutality in the schools.
5. Americans for Democratic Action's "State of the City Report."
6. Franklin Institute study on police manpower requirements.
7. Franklin Institute study comparing Philadelphia's police with police in other cities.
8. Philadelphia Human Relations Commission report on police-community relations.

Civil accountability:

1. The Police Advisory Board Controversy.
2. Appointment of the Police Commissioner.
3. Community Legal Services suit to remove the Police Commissioner.

The Law and Order Issue

1. Proposal to end continuances of trials.
2. Controversy over establishing Community Legal Services, Inc.
3. Restricting the speech of the head of the Philadelphia chapter of the NAACP.
4. Proposals to place the city in a state of "limited emergency."
5. Providing emergency powers for the Mayor during civil disturbances.
6. Controversy over the handling of student demonstrations by the police.
7. Proposal to acquire riot-control vehicles.
8. The Philadelphia Law Enforcement Planning Council's guidelines for lawful demonstrations.
9. Proposed ban on the open display in streets or meetings of any weapon with a cutting edge.
10. The Defender Association controversy.
11. Restricting an anti-war rally.
12. Proposed ban on the carrying of weapons in colleges and universities.
13. Controlling juvenile gangs and criminal repeaters.

Police and Community

1. The North Philadelphia Congress project.
2. The Philadelphia General Hospital controversy.
3. Establishing the Philadelphia Law Enforcement Planning Council.

4. Controversy between the police and the Board of Education on law-enforcement in the schools.
5. Establishing police-community workshops.
6. Establishing a committee to coordinate emergency services during disorders.
7. Permitting police examinations in the Spanish language.
8. Proposal permitting police to enter colleges and universities unasked on evidence of persons bearing arms.
9. Police-community relations program sponsored by the Human Relations Commission.
10. The United Fund controversy.
11. Proposals to control juvenile gangs.

APPENDIX C. DECISION-MAKING CASES IN CHICAGO, 1966-1969

Civil Review and Accountability of Police

Civil review:

1. Citizens committee study called "Police and Public, A Critique and a Program."
2. The Chicago Bar Association report on police brutality.
3. The Cook County grand jury investigation into police tire-theft operations.
4. Nine-member city committee investigation of the Chicago riots of April, 1968.
5. Hearings by the Illinois Advisory Committee of the U.S. Commission on Civil Rights.
6. U.S. Justice Department financed study on police and the slums.
7. The Walker Report to the National Commission on the Causes and Prevention of Violence—"Rights in Conflict."
8. City of Chicago Report on the Democratic Convention Disturbances—"The Strategy of Confrontation."
9. U.S. grand jury investigation of the Democratic Convention disturbances.
10. Cook County Coroner's jury investigation of a police raid on the Black Panthers.

12. The American Civil Liberties Union Report—"Dissent and Disorder."

Civil accountability:

1. Establishing a registrar of complaints against the police.
2. A proposal for an inquiry into charges of favoritism in police civil service promotions.
3. The appointment of the Police Superintendent.
4. A proposed investigation of charges of police harassment of the President of the Afro-American Patrolmen's League.

The Law and Order Issue

1. Establishing a police suspect file.
2. Authorizing the police to "stop and frisk."
3. Proposed emergency ban on civil rights demonstrations.
4. Legal suits against ordinances governing disorderly conduct and proposed new provisions for regulating disorderly conduct.
5. Calling out the National Guard and federal troops during civil disturbances.
6. Establishing and effecting emergency powers to deal with civil disturbances.
7. Legal suit to restrain Chicago police from interfering with news gathering.
8. Legal suit challenging police search warrant procedures.
9. Proposed use of black police in black neighborhoods during civil disorder.
10. Establishing police-security guidelines in the public schools.
11. Proposed curfew on whites in black neighborhoods.

Police and Community

1. Establishing a program to educate the police in the Spanish culture and language.

2. Controversy over police membership in the Ku Klux Klan.
3. Setting up District Community Service Sergeants in police districts.
4. The Blackstone Rangers controversy.
5. Proposal to end the police gang intelligence unit.
6. Proposing School Board cooperation with law enforcement agencies.

Notes

1. On this matter, see The President's Commission on Law Enforcement and Administration of Justice, *The Challenge of Crime in a Free Society* (New York: Avon Books, 1968), pp. 283, 284.
2. *The Politics of Protest*, (Washington, D.C.: U.S. Government Printing Office, 1969), p. 213.
3. *Ibid.*
4. Robert Dahl, *Who Governs?* (New Haven and London: Yale University Press, 1961), p. 124. Our method of looking at decisions is essentially similar to Dahl's except that we look at one major policy area—i.e., the police area—rather than three different ones and we compare three cities instead of observing one. See Appendix B., Section V, *ibid.,* pp. 332-334.
5. See the article by Peter Bachrach and Morton S. Baratz which is critical of Robert Dahl's methods. "Two Faces of Power," *The American Political Science Review,* LVI, 4 (December, 1962), 947-952.
6. The interview method posed some very real difficulties in our three sample cities because of resistance and suspicion by those most directly involved in police affairs.
7. *The Philadelphia Bulletin,* April 21, 1969.
8. *The New York Times,* December 13, 1967.
9. See *Rights in Conflict* (New York: Bantam Books, 1968). An excerpt can be found in Chapter III of this book.
10. Testimony of Virgil Penn, Recording Secretary of the Fraternal Order of Police in Philadelphia. Samuel Lubell confirms the importance of the Tate strategy in his data on racial polarization in Philadelphia in *The Hidden Crisis in American Politics* (New York: W. W. Norton and Co., 1970), pp. 92-95.
11. *The New York Times,* April 17, 1968.
12. See, for example, *Report of the National Advisory Committee on Civil Disorders* (New York: Bantam Books, 1968), chap. 11; *Task Force Report: The Police,* (Washington, D.C.: U.S. Government Printing Office, 1967), chap. 6.

13. *Machine Politics, Chicago Model* (Chicago: The University of Chicago Press, 1968).

14. *Ibid.*, p. x.

15. *Ibid.*, pp. x, xi.

16. The history of this is traced by James Priest Gifford in "The Political Relations of the Patrolmen's Benevolent Association (1946-1969)" (unpublished Ph.D. dissertation, Columbia University, 1970), pp. 277-282.

17. On this subect see James Reichley, *The Art of Government* (New York: The Fund for the Republic, 1959).

18. This has been well documented in a number of studies. See particularly Edward C. Banfield, *Political Influence* (New York: The Free Press, 1961); Martin Meyerson and Edward C. Banfield, *Politics, Planning and the Public Interest* (New York: The Free Press, 1955); Mike Ryko, *Boss: Richard J. Daley of Chicago* (New York: E. P. Dutton and Co., 1970).

19. *Machine Politics, Chicago Style, op. cit.*, p. vii.

20. The four largest associations are the Chicago Patrolmen's Association, the Fraternal Order of Police, the Confederation of Police, and the Chicago Policemen's Annuity and Benefit Fund Protective Association. The Chicago police department officially does not recognize the existence of these organizations.

21. *Op. cit.*, p. 10. For a careful analysis of the nature of dissatisfactions comparing whites with blacks in fifteen cities including Chicago, Philadelphia, and Brooklyn (in New York City), see Howard Schuman and Barry Gruenberg, *The Impact of City on Racial Attitudes* (Ann Arbor, Michigan: Institute for Social Research, The University of Michigan, 1970).

22. A view of police history in the communities studied reveals a third role for the commissioner/superintendent which can be called the "professional cop." The behavior pattern here is one which emphasizes independence from environmental interests including the mayor and the police bureaucracy while stressing reform standards.

SELECTED REFERENCES ON THE POLICE

Abbott, David W., Louis H. Gold and Edward T. Rogowsky. *Police, Politics and Race: The New York City Referendum on Civilian Review*. New York and Cambridge, Mass.: The American Jewish Committee and Harvard University Press, 1969.

Alex, Nicholas. *Black in Blue: A Study of the Negro Policeman*. New York: Appleton-Century-Crofts, 1969.

Banton, Michael. *The Policeman and the Community*. New York: Basic Books, 1965.

Bayley, David H., and Harold Mendelsohn. *Minorities and the Police*. New York: The Free Press, 1969.

Becker, Theodore L., and Vernon G. Murray. *Government Lawlessness in America*. New York: Oxford University Press, 1971.

Berkley, George E. *The Democratic Policeman*. Boston: Beacon Press, 1969.

Black, Algernon. *The People and the Police*. New York: McGraw Hill, 1968.

Bordua, David J. *The Police*. New York: John Wiley and Sons, 1967.

Chevigny, Paul. *Police Power: Police Abuses in New York City*. New York: Pantheon Books, 1969.

Clark, Ramsey. *Crime in America*. New York: Simon and Schuster, 1970.

Cray, Ed. *The Big Blue Line: Police Power v. Human Rights*. New York: Coward-McCann, Inc., 1967.

Gardiner, John A. *The Politics of Corruption: Organized Crime in an American City.* New York: Russell Sage Foundation, 1970.

Gifford, James Priest. *The Political Relations of the Patrolmen's Benevolent Association in the City of New York (1946-1969).* Unpublished Ph.D. dissertation, Columbia University, New York, 1970.

LeFave, Wayne R. *Arrest.* Boston: Little, Brown and Company, 1965.

Lane, Roger. *Policing the City:* Boston 1822-1885. Cambridge, Mass.: Harvard University Press, 1967.

Lipsky, Michael (ed.). *Law and Order: Police Encounters.* Chicago: Aldine Publishing Co., 1970.

Masotti, Louis, and Don R. Bowen (eds.). *Riots and Rebellion: Civil Violence in the Urban Community.* Beverly Hills, Cal.: Sage Publications, 1968.

Miller, Frank W., *et. al. The Police Function.* Mineola, New York: The Foundation Press, Inc., 1971.

National Commission on the Causes and Prevention of Violence. *To Establish Justice, To Insure Domestic Tranquility.* Washington, D.C.: U.S. Government Printing Office, 1969.

National Commission on the Causes and Prevention of Violence. *Rights in Conflict.* Washington, D.C.: U.S. Government Printing Office, 1968.

National Commission on Law Observance and Enforcement. *Report on the Police.* Washington, D.C.: U.S. Government Printing Office. 1931.

Niederhoffer, Arthur. *Behind the Shield: The Police in Urban Society.* New York: Doubleday and Company, 1967.

President's Commission on Law Enforcement and Administration of Justice. *The Challenge of Crime in a Free Society.* Washington, D.C.: U.S. Government Printing Office, 1967.

President's Commission on Law Enforcement and Administration of Justice. *Task Force Report: The Police.* Washington, D.C.: U.S. Government Printing Office, 1967.

Reiss, Albert J., Jr. *The Police and the Public.* New Haven: Yale University Press, 1971.

Richardson, James F. *The New York Police: Colonial Times to 1901.* New York: Oxford University Press, 1970.

Saunders, Charles B. *Upgrading the American Police*. Washington, D.C.: Brookings Institution, 1970.

Skolnick, Jerome H. *Justice without Trial: Law Enforcement in Democratic Society*. New York: John Wiley and Sons, 1966.

Skolnick, Jerome H. *The Politics of Protest: Violent Aspects of Protest and Confrontation*. A Staff Report to the National Commission on the Causes and Prevention of Violence. Washington, D.C.: U.S. Government Printing Office, 1969.

Steadman, Robert F. (ed.). *The Police and the Community*. Baltimore: The John Hopkins University Press, 1972.

Tolchin, Susan J. *The Police Policy Area as a Subsystem of New York City Politics*. Unpublished Ph.D. dissertation, New York University, New York, 1968.

Turner, William. *The Police Establishment*. New York: G. P. Putnam's Sons, 1968.

U.S. Riot Commission. *Report of the National Advisory Commission on Disorders*. New York: Bantam Books, 1968.

Westley, William A. *Violence and the Police*. Cambridge, Mass.: The MIT Press, 1970.